OCCIDENTAL ESCHATOLOGY

Cultural Memory
in
the
Present

Mieke Bal and Hent de Vries, Editors

OCCIDENTAL ESCHATOLOGY

Jacob Taubes

*Translated with a Preface
by David Ratmoko*

STANFORD UNIVERSITY PRESS

STANFORD, CALIFORNIA

Stanford University Press
Stanford, California

Printed in the United States of America on acid-free, archival-quality paper

Library of Congress Cataloging-in-Publication Data

Taubes, Jacob.
   [Abendländische Eschatologie. English]
   Occidental eschatology / Jacob Taubes ; translated with a preface by David
Ratmoko.
      p.   cm. — (Cultural memory in the present)
   "Occidental Eschatology was originally published in German in 1947 under the
title Abendländische Eschatologie."
   Includes bibliographical references.
   ISBN 978-0-8047-6028-7 (cloth : alk. paper) — ISBN 978-0-8047-6029-4 (pbk. :
alk. paper)
    1. Eschatology—History of doctrines.   I. Ratmoko, David, 1968-   II. Title.
III. Series: Cultural memory in the present.
   BT821.T21213 2009
   236.09 — dc22   2009022417

Typeset by BookMatters in Garamond 11/13.5

To my parents

Contents

Preface

DAVID RATMOKO

Over sixty years after it first appeared, *Abendländische Eschatologie*, the astonishing doctoral thesis of Jacob Taubes (1923–87), finally becomes available in English under the title *Occidental Eschatology*.[1] Written at the age of twenty-three, it was the only book by Taubes published in his lifetime, and it was, in many ways, a blueprint for a lifelong endeavor or at least a preview of a larger study: "I had to radically shorten [the book] by two hundred pages, for the publishers were unwilling to print it otherwise," Taubes explains to Gershom Scholem in a letter of 1947. He adds, "I did not read the proofs myself, but friends did, for the proofs came only a week ago, when I left for London. I'm not responsible for any typos."[2] In spite of the occasional typographical error, some missing notes, and an incomplete bibliography, the book was republished in 1991 without any modifications, leaving the editorial task to the Italian edition of *Escatologia occidentale* (1997).[3] For nearly half a century, then, from the first to the second edition, *Abendländische Eschatologie* remained out of print and virtually forgotten, despite an early reference to it in 1949 by Karl Löwith in *Meaning in History*.[4]

I

A charismatic speaker and great polemicist, Taubes is often said to have had his greatest impact as a teacher. Although his oeuvre is thought to be notoriously small, he was in fact a prolific writer, seeing the publication of sixty-nine essays during his life. Unfortunately, only twenty-two of them were republished, in a collection called *Vom Kult zur Kultur* (From Cult to Culture; 1996). The topics range from religion to history, philosophy, art, psychoanalysis, and political theology; the essays, though dispersed in various journals, constitute the bulk of his published work.[5] Previously, a collec-

tion of materials on Carl Schmitt came out in 1987, followed by an edition of
Taubes's lectures on St. Paul in 1993, the translation of which, *The Political
Theology of Paul*, has been his only book available in English to date.[6] The
recent wave of interest in Taubes also saw the publication of his letters to
Scholem, along with essays concerning Scholem's messianism and a seminar
on Benjamin's "Theses on the Philosophy of History," first in Italian and
then in German under the title *Der Preis des Messianismus* (The Price of
Messianism).[7] A complete bibliography exists only up to the year 2000.[8]

II

Born in Vienna in 1923, Jacob Taubes moved to Zurich in 1937 when his
father was appointed chief rabbi, and there they survived the Nazi persecution. Ordained a rabbi himself in 1943, Taubes completed his studies in philosophy at Zurich and published *Abendländische Eschatologie* in 1947. During
those years, he often attended the lectures of Hans Urs von Balthasar, whose
Catholic *Apokalypse der deutschen Seele* (Apocalypse of the German Soul)
(1937–39) arguably provoked Taubes's Jewish account of the apocalypse in
response.[9] The following year Taubes moved to the United States, obtaining
a post at the Jewish Theological Seminar in New York, but by 1950 he had
already left for Jerusalem as a research fellow under the patronage of Scholem,
who was impressed by Taubes's doctoral thesis. After an irreparable break
with Scholem, he returned to the United States in 1953 and spent two years at
Harvard University on a Rockefeller scholarship. He taught at Princeton
University in 1955–56, and was appointed professor of history and philosophy
of religion at Columbia University, where he stayed for ten years. There, he
met Peter Szondi and Theodor Adorno. In 1966, Taubes accepted the chair of
Jewish studies at the Freie Universität in Berlin, before taking charge of the
Department of Hermeneutics created especially for him. During this period,
he was also a regular guest lecturer at the Maison des Sciences de l'Homme in
Paris, where he met Derrida, Lévinas, and others. In those days Taubes not
only became an icon of the student movement in Berlin, but he also held one
of the most influential positions in German intellectual life, that of coeditor
of the Theorie series at Suhrkamp, together with Jürgen Habermas.[10] His
own materials on Carl Schmitt, ironically, were published at Mervé, a small
Berlin publisher. Declining Schmitt's invitations for thirty years, he met his
"arch-enemy" only in 1978, after Alexander Kojève ventured to Plettenberg,
to Schmitt's place of "inward exile."[11] Taubes died in 1987, following his

Heidelberg course of lectures on Paul, and he is buried at the Jewish cemetery in Zurich, the city where he composed *Abendländische Eschatologie*.

III

Eschatology, the doctrine of "last things" (gr. *eskhatos*), is originally a Western term, referring to Jewish and Christian beliefs—and characterizing the entire "Aramaic world" (22)—about the end of history, the resurrection of the dead, the Last Judgment, and related matters.[12] And yet, neither *Western* nor *occidental* fully renders the meaning of *abendländisch* in the German title, which denotes not only the "Western hemisphere or culture of the West" (*OED*), but more specifically the "cultural union of Europe as formed through antiquity and Christianity."[13] At stake in Taubes's title, therefore, is precisely the historical synthesis and spiritual legacy of the West that Taubes seeks to renegotiate through his study of eschatology. Apropos of Hegel, for whom the "history of the spirit is complete" (93), Taubes notes, "Once the framework of the modern age is smashed, the aeon demarcated by the milestones of Antiquity–Middle Ages–New Age comes to an end.... Hegel's fulfillment, however, is a reconciliation of destruction, for it is the final act before a great reversal, before the complete break with the classical, Christian Western tradition" (191).

Crucial for the work of eschatology is the direction and end implied in the noncyclical concept of time as established by the Judeo-Christian tradition. As Taubes noted of apocalypse in a 1987 interview, "Whether one knows it or not is entirely irrelevant, whether one takes it for fancy or sees it as dangerous is completely uninteresting in view of the intellectual breakthrough and experience of time as respite [*daß Zeit Frist heißt*]. This has consequences for the economy, actually for all life. There is no eternal return, time does not enable nonchalance; rather, it is distress."[14]

Occidental Eschatology is divided into four books. Book I, "On the Nature of Eschatology," outlines the elements, nature, and metaphysics of eschatology; it gives an extremely rich account of how history based on linear time evolved from the situation of exile as characterized by Exodus, Hebrew prophecy, apocalypticism, and gnosis. Book II continues the chronology by tracing the "history of apocalypticism" from Daniel to Jesus, Paul and John, through to early Christianity, Augustine, and Joachim. Drawing out the implications for history, Taubes shows how the four successive empires in Daniel enable "our" transdynastic or universal concept of history, how Jesus and Paul divide "our" time into a before and after Christ, how the "history of Christendom is founded upon the delayed Second Coming" (56), the "nonoccurring event" (56), and how Joachim's Trinitarian prophecy of the three ages (of the Father, the Son, and the Spirit) inaugurates "our" tripartite division of history into antiquity, Middle Ages, and modernity. Recording the fate of the "theological eschatology of Europe," Book III focuses on the marginal but explosive tradition of spirituality or *pneumatics* after the chiliasm of Joachim, from the Franciscan Spirituals to Thomas Müntzer and the Anabaptists.

The beginnings of "the philosophical eschatology of Europe" are marked by the Copernican turn, "the loss of heaven" (107), and Book IV discusses Lessing, Kant, Hegel, Marx, and Kierkegaard in this regard. Seeking to restore a link to the beyond, Lessing "associates the Eschaton with subjective spirituality" (131), while for Kant "metaphysical Christian statements become the *as ifs* of transcendental eschatology" (139). Hegel, like Joachim, constructs "world history from the perspective of an end to fulfillment. They both consider the history of the spirit to be synonymous with the course of history" (161). More specifically, "the confusion surrounding Hegel is substantively caused by the fundamental ambivalence of *sublation* [*Aufhebung*], an ambivalence which it shares with Joachim's *transire*" (165). Although breaking with Hegel, Marx and Kierkegaard, two of his prominent successors, share in the philosophical eschatology: "Once self-alienation is revealed to be the leitmotif in the analyses of Marx and Kierkegaard, then elements inevitably emerge which determine the eschatological drama of history in each of their views. The entire socioeconomic catalog of Marx's analyses simply serves as the orchestration of the theme of self-alienation—the fall into exile and the path to redemption. *Social economy* is for Marx the *economy of salvation*. Kierkegaard, for his part, seeks to eclipse eighteen centuries as if they had never existed and to live as Christ's contemporary. With Kierkegaard the apocalypticism of early Christianity [*urchristliche Apokalyptik*] becomes reality again" (183).

Ending his tour de force, the young Taubes continues to speak through the voices of Hegel, Marx, and Kierkegaard, up to the final paragraph of the Epilogue, when he regains the Gnostic, apocalyptic voice of Book I: "the holy is separation [*Aussonderung*] and setting apart [*Absonderung*]; being holy means being set apart. The holy is the terror that shakes the foundations of the world. The shock caused by the holy [*das Heilige*] bursts asunder the foundations of the world for salvation [*das Heil*]" (193).

IV

Over and above purely theological concerns, Taubes's study shows apocalypticism to be a revolutionary force in Western history, springing from situations of *exile*—the "base word [*Urwort*] of apocalypticism" (26)—in Exodus and the apocalyptic book of Daniel, and driving the philosophies of history of Joachim, Hegel, and Marx. "Taubes is right," Carl Schmitt concurs, "today everything is theology, except that which theologians speak about."[15] What might appear to be a simple case of secularization, from theology to philosophy, in fact exhibits a desire to break "out of the cycle of nature into the realm of history" (5) and to reach the end (*telos*) of history as its fulfillment (*pleroma*).

Signifying an emphatic "turn" or "turning point," *Wende*, *Umschlag*, and *Umkehr* are the key terms Taubes employs for his history of apocalypticism, reconciling the religious meanings of the Hebrew *schuwu*, Greek *metanoia*, and Latin *conversio* with the political sense of revolution and the epistemological meaning of the Copernican turn. On the nature of this "turning around" he clarifies: "The *metanoia* which the messengers of Jesus are to preach is not a message of repentance intended purely to provoke inner remorse. The disciples go throughout the land and with their *schuwu*, their "turn around" [*kehret um*], demand an *act* which turns human life upside down [*grundlegend umstürzt*]" (54). "God is the powerful promise of a turning point [*Wende*]" (10). Locating the origin of this "turning" in history, he notes, "The historical place of revolutionary apocalypticism is Israel. Israel aspires and attempts to "turn back" [*Umkehr*]. Turning back on the inside [*des Innen*] has a parallel effect on the outside [*des Außen*]" (15). *Umkehr* is also the effect of prophecy on the Roman Empire: "But the message of the Kingdom of God is particularly *good* news to the poor. This is because it brings repentance [*Umkehr*] and reversal [*Umkehrung*]. In Rome each year at the Feast of Saturnalia, the '*topsy-turvy world*' [*verkehrte Welt*] was enacted for the masses." Analyzing post-Hegelian philosophers, he traces the same distinctions: "Inwardness and outwardness are divided between Marx and Kierkegaard into worldly revolution [*weltliche Umkehrung*] and religious repentance [*religiöse Umkehr*]" (190). This ambivalence seems to be programmatic, running like a thread through the entire book, and, by and large, it expresses an antinomian desire.

Any notion of a "Christian Occident," therefore, derived solely from the conversion of pagan Rome or individual "repentance," disregards the continuing apocalyptic force of *Wende* and *Umkehr* as identified by Taubes. Likewise, any study of "tropes" would benefit from Taubes's inner history of "turns."[16] Arguably, the only one that comes close is Erich Auerbach's analysis of *figura* in *Mimesis*, showing Western realism to originate in typological interpretations of history. Also published in Bern, one year before Taubes's study, Auerbach's *Mimesis: Dargestellte Wirklichkeit in der abendländischen Literatur* (*Mimesis: The Representation of Reality in Western Literature*), takes its bearing from the apocalyptic events surrounding Christ—without ending in a Christology and thus avoiding the split into a New and an Old Testament.[17] Not surprisingly, Taubes was a lifelong admirer of Auerbach's work.

V

The fact that theological concepts underlie the project of modernity, understood in the chiliastic sense of the "new age," was amply demonstrated by Carl Schmitt in 1922 ("all significant concepts of the modern theory of the state are secularized theological concepts"), and by Karl Löwith in 1949 ("the philosophy of history is entirely dependent on theology of history, in particular on the theological concept of history as a history of fulfillment and salvation").[18] Not only is this relevant because of secularization, but also because the lynchpins of Taubes's study are "political theology," a term coined by Schmitt, and "philosophy of history." Of the three thinkers, however, only Taubes endorses the eschatological tradition from the view of the oppressed. Schmitt, an "apocalyptician of counterrevolution,"[19] shares an eschatological view of history, but he advocates *translatio imperii*—the succession of the Roman Empire by the Holy Roman Empire and the Third Reich—along with the retarding force of the katechon, described in *The Nomos of the Earth* as "the restrainer [who] holds back the end of the world."[20] Schmitt's view of history can thus be said to be *katechontic*, seeking divine legitimation of power, while Taubes's is emphatically *apocalyptic*, seeking "a theological *delegitimation* of political power as a whole."[21]

As for "philosophy of history," Löwith discusses the same genealogy of theological accounts of history in *Meaning of History* as Taubes does in *Occidental Eschatology*—the biblical view, Daniel, John, Jesus, Augustine, Joachim, Hegel, and Marx—but he does so in reverse order.[22] At first glance, many of the analyses and findings are strikingly similar, which is partly explained by the fact that the authors had read each other's work. Löwith

Catechontic

that which withholds

mentions *Abendländische Eschatologie* twice, first referring to it as a "penetrating study" and then summarizing it, in a note on Joachim, as "a comparative analysis of Hegel's philosophy of "spirit" with Joachim's prophecy."[23] Likewise, Taubes had read Löwith's study *Von Hegel bis Nietzsche* (From Hegel to Nietzsche; 1941), recalling the epiphany as follows: "The scales fell from my eyes when I understood Löwith's line [*Kurve*] from Hegel to Marx, Kierkegaard, and Nietzsche. Everything I had so far read and heard about the spiritual and intellectual history of the nineteenth century felt stale and irrelevant in comparison."[24]

The main point which distinguishes Taubes from Löwith is that the latter, through "the methodical regress from the modern" to "the ancient religious pattern," undertakes a *critique* of the secularizations of eschatology, deploring the emergence of the philosophy of history from the history of salvation. The full title, *Meaning in History: The Theological Implications of the Philosophy of History*, itself makes a programmatic distinction that seeks to purge the science of history from theological influences. Löwith's concerns, as he repeatedly points out, are shaped by his own times, when chiliasm, among other doctrines, was misappropriated by totalitarianism—for instance, when the title of *Duce* was transferred from St. Francis and ultimately from Joachim's vision of the *novus dux*.[25] What Löwith seems to confuse, however, is precisely the spiritual, apocalyptic tradition with the imperial, "katechontic" one.

This distinction is vital for apocalypticism in order to avoid the fatal cul-de-sac in which Schmitt ended up and against which Löwith warned.[26] And yet, in 1972, Taubes cautions: "If the messianic idea in Judaism is not interiorized, it can turn the 'landscape of redemption' into a blazing apocalypse. . . . For every attempt to bring about redemption on the level of history without a transfiguration of the messianic idea leads straight into the abyss."[27] Already in *Occidental Eschatology* he warns, "If the telos of the revolution collapses, so that the revolution is no longer the means but the sole creative principle, then the destructive desire becomes a creative desire. If the revolution points to nothing beyond itself, it will end in a movement, dynamic in nature but leading into the abyss [*ins leere Nichts*]" (11).

Thus, freed from the suspicion of inevitably disastrous consequences, the apocalypticism of Taubes vindicates the perspectives of *political theology* and of *philosophy of history*. As a means of critical intervention and analysis, they have remained viable for *Occidental Eschatology* in the twentieth-century tradition of Georg Lukács, Ernst Bloch, and Walter Benjamin.

VI

Rarely does Taubes reflect on his methods in *Occidental Eschatology*, but his historico-philosophical perspective allows him to reflect on two main traditions: "Theistic-transcendental metaphysics shifts the absolute freedom of eternity beyond the constraints of interdependence implied in the infinite modifications of freedom. The pantheistic-immanent viewpoint of late antiquity and German Idealism frames the relationship of interdependence as the Absolute" (6). Where his methods cannot be inferred from the argument or from his polemics, they might be mistaken for inconsistent. Thus at the very beginning, "On the Nature of Eschatology," the reader is first presented with the inside perspective of a transcendental philosopher—"The subject of inquiry is the essence of history"—immediately followed by the words of a poststructuralist *avant la lettre*: "What is the sufficient condition on which history as possibility rests?" The second paragraph then concludes from the viewpoint of a Gnostic: "It is in the Eschaton that history surpasses its limitations and is seen for what it is" (3).

Much later, in a colloquium on gnosis and surrealism in 1966, Taubes answers questions on method, as posed by Iser, Jauss, Kracauer, and Blumenberg, in what can be taken to be a late reflection on *Occidental Eschatology*: "As far as methods are concerned, I am moving between the Scylla of an individualizing interpretation and the Charybdis of an archetypal one. . . . It would be misleading to conclude from the return of Gnostic mythology that the Gnostic structure was a timeless, eternal, archetypal idea, which manifests in language without any particular historical detonator [*Zünder*]. It remains decisive *when, how* and *where* the Gnostic structure, which emerged from a particular historical situation in late antiquity, becomes 'citable.'"[28] Unmistakably, Taubes draws on Benjamin's "now time [*Jetztzeit*]," or "the now of cognizability [*Jetzt der Erkennbarkeit*]," "an enormous abbreviation of messianic time,"[29] as a way of enabling historical cognition and historiography: "only for a redeemed humanity has its past become citable in all of its moments."[30]

Applying this to *Occidental Eschatology*, we can see that the original apocalyptic-Gnostic situation is continually being "restored," though not unchanged, throughout the history of Western spirituality by dint of particular historical "detonators." These are Exodus, the Babylonian Exile, the Maccabean revolt against Hellenization, and the struggle of the Zealots against the Roman Empire, to name only the "detonators" of antiquity. The

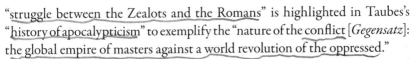

"struggle between the Zealots and the Romans" is highlighted in Taubes's "history of apocalypticism" to exemplify the "nature of the conflict [*Gegensatz*]: the global empire of masters against a world revolution of the oppressed."

Such are the sites of historical struggle, the particular "*when, how,* and *where,*" from which apocalypticism reemerges, constituting a *Jetztzeit.* It is blatantly clear that Taubes does not undertake a history of ideas, a study of motifs, or a study in religious anthropology. His is rather an extensive *Wirkungsgeschichte* ("effective history") of apocalypticism or revolutionary spirituality in the West, one which is matched in scope and audacity only by Freud's *Moses and Monotheism* (1939), the amazing history of the Jewish "phylogenetic heritage" with its work of "awakening memory-traces."[31] A discussion of and lengthy quotation from *Moses and Monotheism* concludes Taubes's lectures on Paul shortly before his death. Even though Freud is mentioned by name nowhere in *Occidental Eschatology,* psychoanalysis is "omnipresent" not only in the Gnostic struggle between *pneuma* and *psyche,* but also in the salvation history of spirituality, considering that *Heilsgeschichte* (salvation history) also implies *Heilungsgeschichte* (story of healing or healing process). Significantly, Freudian terminology is deployed in *Occidental Eschatology* at the key moment (*kairos*) when the political theology of Rome, the "Caesarian superego," was briefly superseded by early Christianity:

> In the Christian community the man of late antiquity blots out his own ego in favor of the *superego* [*Über-ich*], which, coming from beyond, descends to the people. That superego is one and the same in each member of the community, so that the community represents a collective of the spirit [*das pneumatische Wir*]. The spiritual center of man is the superego of the beyond [*das jenseitige Über-Ich*]: "It is not I who live, but Christ who lives in me."
>
> The superego of Christ is seen by the masses as opposing Caesar [*Anti-Cäsar*]. It outshines and devalues the Caesarian superego [*cäsarisches Über-Ich*]. (65)

VII

Finally, a note on the translation is in order. The difficulties in the task of translation were formidable, and only at times does the translation rise to the challenge. The nature of the difficulties can be glimpsed in the complex connotations of German words that seem easy to translate, like *abendländisch* (occidental), *Neuzeit* (modern age), or *Heilsgeschichte* (history of salvation). So whenever the English translation lacks precision or is felt to be inadequate, I have provided German interpolations. And were this practice not to stop the flow of reading, I would have made use of it more often. Needless to say, my English translation never claims to dispense with the need for the German original. I have refrained, moreover, from giving annotations or translator's notes. Failing to give annotations, a brief comment on *Neuzeit* and *Heilsgeschichte* is necessary.

The term "modern age" only inadequately translates the German *Neuzeit*, which according to Joachim begins in the thirteenth century. In fact, the German division of history into the periods of *Altertum* (ancient), *Mittelalter* (medieval), and *Neuzeit* (new or modern) is very much based on the millenarianist or Joachimite view of world history, which Hegel continued.

The scope of the German word *Heil* (salvation) is outlined by Löwith: "'Salvation' does not convey the many connotations of the German word *Heil*, which indicates associated terms like 'heal' and 'health,' 'hail' and 'hale,' 'holy,' and 'whole,' as contrasted with 'sick,' 'profane,' and 'imperfect.' *Heilsgeschichte* has, therefore, a wider range of meaning than 'history of salvation.' At the same time, it unites the concept of history more intimately with the idea of *Heil* or 'salvation.'"[32]

Finally, I am greatly indebted to Peter Routledge for assisting in the early stages of the translation and to Misha Kavka for reading the proofs. Thanks also to Elettra Stimilli for the notes of the Italian translation, which have helped the present English edition. Special thanks go to Tan Wälchli and Susanne von Lebedur for drawing my attention to Taubes long ago. And, last but not least, let me thank Hent de Vries, the series editor, and Emily-Jane Cohen, the acquisitions editor, for making this book possible.

Notes

1. Jacob Taubes, *Abendländische Eschatologie*, Beiträge zur Soziologie und Sozialphilosophie, ed. René König, vol. 3 (Bern, 1947). All page numbers that follow quotations refer to this edition.

2. Jacob Taubes, "Taubes Briefe ad Scholem," in *Der Preis des Messianusmus* ("Taubes's Letters to Scholem," in The Price of Messianism), ed. Elettra Stimilli (Würzburg, 2006), 96. All English translations are mine unless stated otherwise.

3. Jacob Taubes, *Abendländische Eschatologie* (Munich, 1991); *Escatologia occidentale*, trans. Guisi Valent, ed. Elettra Stimilli (Milan, 1997).

4. Karl Löwith, *Meaning in History: The Theological Implications of the Philosophy of History* (Chicago, 1949), 248 and 255–56.

5. Jacob Taubes, *Vom Kult zur Kultur*, ed. Aleida Assmann, Jan Assmann, and Wolf-Daniel Hartwich (Munich, 1996).

6. Jacob Taubes, *Ad Card Schmitt: Gegenstrebige Fügung* (Berlin, 1987); Jacob Taubes, *Die politische Theologie des Paulus*, ed. Aleida Assman and Jan Assmann (Munich, 1993); Jacob Taubes, *The Political Theology of Paul*, trans. Dana Hollander (Stanford, Calif., 2004). For a summary review of the lectures, see David Ratmoko, review of *The Political Theology of Paul*, by Jacob Taubes, *Umbra: A Journal of the Unconscious* (2005): 138–41.

7. Jacob Taubes, *Der Preis des Messianusmus*, ed. Elettra Stimilli (Würzburg, 2006). This is based on an earlier, Italian edition, *Il prezzo del messianesimo: Lettere di Jacob Taubes a Gershom Scholem e altri scritti*, ed. Elettra Stimilli (Macerata, 2000).

8. For a full bibliography of Taubes's oeuvre up to the year 2000, see Josef R. Lawitschka, "Eine neu-alte Bibliographie der Texte von Jacob Taubes," in *Abendlandische Eschatologie: Ad Jacob Taubes*, ed. Richard Faber et al. (Würzburg, 2001), 561–70 (hereafter cited as *Ad Jacob Taubes*).

9. Hans Urs von Balthasar, *Die Apocalypse der deutschen Seele* (Einsiedeln, 1998). On the similarities and differences between the two dissertations, see Ursula Baatz, "Ein Anstoss zur Abendländischen Eschatologie: Hans Urs von Balthasars Apokalpse der deutschen Seele," *Ad Jacob Taubes*, 321–29.

10. Cf. Elettra Stimilli's entry for Taubes in the *Encyclopedia of Religion*, 2nd ed., ed. Lindsey Jones, vol. 13 (Farmington Hills, MI, 2005).

11. Jacob Taubes, *Ad Carl Schmitt: Gegenstrebige Fügung* (Berlin, 1987), 24–25 (hereafter cited as *Ad Carl Schmitt*).

12. S.v. *eschatology*, in *Encyclopedia Britannica* (2005).

13. S.v. *Abendland*, in *Duden: Deutsches Universalwörterbuch*, 3rd ed. (Mannheim, 1996), my translation. The title of Oswald Spengler's *Untergang des Abendlandes*, mentioned by Taubes in connection to Gnosis, gives the full scope of what is entailed in *Abendland*.

14. Florian Rötzer, "Interview mit Jacob Taubes," in *Denken, das an der Zeit ist*, ed. Florian Rötzer (Frankfurt, 1987), 317. The English translation is taken from Joshua Robert Gold, "Jacob Taubes: Apocalypse from Below," *Telos* (2006): 140–56.

15. Carl Schmitt in a letter of August 14, 1959, Jacob Taubes, *Ad Carl Schmitt*, 37.

16. This may apply to even the most celebrated tropologies, such as Hayden White, *Figural Realism: Studies in the Mimesis Effect* (Baltimore, 1999).

17. See Martin Tremel's afterword to *Abendländische Eschatologie* (2007), 286.

18. Carl Schmitt, *Political Theology: Four Chapters on the Concept of Sovereignty*, 2nd ed. (Chicago, 2005); Löwith, *Meaning in History*, 1.

19. Jacob Taubes, "Carl Schmitt: Ein Apokalyptiker der Gegenrevolution," *Ad Carl Schmitt*, 7.

20. Carl Schmitt, *The Nomos of the Earth*, trans. Gary L. Ulmen (New York, 2003), 59–60. For a fine summary of the apocalyptic and catechontic views of his-

tory, see Aleida Assmann, *Zeit und Tradition: Kulturelle Strategien der Dauer* (Cologne, 1999), 20–30.

21. Marin Terpstra and Theo de Wit, "No Spiritual Investment in the World As It Is: Jacob Taubes's Negative Political Theology" in *Flight of the Gods: Philosophical Perspectives on Negative Theology*, 321 (New York, 2000).

22. "The methodical regress from the modern secular interpretations of history to their ancient religious pattern is, last but not least, substantially justified by the realization that we find ourselves more or less at the end of the modern rope. It has worn too thin to give hopeful support" (Löwith, *Meaning in History*, 3).

23. Ibid., 248 and 255–56.

24. Taubes, *Ad Carl Schmitt*, 8.

25. Löwith, *Meaning in History*, 245. For a detailed discussion, see Michael Jaeger, "Jacob Taubes und Karl Löwith: Apologie und Kritik des heilsgeschichtlichen Denkens," *Ad Jacob Taubes*, 485–508.

26. Nowhere in *Occidental Eschatology* does Taubes mention the Shoah.

27. Jacob Taubes, "The Price of Messianism," *Journal of Jewish Studies* 33, nos. 1–2 (Spring–Autumn 1972): 600.

28. Jacob Taubes, "Noten zum Surrealismus," *Vom Kult zur Kultur*, 145.

29. Jacob Taubes, "Carl Schmitt: Ein Apokalyptiker der Gegenrevolution," *Ad Carl Schmitt*, 28.

30. Walter Benjamin, "Theses on the Philosophy of History," in *Illuminations*, trans. Harry Zohn (New York, 1968), 254.

31. Sigmund Freud, *Moses and Monotheism*, vol. 23 of *The Standard Edition of the Complete Works of Sigmund Freud*, trans. James Strachey (London, 1964), 132–33.

32. This is the first note to Löwith's *Meaning in History*, 225.

Works Cited

Assmann, Aleida. *Zeit und Tradition: Kulturelle Strategien der Dauer*. Cologne, 1999.

Baatz, Ursula. "Ein Anstoss zur Abendländischen Eschatologie: Hans Urs von Balthasars Apokalpse der deutschen Seele." In *Abendländische Eschatologie: Ad Jacob Taubes*, ed. Richard Faber et al., 321–29. Würzburg, 2001.

Balthasar, Hans Urs von. *Die Apocalypse der deutschen Seele*. 3 vols. Salzburg, 1937–39.

Benjamin, Walter. "Theses on the Philosophy of History." In *Illuminations*. Trans. Harry Zohn. New York, 1968.

Duden: Deutsches Universalwörterbuch, 3rd ed. Mannheim, 1996.

Encyclopedia of Religion. 2nd ed. Ed. Lindsey Jones. Vol. 13. Farmington Hills, MI, 2005.

Freud, Sigmund. *Moses and Monotheism*. Vol. 23 of *The Standard Edition of the Complete Works of Sigmund Freud*. Trans. James Strachey. London, 1964.

Gold, Joshua Robert. "Jacob Taubes: Apocalypse from Below." *Telos* (2006): 140–56.

Lawitschka, Josef R. "Eine neu-alte Bibliographie der Texte von Jacob Taubes." In *Abendlandische Eschatologie: Ad Jacob Taubes*, ed. Richard Faber et al., 561–70. Würzburg, 2001.

Löwith, Karl. *Meaning in History*. Chicago, 1949.

Ratmoko, David. Review of *The Political Theology of Paul*, by Jacob Taubes. *Umbra: A Journal of the Unconscious* (2005): 138–41.

Rötzer, Florian. "Interview mit Jacob Taubes." In *Denken, das an der Zeit ist*, ed. Florian Rötzer, 317. Frankfurt, 1987.

Schmitt, Carl. *The Nomos of the Earth*. Trans. Gary L. Ulmen. New York, 2003.

———. *Political Theology: Four Chapters on the Concept of Sovereignty*. 2nd ed. Chicago, 2005.

Taubes, Jacob. *Abendländische Eschatologie*. Beiträge zur Soziologie und Sozialphilosophie. Ed. René König. Vol. 3. Bern, 1947.

———. *Abendländische Eschatologie*. Munich, 1991.

———. *Ad Carl Schmitt: Gegenstrebige Fügung*. Berlin, 1987.

———. *Escatologia occidentale*. Trans. Guisi Valent. Ed. Elettra Stimilli. Milan, 1997.

———. *Vom Kult zur Kultur*. Ed. Aleida Assmann, Jan Assmann, and Wolf-Daniel Hartwich. Munich, 1996.

———. *The Political Theology of Paul*. Trans. Dana Hollander. Stanford, Calif., 2004.

———. *Die politische Theologie des Paulus*. Ed. Aleida Assmann and Jan Assmann. Munich, 1993.

———. *Der Preis des Messianusmus*. Ed. Elettra Stimilli. Würzburg, 2006.

———. *Il prezzo del messianesimo: Lettere di Jacob Taubes a Gershom Scholem e altri scritti*. Ed. Elettra Stimilli. Macerata, 2000.

———. "The Price of Messianism." In *Proceedings of the Eighth World Congress of Jewish Studies*, August 16–21, 1981 (Jerusalem, 1982), 99–104.

———. "Taubes Briefe ad Scholem." In *Der Preis des Messianusmus*, ed. Elettra Stimilli, 93–124. Würzburg, 2006.

Terpstra, Marin, and Theo de Wit. "No Spiritual Investment in the World As It Is: Jacob Taubes's Negative Political Theology." In *Flight of the Gods: Philosophical Perspectives on Negative Theology*, ed. Ilse N. Bulhof and Laurens ten Kate, 319–52. New York, 2000.

White, Hayden. *Figural Realism: Studies in the Mimesis Effect*. Baltimore, 1999.

OCCIDENTAL ESCHATOLOGY

ON THE NATURE OF ESCHATOLOGY

Elements

The subject of inquiry is the essence of history. This inquiry does not concern itself with individual historical events—battles, victories, defeats, treaties, political occurrences, economic complexities, artistic and religious formations, or the results of scientific knowledge. The question about the essence of history disregards all that and looks beyond it to a single issue: How is history possible in the first place? What is the sufficient condition on which history as possibility rests?

Amid the confusion over the purpose of history, it is impossible to plumb its depths through individual events. Instead, occurrences must be disregarded and it must be asked: what makes an event history? What is history itself? When the question about the essence of history is posed from the perspective of the Eschaton, we have a position and a yardstick. It is in the Eschaton that history surpasses its limitations and is seen for what it is.

The course of history is borne away in time. Time is the life of the inner realm [*des Innen*]. In order to manifest in the outer realm [*nach Außen*], the light of the inner realm needs time. Time is the order of the world, which is split into an inner and an outer realm. It is the calibration necessary for measuring the distance between these two spheres. The nature of time is summed up by its irreversible unidirectionality [*Einsinnigkeit*].[1] From a geometrical point of view, time runs in a straight line in one direction [*einsinnig*]. The direction of this straight line is irreversible. This unidirectionality is common to both life and time. Unidirectionality and irreversibility are fundamental to their meaning. The purpose of this unidirectionality lies in the direction itself. The direction is always toward an end; otherwise, it would be directionless. The end is essentially Eschaton. This sheds light on the relationship between the order of time and the eschatological order of the world. The irreversible direction of time is grounded in the will. The "I" as will is the time of the "I." The will is directed, determining by its course the direction of time. Because time and the will move in a common direction, the first dimension of time is the future. The will detaches all that is unwanted, causing it to pass away. Likewise, time detaches as past that which is passing away [*das Vergehende*]. The second dimension of time is the past. The order of time arises from the distinction of and decision between past and future. This distinction and decision can only be brought about in *action*. Action occurs in the present, which is the medium of interference between past and future.

Saying that history is borne away in time sheds light on only one aspect of the relationship between time and history. Time and history each require the other's existence. Even time can only come into being in history. The relationship of interdependence is only possible by virtue of an identical origin. The origin of time and history is eternity. Just as history is the *interim* between eternity and eternity, so time is—if this is not too presumptuous—a stage of eternity, corresponding to that interim of history. Time emerges when the eternity of the origin is lost and the order of the world is gripped by death. The face of death is the sign of this world. Time is the Prince of Death, just as eternity is the Prince of Life. The entanglements [*Ineinander*] and disentanglements [*Auseinander*] of death and life take place in history. To conquer time eternity has to enter the temporal zone [*zeitliche Ort*] of history. History is the place where the substance of time and the substance of eternity, death and life, cross paths.

Apocalypse means, in the literal and figurative sense, revelation. All apocalypse tells of the triumph of eternity. This telling is receiving the signs of eternity. What is complete [*das Vollendete*] is glimpsed in the first sign, and what is glimpsed [*das Erschaute*] is boldly put into words in order to gesture ahead of time toward that which is not yet fulfilled. The triumph of eternity is played out on the stage of history. When, at the end of history, time, the Prince of Death, is overthrown, the *End Time* begins. The End Time is the end of time. The end is the full-filment [*Voll-endung*], as the order of time has been sublated [*aufgehoben*]. Seen from the perspective of the course of history, the end is a temporal end. Seen from the perspective of complete *full-fillment*, this temporal end is eternity. In the order of eternity, being is sublated as time. Endless infinity characterizes indifferent happening [*das gleich-gültige Geschehen*] that does not call for decision. History separates itself from this indifferent happening by placing one into the decision for truth.

History and truth have a common origin in the essence of freedom, and this binds them together. As early as Hosea, we see history described as the tragedy of freedom:

When Israel was a child, then I loved him, and out of Egypt I called my son. But when one calls them now, they turn away. . . . My people are tired of turning to me, and when one preaches to them, not one of them turns around. What should I make of you, Ephraim? Should I protect you, Israel? How can I make you like Admah? How can I treat you like Zeboiim? My heart recoils within me; my compassion grows warm and tender. I will not execute my fierce anger; I will not again destroy Ephraim: for I am God and no mortal, the Holy One in your midst, and I will not come in wrath.[2]

History contains the tragedy between God and the world as seen in mankind. Nicolay Berdyayev, whose work marks a significant point of intersection between East and West, explains the only reason for history: "God wanted freedom, because the world's original mystery, its original drama . . . is . . . the mystery and drama of freedom. That original, irreducible freedom is the key to the enigma of world history. In that freedom, not only does God manifest himself to mankind, but mankind, in response, manifests itself to God, because freedom is the source of movement, processes, conflicts, and internally experienced contradictions. Therefore, the connection between . . . freedom and . . . history is indestructible."[3]

The essence of history is freedom. History is not at the mercy of anything, because freedom is not made subservient; rather, freedom, as foundation, possesses all that is founded upon it. Freedom alone lifts mankind out of the cycle of nature into the realm of history. To exist in freedom is the only way that mankind becomes part of history. Nature, and mankind embedded in nature, have no history. Freedom, however, can only reveal itself in apo-stasy [*Ab-fall*]. For as long as freedom is caught up in the divine cycle of Nature, it is subject to the necessity of God and Nature. A *non posse peccare* is no different from a compulsion to do good. Only mankind's answer [*Ant-wort*] to the word of God, which is essentially a negative one [*ein Nein*], is evidence of human freedom. Therefore, the freedom of negation is the foundation of history.

Just as the essence of history is founded on freedom, so is the essence of truth.[4] Freedom is the act of revealing the mystery. Since truth is founded on the essence of freedom, concealment and obscurity become possible, too. Forgetting the mystery, the world is fashioned according to the latest designs; the constructions of the world block the path to the mystery, so that there is no escape from the labyrinth of constructed routes. The labyrinth of this world is the state of error [*Stätte der Irre*]. We have not just begun to err, but are constantly doing so, because we have always been in error.[5] Error is not some well-defined district on the outskirts, but is part of the world's very constitution. But if this error which holds sway throughout the world is experienced for what it is, then the way to avoid it [*sich nicht zu beirren lassen*] becomes clear.[6] Knowledge of error, as error, is the pathway to escaping from error on the way to the revelation of the truth.

The relationship of interdependence between time and history, the identical origin of which has been recognized as eternity, can now be completely unsealed. This relationship is rooted in the true essence of freedom. It follows that eternity is the element of freedom. Being free means, above all, to be free "for oneself" [*frei 'für sich' sein*]. Everything which is not free in itself is shaped by freedom. But being free means, fundamentally, to be free "from something." Everything which is free is, in this sense, based on necessity. Ultimately, therefore, freedom is inextricably constitutive and constituted.[7] The question is: How does finite freedom, which is an element of time, relate to absolute freedom, an element of eternity? This relationship can be determined in theistic-transcendental, pantheistic-immanent, and atheistic-materialistic terms.

Theistic-transcendental metaphysics shifts the absolute freedom of eternity beyond the constraints of interdependence implied in the infinite modifications of freedom. The pantheistic-immanent viewpoint of late antiquity and German Idealism frames the relationship of interdependence as the Absolute.[8] The atheistic-materialistic ideology shatters the pantheistic fusion of Idealism, separating liberal reason from the necessity found in reality [*notwendige Wirklichkeit*]. The Hegelian left sees reality as sublogical and subjects the necessity found in reality to the constraints of interdependence of both kinds of freedom found in eternity. The necessity found in reality must first of all come into line with liberal reason.

Late antiquity and German Idealism merge God and the world in an aesthetic-religious way, resulting in a strange interchangeability of "possible" and "real" that characterizes Plotin as well as Fichte and Hegel.[9] The possible has already become a reality, even if only "as a concept." Theistic-transcendental and atheistic-materialistic philosophy are apo-calyptic because they are only complete when revelation has taken its course. From a theistic-transcendental viewpoint, the Eschaton reveals the central point of God and the world from above; from an atheistic, materialistic viewpoint, the center is revealed from below. Both perspectives require a *leap*: from above into the absurdity below; from below, the realm of necessity, up into the realm of freedom. The situations of Marx and Kierkegaard correspond to one another in this way. Knowledge of causal necessity and belief in freedom are irreconcilable, yet necessity and freedom "must" meet in a moment uncoupled from time. Some*where* freedom *must* break the closed circle of the world. However, in both modifications "must" [*das Muss*] assumes a different meaning, depending on which one applies. Marx wants to create the absolute out of a mankind subject to natural frailty; Kierkegaard relies on a God with Whom nothing is impossible.[10]

Revelation is the subject of history; history is the predicate of revelation.[11] Revelation is the fire which casts light upon the clearing [*Lichtung*] between God and the world. The burning fire reaches the center of heaven; the world is darkness and gloom. The voice of God, which is the very essence of revelation, is to be *heard* in this fire, but has no visible form. It sprays flames of fire. Mankind cannot break through to God without being scorched. It can only see God from behind, but not face to face. Nobody can see the face of God and live.

God is seen face to face in the light of the creation in paradise, "where that which is separated in nature and history burns in eternal and original unity with one flame"[12] and must, in the aeon of sin, forever seek flight between creation and redemption. The separation of nature and history is indicative of the state of sin, as the oneness of God and the world is torn apart, and the face of death weighs heavily on the world. The face of Adam Kadmon is destroyed. He is afraid and knows he is naked and exposed before the face of God. Not until after he has sinned, when the glow of the original state of paradise has cooled, does Adam *hear* God's voice.[13] God stands at the gate of the world and throws questions into the world. The heavenly voice calls out to the world.[14] The word of God is the call which, in the aeons of the night, awakens mankind from sleep, because the heavenly voice recalls the origin of Adam, that which was before history [*das Vor der Geschichte*], and promises redemption, the sequel to history [*das Nach der Geschichte*]. In the state of sin, in the interim between creation and redemption, Adam can only "hear" and "believe."[15] Revelation is the light in the aeon of sin, since Adam only knows in part, because he now sees through a glass in a dark word.[16] In the light of redemption, Adam recognizes, just as he himself has been recognized, face to face.[17]

History is the source of revelation for mankind and his pathway through time.[18] In the aeon of sin, existence begins as time, aiming toward death. Time contains the principle which brings death. Time is fragmented into past, present, and future.[19] Like specters, the separate parts rise up and devour each other. The present becomes an unreal boundary between the "no-longer" of the past and the "not-yet" of the future. Time is not the place of life, but contains the pestilential smell of death, and plunges life into the Sheol of the past. Not until the End Time, at the end of time, when transience itself passes away, will eternity triumph over the deadly principle of time. It is the work of magic, whose last offshoot is art, that ties an eternal moment to the present time. In the aeon of sin, paradise is conjured up, and the cherubim keeping watch at the gate are disregarded. From this perspective, both reality and its very significance are overlooked. From this perspective, everything can be internally reconciled, because no action is needed to break the spell of interiority [*Innerlichkeit*].

It is in their critique of the "world" that the transcendent-theistic and the atheistic-materialistic philosophies of Kierkegaard and Marx intersect again. Their critique engages with the concept of reality as Hegel formulated it, and strikes at the world of bourgeois society. Kierkegaard constantly opposes the claims of idealistic philosophy that reality can be grasped through reason: "Whenever one hears philosophers speak about reality, it is just as misleading as when one looks through the window of a junk-dealer and reads the words on a sign: 'Get your washing wrung here.' If you wanted to have the washing put through the wringer, you would be deceived. The sign is only there to be sold."[20] Kierkegaard is always at variance with Hegel on the same topic: reality cannot be pressed into a system; any section of text that treats reality within a system is absurd. This is the very point with which Marx engages in his critique of Hegel. His arrows are aimed at the alleged unity of reason and reality, of being [*Wesen*] and existence. Hegel reconciles idea and reality, but only as concepts. In so doing, existence becomes mystified into an idea, and Hegel's "idealistic" exposition changes into the "most crass materialism."[21] "When philosophy imposes its intellectual will on the phenomena of the world, it reduces the system to an abstract totality... breaking down spiritual and intellectual autonomy [*innere*

Selbstgenügsamkeit]. What was inner light becomes a consuming flame turned outward."[22]

When Marx philosophizes in the *absence of* God [*ohne Gott*], and Kierkegaard in the *presence of* God [*vor Gott*], they have one mutual premise: the disintegration of God and the world. World-history, which Hegel still understands as theo-dicy, is understood by Marx and Kierkegaard as history of the "world." In the presence of *kairos*, world history is downgraded to prehistory. The End Time and primordial time intersect in *kairos*. Because the history of the Christian world is at an end, Kierkegaard believes it possible to connect with the early age of the Christian aeon. Only after Christ, after the end of the Christian era, is the *following after* Christ [*Nach-folge Christi*] possible. For Marx the "early communist community" is realized in the "realm of freedom." However, this realm of freedom does not evolve "naturally" out of the realm of necessity. Kierkegaard and Marx require a miraculous *leap*. For Kierkegaard this is a leap back over the chasm of world history, "disposing of eighteen hundred years as if they had never existed," so as to become spiritually and intellectually [*innerlich*] "contemporary" with Christ.[23] For Marx this is a leap from the realm of necessity into the realm of freedom.

Freedom and Revolution

The question of freedom is the fundamental theme in apocalypticism, and all of its motifs point to the turning point, when the structure of this world prison will burst apart. This turn does not refer in the first instance, or exclusively, to the existing social order. Apocalypticism is at first not concerned with changing the structure of society, but directs its gaze away from this world. If revolution were to mean only replacing an existing society with a better one, then the connection between apocalypticism and revolution is not evident. But if revolution means opposing the totality of this world with a new totality that comprehensively founds anew in the way that it negates [*neu stiftet wie sie verneint*], namely, in terms of the basic foundations, then apocalypticism is by nature revolutionary.

Apocalypticism negates this world in its fullness. It brackets the entire world negatively. Law and fate are the foundations of the cosmos. But since classical antiquity, the cosmos has always been represented as a harmonious structure.[24] And because law and order rule the cosmos, because fate is the highest power in the cosmos, *for this reason*, concludes apocalypticism in a monstrous inversion [*ungeheurer Umkehrung*], the cosmos is an abundance of that which is bad. The world is a totality which keeps itself distinct from the divine, forming an auto-nomy in relation to God. Therefore, the world has its own spirit, its God. As the world does not contain its real source of power but is determined by an opposite pole, God is also held in tension at a distance from it. This relationship of tension is mutual and determines both poles. The world is that which stands in opposition to God [*das Gegengöttliche*], and God is that which stands in opposition to the world [*das Gegenweltliche*].[25] God is an unknown stranger. When he appears in the world, he is *new* to the world. The "new God" is the unknown God, a stranger in the world. He is nonexistent in the world. The "new God" is, according to Basilides, the "nonexistent" God. God thereby does not vanish into empty abstractions, because the "nonexistent" God has enormous power. The "nonexistent" God is an annihilating God [*nichtender Gott*] who crushes the world [*umklammert und ver-nichtet*].[26] The "nonexistent" God puts the being of the world in question by contesting the entire validity [*Gültigkeit*] and finality [*Endgültigkeit*] of what exists. Therefore, the gospel of the God who is distant, unknown, and even nonexistent, as proclaimed by Gnosticism, can be the universally stirring slogan for nihilistic, revolutionary longing.[27] The "nonexistent" God in the world and against the world sanctions the nihilistic viewpoint mankind has of the world. The "nonexistent" God, and that means the "not-yet-existing" God, is the powerful promise of a turning point. God will annihilate the world and then appear in his might.

Apocalypticism is revolutionary because it beholds the turning point not in some indeterminate future but entirely proximate. Apocalyptic prophecy thus focuses on the future and yet is fully set in the present. The telos of the revolution binds the forces of chaos, which otherwise would burst all forms and overreach established boundaries. Even revolution has its forms and is "formalized," particularly when it shatters the rigid structures of the positivity of the world. The apocalyptic principle combines within it a form-destroying [*gestalt-zerstörend*] and a forming [*gestaltend*] power. Depending on the situation and the task, only one of the two components emerges, but neither can be absent. If the demonic, destructive element is missing, the petrified order, the prevailing positivity of the world cannot be overcome. But if the "new covenant" fails to shine through in this destructive element,[28] the revolution inevitably sinks into empty nothingness [*leere Nichts*].

If the telos of the revolution collapses, so that the revolution is no longer the means but the sole creative principle, then the destructive desire becomes a creative desire. If the revolution points to nothing beyond itself, it will end in a movement, dynamic in nature but leading into the abyss [*ins leere Nichts*]. A "nihilistic revolution" does not pursue any goal [telos], but takes its aim from the "movement" itself and, in so doing, comes close to satanic practice.[29]

But this also reveals the tragic nature of genuine revolution. While pursuing the absolute telos, it finds no adequate shape or manifestation. And yet utopia can only become reality in topos. The revolutionary principle lurches from one manifestation to the next. Each time something is implemented in reality, it threatens the absolute demand of telos. It is the absolute nature of the demand which brings about a state of "permanent" revolution. The feelings of agitation which the revolutionary principle generates are shared by its supporters. It drives prophets and apocalypticists from place to place. The many journeys of Jesus present the greatest of difficulties for exegetes.[30] It would also be superficial to attribute the continuous displacement of modern revolutionaries solely to the eviction orders received from the police. Fate is operating unseen behind the rational surface of events and the expediencies of the moment.

Spirit and History

A critical turning point arises when the whole gamut of Israel's history is thrown into relief against the mythological realm of the ancient Orient and classical antiquity. All myth reverberates with the cycle of birth and death. Life runs its course between birth and death, and death is already implanted at birth: "Wherever your birth comes from, there your death returns by necessity."[31] In the cycle of life only that which comes from and returns to the origin can come to fruition. Myth is the "narrative" of origin. Myth answers the question of *whence*.[32] The questions of whence and whither coincide in the eternal return of the same. Origin, conceived as the coincidence [*Ineins*] of whence and whither, designates the very center of the mythical world. The all-embracing power of origin is nature, because it keeps [*bannt*] all events within a cycle in which everything flourishes and fades. The gods of nature are the Baals, and the most holy of the gods of Baal is Dionysus.

Animal life is founded upon the vegetative basis of origin. It, too, runs its course in the cycle of birth and death. Equally, mankind is a *zoon politikon*, and its social organization is grounded in blood and soil [*Blut und Boden*]. Blood and soil are elements of nature. The cycle of nature is driven by the power of origin. The bounds can be drawn narrower or wider, but the cycle remains. So, in the mythical world, time is under the dominance of space. But when time is seen as a cycle, or as a circle among circles, its essence is not evident. For it is the essence of time to move forward, irreversibly straining toward something new while inquiring into its purpose.[33] To inquire into the purpose is to break the cycle of nature and burst apart the structure of the eternal return.

The spirit inquires into the purpose of things [*das Wozu*], as it is not confined by the power of origin. The eternal return of the same is dominated by eros, which draws together what is above and what is below, and completes nature's cycle. By contrast, in the realm of time moving irreversibly in one direction, it is the *spirit* that rules, as it presses forward. Therefore, the spirit is strictly bound up with time.

It explains that the *age of the Spirit* [*Geist-Zeit*] (Joachim and the Spirituals) and the *spirit of the age* [*Zeit-Geist*] (Hegel and left-wing Hegelians) have their foundations in the essence of history. It follows that history is the element of the spirit. Just as history is the element of the spirit, so too is the spirit the element of history. History only comes into being in the spirit. Spirit and history are necessary for each other's existence. This relationship of interdependence is only possible because, in spirit, eternity is visible in time.

Mankind shares the condition of being thrown into existence [*Geworfenheit des Ursprungs*] with nature and its cycle of necessity. But we confront this condition of being thrown with the pro-ject [*Ent-wurf*] of the spirit. This project is human *freedom*, of which the spirit is an essential component [*im Element*]. History is the project of the spirit; it surpasses the bounds of nature. The power of the origin and rootedness in space break down when it comes to Israel. Thus, Israel is able to become a "people without space" [*Volk ohne Raum*]. It does not perish because it knows itself to be a "people of time" [*Volk der Zeit*] who have been uprooted from their rootedness in space.[34] Here time comes into its own and is elevated beyond space. Time is directed toward something which has not yet been but will be, and which, when reached, will not be lost again. The world as time is moving toward a "new heaven and a new earth." The *novum* [*das Neue*] exceeds the cycle of origin. The *novum* is in the element of history. Seen from the perspective of history, origin becomes the *beginning*, followed by the middle and the end.[35] History itself is the center between creation and redemption.

The world as history has its roots [*Schwerpunkt*] not in the eternal present of nature but rather is nurtured by the original creation and directed toward the final redemption. The individual event serves the passage from creation to redemption. It does not have any significance in itself, but reveals a glimpse of the order of creation, pointing forward to the order of redemption. An event is always related to the Eschaton. The Eschaton is the *once* [*das Einst*] in a double temporal sense: the that-which-once-was [*das Einst*] of the creation, axiology, and the that-which-one-day-will-be [*das Einst*] of redemption, teleology.

An event is never just axiological or teleological in relation to its Eschaton, but is inextricably a union of both. The dialectical relationship between axiology and teleology, the focal points of the eschatological ellipse, is constantly threatened by the two poles gaining independence. On the one hand, the axiological pole of creation can be released into the objective sphere of eternal value.[36] Historicism, while indulging in convoluted language and theological embellishment, tends to equate axiology and value: all ages are equally near to God. This statement always collapses into another: all events are of equal value [*gleich gültig*] and therefore indifferent [*gleichgültig*]. This indifferent proximity to God overlooks the essence of history as the pathway to redemption. The ideology of progress, on the other hand, isolates the teleological pole when it devalues each moment of history in favor of an ideal, which it finds in the infinite instead of in the eternal.[37] The ideology of progress overlooks the essence of history, which is the pathway from creation. Apocalyptic ontology is only possible in the dialectic of axiology and teleology. An event always allows the once-was [*das Einst*] of creation to shine through: an axiological relationship. Because that once-was [*Einst*] of creation is glimpsed in the event, it also points forward to the one-day [*Einst*] of redemption: a teleological relationship. Therefore, history is in the middle between creation and redemption. History only reveals its essence as eschatology. In the once-was of creation history has its beginning, and in the one-day of redemption it comes to its end. The interim between creation and redemption is the pathway of history. The *procedere* from creation to redemption is salvation. History, therefore, is necessarily the history of salvation [*Heilsgeschichte*].

Memory is the foundation of history. Because without it present, past, and future would be cut off forever. Historical knowledge is an act of memory. The outward objective event is internalized by memory: man recalls within himself the depths of time. Like a gramophone record he captures all the heights and depths, each *forte* and *piano* of world history. History does not just happen objectively in macrocosm, it also comes about in man as microcosm. Subject and object receive their identity from history.[38] All revolts, wars, victories, and defeats, all storms, fires, and earthquakes, are just mankind's stage [*aufgeschlagene Bühne des Menschen*]; they are instrumental in bringing about the genesis of mankind. The memory is the organ which embeds man into history. Memory mirrors the confrontation of time and eternity on the battlefield of history and recalls the final victory of eternity. That is why memory is an eschatological area, a powerful force in the drama of eschatology.

During Israel's festival of the New Year, which resounds with the ancient celebration of Yahweh's enthronement, God is celebrated as King of the World. The drama of the enthronement of God is played out in three acts: coronation, commemoration, redemption. The second act of the drama of the enthronement of God is "commemoration," from which the day gets its name: the Day of Commemoration. God, who is called to be king, recalls His covenant with man and redeems him. God is the absolute memory and with Him there is no forgetting. Remembering is the positive principle, against which forgetting stands as the negative principle. Remembering belongs to Israel, the masculine pole, whereas forgetting corresponds to the feminine pole. *Sikaron*, memory, is related to *sakar*, masculine; and *nakab*, containing many holes like a sieve, is related to *nkeba*, feminine.

Memory bursts the bounds set by mortal nature. "Through memory" ["*Zum Gedächtnis*"] mankind goes beyond mortality. The drive toward immortality is closely associated with memory. The drive toward immortality produces the fear of death. Memory uncouples an event from the stream of time. An event can be released from the time element in this way because it is set fast and does not disappear in the course of time. Through memory we are aware that time is *passing*; this is only possible because time is conquered by memory. Because memory stands *outside* time, it can be aware of its transitory nature. Without eternity there would be no capacity to reflect on time in this way.

 In eschatology memory represents the principle which enters into battle with time in the name of eternity. In Israel, to forget means falling away and dying. The message of Deuteronomy turns on the theme of forgetting: "Beware lest you forget the Lord who led you out of slavery into the land of Egypt."[39] "Remember and do not forget" is the leitmotif of Moses' speech in Deuteronomy and of all prophetic speech.

History is the plane on which God and the world intersect. History is the path of God and He shows Himself at work in it. History is also world history. As the midpoint between God and the world, mankind thus becomes the agent of history. Revelation of the world and revelation of God is in its precise sequence only a story, like a spark jumping from pole to pole: the unveiling of mankind.[40] The story aims at union with God. Only the world which restricts God can reveal the principle of freedom. The world was created for the express purpose of revealing freedom. God's totality [*das All Gottes*] should become world, so that in *freedom* God may be all in all. Mankind is to entrust the world to God, who abolishes all worldly dominion, authority, and power. But when everything is subject to mankind, from that moment it will also be subject to Him who has subjected everything to mankind, so that God may be all in all.[41] Only through the process of redemption does God become the *all in one* for which man has been searching.[42] Man has always claimed its presence and has been engaged in this search throughout the ages and in all places, but could never establish whether it existed because it was nowhere to be found and did not yet exist.

Dialectic is the signpost on the pathway of history, from creation to redemption. The inherent possibility of dialectic springs from the essence of freedom. Freedom only exists where it allows for the freedom of negation. History is dialectical because it reveals the "enormous power of negation."[43] The power of negation compels one to accept the antithesis, and explains why the Kingdom of God is not realized at the stage of the thesis. The difference between the thesis of the omnipotence of God, *deus sive natura*, and the synthesis, that God may be *all in all*, is the principle of freedom. The gap between thesis and antithesis reveals the principle of freedom as history. The thesis is the totality [*das All*], when God and the world are not yet differentiated. The antithesis is the separation of God and the world: synthesis is the union of God and the world through mankind, so that in *freedom* God may be all in all.

god or nature
Spinoza's
Pantheism

Israel as the Place of Revolution

The historical place of revolutionary apocalypticism is Israel. Israel aspires and attempts to "turn back" ["*Umkehr*"]. Turning back on the inside [*des Innen*] has a parallel effect on the outside [*des Außen*]. The pathos of revolution defines Israel's attitude to life.[44] Israel's hope culminates in the sovereignty of God alone. In the introduction to the ceremonial enthronement of God as king, at the beginning of the year and at the end of every service, the

Jewish community prays: "We hope that we will change the world through the rule of the Almighty."[45] God's voice resounds as a call to action, to make ready the wilderness of this world for the Kingdom.[46] Saying "we want to act and hear," the tribes seal the Covenant with God on Sinai.[47]

 If Hellas is called the "eye of the world," Israel can be said to be the "the ear of the world."[48] Israel hears God's voice in revelation. Moses addresses the tribes with "Hear, O Israel." In the *keriath schma*, in "the calling to hear" the Jew daily assumes the "yoke of the Kingdom of Heaven."[49] The true story of Israel is one of vacillation between obedience and disobedience toward God.

Israel is the restless element in world history, the leavening that first actually produces history. It is initially released from sojourn in Babylon and Egypt. The cultures on the banks of the Nile and in Mesopotamia seem to have arisen once and for all. Mesopotamia resembles a stone wall that is continually being repaired but that essentially remains the same. Egypt seems to have fossilized into a stone hieroglyph. It is not as if there has been a dearth of events. Cruel events abound throughout these countries, but the spiritual and intellectual repercussions of these fateful happenings are extremely slight. Life is caught up in the eternal recurrence of the same [*die ewige Wiederkehr des Gleichen*]. At the *end* of Europe's history, when the Christian, apocalyptic reserves have been exhausted, the symbol of the eternal recurrence of the same comes up again. Israel breaks through the cycle of this endless repetition, opening up the world as history for the first time. History is for Israel the pivot around which everything revolves. The festivals which Israel retains from its Egyptian, Babylonian, and Canaanite ambit assume a totally new meaning because of their historical foundations.[50] Oriental mythology, which describes the endless repetition of nature's cycle, is inscribed into Israel's historical fate. Some of the motifs of these myths are used for a sketch of the history of mankind. The world's ages within the cosmic year, taken from the realm of astral mythology, are recast as aeons of a *unique* strand of history.[51] In apocalypticism the aeons are stages in the drama of history which lead up to the end. Even the correspondence between primeval times and End Time is found in the Oriental myths depicting the eternal cycle. The yearnings and hopes of apocalypticism echo these mythological motifs. However, these mythological motifs merely grace the one purposeful path of history; they are only functional parts of the world historical drama. Apocalypticism exploits the whole Oriental world of fairy tales to give substance to its ideas. It compresses torn, fragmentary motifs, complete stories, individual pieces from myths into a tragedy of the world's fate, encompassing all [*das All*]: God, mankind, and the world.

Paganism [*Heidentum*] is nationhood [*Völkertum*]. That is the essential meaning of the Hebrew and Greek words used to translate it. The rise of different peoples, confusion over language, and the birth of the gods are all linked with one another.[52] Genesis associates the rise of different peoples with the appearance of different languages.[53] The formation of different nations is seen to result in a confusion over language. Mankind foresees the division: "Let us build a town and a tower, the top of which will reach to heaven, so that we make a name for ourselves! Otherwise, we will be scattered over all the lands." "To make a name for oneself" means nothing more than "to become one people."[54] But there is no escaping fate: human language becomes confused, and the peoples scatter across all the lands. "It is not a thorn prick from the *outside*, but one of inner turmoil, the feeling of not being the whole of humanity but only a part of it; not belonging anymore simply to the One but being passed on to a particular god or gods. That was the feeling which drove the nations on from country to country, from coast to coast, till each one felt individually isolated and separated from all that was foreign, and had found the place intended and suitable for it."[55]

The revelation of God can no longer take place in humanity, because the latter is so torn and scattered [*zerstreut*]. Nor can it take place in a nation [*Volk*] because everything bearing that name has fallen prey to other gods. It can only happen in one race [*Geschlecht*] which has not trodden the same path as other nations, and knows it is still covenanted to the God Who was there at the beginning of time.[56] The revelation of God wrenches the race of Abraham from its homeland, its birthplace and ancestral home, and promises a land "which I shall show you."[57] Abraham is a stranger on this earth, a foreigner to the lands and nations he meets. Abraham's race regards itself not as belonging to the nations, but as a nonnation. This is exactly what the name Hebrew means. "Abraham who is called *Ibri*, that is: Abraham, belonging to those who pass through, having no fixed abode, living as a nomad as the patriarch was still known in Canaan: because he who does not bide a while anywhere, is only a stranger, a wanderer."[58] This *opposition* to the world, if it was not intended to be built on air alone [*im leeren Nichts gründen*], had to be supported by a God who was also estranged from the world.[59]

The revelation of God takes place in the *wilderness*. It is there that Israel becomes the people of God. It is there that its fate is forged and the people of the wilderness become the pioneers of Israel's path to the Kingdom of Heaven in history.[60] Canaan is always a Promised Land for Israel—their promise. The tribes are continually surrounded and infiltrated by other nations in Canaan, but the message of prophecy keeps the nomadic ideal alive. Israel is constantly reminded that it is not "Lord" of the land. The word of prophecy continually threatens Israel with exile.

Exile is the wilderness state of the nations in which Israel wanders till the end of its days. In fact, exile repeats the wilderness state because the tribal groups, which were the basis of community prior to becoming settlers, reemerge. Just as in the wilderness the desert tribes focused on the Promised Land, so too was life in exile only possible through the hope of redemption.[61] Israel is torn from the earth in exile and, contrary to natural growth, its roots are planted upward. Its God is also torn from the earth in exile, and all ties are severed which linked him with the Canaan-Palestinian folk religion, with the numerous local gods, ancestral cults, and holy prostitution. In exile, the invisible God of the wilderness becomes the God of the world who directs world history. Jewish apocalypticism receives its eschatological impetus from the fact that the God of the world also remains Israel's God.

The threads of prophecy, apocalypticism, and law merge in Ezekiel, the prophet of exile. Ezekiel's work continues that of Ezra, whom the Talmud tradition compares to Moses: "Ezra was worthy to have brought the Torah, had Moses not preceded him."[62] Modern literary criticism tries to show that Ezra wrote the Torah.[63] Like Moses, Ezra molds Israel. The Torah becomes the foundation of the Jewish community. It was Muhammad who was the first to say so and the Jews have been the people of the book ever since, a people rooted in the logos: the word. Philo praises the law of Moses because it is the law of the wilderness, set apart from all natural criteria. The yardstick of the law, which was revealed in the wilderness, is the will of God, not a human calibration [*Vermessung*].

When Josephus describes Israel's law as applied to state and society, he coins a word which admirably encompasses Israel as a political idea: theocracy.[64] In Israel, God claims lordship over the whole of life, proclaiming his will in a law which, while regulating cult and custom, determines state and society.[65] Concerning its idea of theocracy, Israel shares common ground with Arabia, where there is a similar tendency to rebel against any form of human authority. The Bedouin tribes in particular, the desert nobles, share this characteristic belligerence against social order. They are organized into a "community without authority," in a similar fashion to Israel's theocratic community.[66] A Bedouin chief never calls himself king; at the very most he can be *Said al Arab*, spokesman of the Arabs. According to an early Islamic viewpoint, God alone is worthy of having dominion over mankind.[67] A human *mulk*, a monarchy, would be anti-God. Even at the time of the Abbasid, the caliphate's lawyers had to seek refuge in legal fiction to reconcile the concept of a hereditary monarchy with feelings deeply embedded in the nation's consciousness.

The Bedouin characteristics of the seminomadic tribes of Israel which migrated from Egypt explain why they did not elect their human leader as king. Theocracy is built upon the anarchical elements in Israel's soul.[68] It expresses the human desire to be free from all human, earthly ties and to be in covenant with God. The first tremors of eschatology can be traced to this dispute over divine or earthly rule.[69] The concept of theocracy can stir up passionate action. Viewed in terms of immanence, theocracy is a utopian community. Israel played a leading part in the revolutionary movement because the transcendent, political concept of the nation was inevitably geared to the life of the world. It had the religious resources needed for the passion of revolution. At the time of the ghettos, when the Jews were cut off from the spiritual life of Europe, the Old Testament was the foundation for all religious, revolutionary movements, up to their liberation [*Emanzipation*]. It was closer to the revolutionary sects of the late Middle Ages than to the New Testament. There is evidence that the Old Testament was preferred by the Taborites right through to the Puritans.[70] Since the liberation, the part played by the Jews in the revolutionary movement has been decisive, as names like Moses Hess, Karl Marx, Ferdinand Lassalle, Rosa Luxemburg, Max Adler, Otto Bauer, Eduard Bernstein, and Leo Trotsky attest.

In the world seen as history, mankind stands in the middle between God and the world. As far as the world is concerned he is oriented entirely toward God; as far as God is concerned, he is oriented entirely toward the world. The nature of mankind is determined by this duality [*doppelte Fluten*] within him: with God he is entirely divine, with the world he is entirely worldly; he is betwixt and between. Mankind is bound to the world by "the ties of nature." He is bound to God by a *Covenant*. He is placed midway between the ties of nature and the divine Covenant.

The Sinai Covenant is a royal covenant.[71] Israel chose Yahweh not just as a god to protect the federation, but as a king. God as king is the God with us [*mit-gehende Gott*], the guide along the path: an idea which is associated with kingship in the Orient. Baal is the owner and inhabitant of a place, but Yahweh wanders with the tribes in the wilderness. The "Lord of Hosts" leads the earthly and heavenly hosts,[72] and is not confined to any place.[73] Prophecy recalls the period in the wilderness when Yahweh himself as king led the Israeli flocks and Israel placed no reliance on horses or their riders. In the wilderness period, when Israel was a community without sovereign power, prophecy was the norm. In the dispute with earthly kingship the prophetic formula of "King Yahweh Sabbaoth," "Lord of Hosts," already includes the claim that Yahweh alone is the legitimate king in Israel.[74] Yahweh as King of Israel extends, without any loss of meaning, to King of the World. The contradiction between the reality of the godless world and the idea of the Kingdom of God in the world brings forth eschatology.[75]

The dispensation of the Covenant defines the community of Israel, which Max Weber describes as a confederacy bound by an oath [*Eidgenossenschaft*].[76] Bands of seminomadic tribes easily split up and it is only the binding Covenant which proves to be a workable foundation for political and social organization.[77] This form of covenant community brings about the ethos of freedom which is commensurate with priestly and Talmudic law. The Code of Hammurabi lays down that a slave who tries to run away shall have his ear cut off.[78] In the Torah the law concerning slavery decrees that an Israelite slave who has no intention of leaving his master after six years because he says, "I love my master, my wife and my children, and I will not go out a free person," so shall his master keep this slave at his "door and doorpost" and pierce his ear with an awl, and he shall serve him for life."[79] The Talmud explains this law:[80]

What makes the ear different from all other parts of the body? The Holy One said: the ear heard my voice on Sinai when I said: "the people of Israel are servants,"[81] but not the slaves of slaves, therefore the ear of him shall be pierced who went and placed himself under a lord. What is the difference between the door and the doorpost and all the other objects in the house? The Holy One said: door and doorpost bore testimony in Egypt of how I passed over the lintel and the two doorposts and I said: "for the children of Israel will be my servants,"[82] not the slaves of slaves. I led them out of slavery into freedom, but this slave went and placed himself under a lord, that is why he shall be pierced before them.

The Covenant between God and Israel is also present whenever misfortune threatens to undermine their faith, because all misfortune derives from the will of God. Yahweh also uses the opponents of Israel as instruments so that the humiliation or even the collapse of Israel cannot be construed as defeat for Yahweh. This conclusion may appear simple, but it is by no means obvious; on the contrary, it is revolutionary and new.[83] One might have anticipated that the normal reaction would be: the foreign gods are stronger or Yahweh can no longer help his people.

Prophecy abandons this popular conception and sets out how Yahweh himself deliberately brings misfortune upon his people. The theodicy of misfortune within prophecy takes for granted the Covenant and rebellion against it. The concept of rebellion does not otherwise occur in the Middle Eastern world.[84] Covenant-rebellion-misfortune are syllogisms of the prophetic message. But misfortune [*Unheil*] never means the end; prophecy never fails to predict salvation [*Heil*], even if it is far off and only comes to a remaining few.[85] Israel's popular eschatology, which revolves around the day of Yahweh with a possible echo of the memory of Sinai, is primarily an expectation of salvation. The dark side of salvation is also present but it is relegated to other nations. It is not until the prophetic message arrives that the old equation is broken down: Israel = salvation, the other nations = disaster. This recasts eschatology as a sketch of history, comprising a chain of unfortunate and fortunate events [*Unheil und Heil*].[86] Prophetic eschatology, with its definite imminence,[87] differs from the vague indefiniteness of popular eschatology, which does not affect daily life. In prophecy disaster is near at hand; in the belief that the world is coming to an end, prophecy devalues the life and ways of this world.[88] "Whenever they advise against alliances, whenever they turn against the vain, proud nature of this world, when Jeremiah is celibate, there is the same underlying reason as in the commandment of Jesus: render unto Caesar what is Caesar's, and unto God what is God's. Paul's commandment is similar when he says that each should remain in the state he is in, and that they should remain married or unmarried; those who have a wife should act as if they did not. All these present things are completely inconsequential because the end is imminent."[89] The expectation of the end molds the essence of prophecy and gives power to its proclamation. Even though salvation is delayed, whoever announces that the end is coming shares the same passionate faith as the others who have done so—from Daniel to Jesus and from Bar Kochba to Sabbatai Zvi. The world of apocalypticism is to be found in this forward-looking expectation [*Spannung nach vorn*]. These passionate people, whom Israel produced, live in a state of constant expectation [*steten Harren*].[90]

The Orbit of Apocalypticism

A new principle is announced in the prophecy of Israel: the spirit of apocalypticism. This new canon expresses itself in apocalyptic visions and the formulations of Gnostic systems.[91] The apocalyptic attitude to the world [*Weltgefühl*] bursts with enormous force into the wide sphere of Aramaic languages at one and the same time.[92] This apocalyptic principle struggles for new expression, but its fate is dependent on the influence of Hellenism, which it encountered in its Western offshoots.[93] To a large extent, therefore, this new way of experiencing the world is not formulated independently through its own symbols. The spirit of apocalypticism and gnosis has to construct its symbolism out of the already sterile bank of concepts available within Hellenism.[94] The Hellenistic veneer over the Aramaic world threatens the development of the apocalyptic logos, which thus takes a long time to become aware of itself. This veneer [*Überlagerung*] still makes it difficult to recognize clearly the apocalyptic, Gnostic spirit, and even now many scholars are misled by the implications arising from the use of the Greek alphabet.

The area influenced by apocalypticism and gnosis spreads further eastward via the heathen, Greek group of Hermetic and Neoplatonic philosophy, the Christian Greek group of nonsynoptic writings in the New Testament, the fathers of the early Church in their battle against heresy, and various apocryphal apocalypses. In the centuries around the turning point of history [*die Wende der Zeiten*], Mandaean and Manichaean literature arises against a background of turmoil in the East. This literature belongs to the sphere of the Aramaic languages. However, fragments of Manichaean material find their way to Central Asia, and even to China, in the course of the Manichaean mission. This Eastern literature is significant because it attests to an apocalyptic, Gnostic stratum which was not subject to the "pseudomorphosis" [*Pseudomorphose*]. At the same time, this reference to the "pseudomorphosis" recalls Oswald Spengler's *Problems of the Arabian Culture* [*Probleme der arabischen Kultur*].[95] The "controversy over Spengler," which largely referred to his thesis in *The Decline of the West* [*Untergang des Abendlandes*], overshadowed his deep insight into the apocalyptic, Gnostic world. As important a scholar as Hans Jonas said quite rightly that Spengler's essay on the apocalyptic, Gnostic world is "the best and most conclusive ever written on the subject."[96] Academic research into the subject of Oriental-Hellenistic syncretism only saw the *fading* of old traditions, a sterile mixture which amounted to its death knell [*Ausklang*]. Spengler, on the other hand, discovered in all this the *birth* of a cohesive new form of experience, whose universality he recognized. He rightly perceived that the center of the apocalyptic, Gnostic principle lay in the eschatological myth of the "redeemed redeemer." With his concept of "pseudomorphosis," Spengler aptly established the link between the new spirituality [*Seelentum*] and the Hellenistic universal milieu. It is not surprising that Spengler's ideas in this field of research have left no trace, but it does show the boundaries of academic research in a harsh light. It is thanks to Hans Jonas that Spengler's proposals, "to which [Jonas] is mainly indebted for his understanding of the history of the ideas of Gnosis,"[97] have found their way into the body of accepted knowledge. Spengler still regarded "pseudomorphosis" as a misfortune. Western history has this fact alone to thank for its continuity. This should be borne in mind, despite Spengler's objections, which one should take very seriously, and against those who imitated or plagiarized him, who should be taken less seriously.

Several nations clearly come under the influence of apocalypticism. But, just as the Greeks and Romans are prominent in ancient culture because they most purely represent the characteristics of the classical world, so in the regions where Aramaic is spoken there are only a few nations in which the spiritual nature of the Aramaic world is markedly evident. In the "leading nations" the establishment of a particular pattern of life is most clearly expressed, because in them the different elements of this part of the world are visibly blended. It helps a great deal in the understanding of the Aramaic, apocalyptic world when one sees that Jews and Persians played the same role here as the Greeks and Romans did in the ancient classical world. The comparison can be taken even further: the Jews are the "Greeks" and the Persians are the "Romans" in the context of apocalypticism in the Aramaic region. It is with the Jews and the Persians that the spirit of apocalypticism is revealed, a spirit which interprets the world as history, the point where the principle of good and evil meet. The spirit of the original vegetative state, characteristic of the Asiatic cultures, is superseded in these two nations. The spirit imprisoned in nature seeks release and understands itself as history. Even if Jews and Persians have the same metaphysical foundations, they are essentially different in the way they relate to the reality of the world.

The Persians are the rulers of the Aramaic region, whereas the Jews eke out a politically unimportant existence, dispersed as they are across the western periphery of this world. This is a significant fact which accounts for the seat of apocalypticism. Admittedly, the Persians provide the scaffolding for apocalypticism. The symbols of the Son of Man, Satan and the angels, the books of God and the Divine Host, individual judgment after death, and the Judgment of the World, are Persian versions of apocalyptic symbolism.[98] But when the Persians become the successors of Assyria and Babylon, the anti-world [*gegenweltliche*] principle of apocalypticism subsides, while the tribulation and persecution of the Jews nurture the apocalyptic seed in them.

The Jewish situation is the ideal climate for the spiritual state of apocalypticism. The apocalypses and the messianic expectations come about at this time of great divisive tension. The oppression of Antiochus Epiphanes gives rise to the Apocalypse of Daniel. It is under the yoke of Roman rule that the Apocalypses of Baruch and the Fourth Book of Ezra emerge. The Johanine Apocalypse is written by a martyr for martyrs. The Christian Church has always preserved the connection between the coming of Jesus and its occurrence *sub Pontio Pilato*. The messianic tide in Israel from Jesus, Menahem, Bar Kochba to Molcho, Sabbatai Zvi, and Frank is closely related to the "horrors of devastation."

In the area bound by Aramaic languages, a new idea of *the nation* emerges, in which the bond between a people and their territory [*Volk und Boden*] is loosened. It is this new concept of nationhood that causes difficulty for modern scholars and contributes to the fact that the Jewish nation is often presented as an "exception." In fact, as will be shown in more detail, the general Aramaic idea of the nation is fundamental to the Jewish nation. Even before the fall of Samaria, Israelites settled outside the frontiers of their land. They were taken prisoner in many wars and often the subjugated groups embarked on the journey to exile.[99] Back in the seventh century, there were, as the Elephantine Papyri show, Israelite settlements in Egypt.[100] With the decline of the Northern Kingdom the ten tribes were driven into exile. But the remaining Judeans could not forget them, and the remnants of the Israelites who had been dispersed joined together with the recently banished Judeans in exile in Babylon.[101]

Israel in exile is in *statu nascendi*, a situation which is parallel to their wanderings in the wilderness. The Exile is the wilderness of the nations, where there is no sense of being rooted to the land or any adherence to a state. But the prophecy can only unfold because the institutions and powers which hindered it in their own land are absent in the Exile. Prophecy works on and remolds the strains of disintegration [*zerfallenden Ton*] that afflict the nation. Ezekiel, the prophet of the Exile, is convinced that putting down roots in the state and in the earth was misguided. Therefore, he completely uproots the tree of the nation from the old earthly kingdom and—in a monstrous inversion [*in ungeheurer Umkehrung*] of the laws of natural growth—replants it with its roots pointing upward. Israel's history culminates in Ezekiel. He is both priest and prophet, a scribe and a bearer of apocalypticism. He combines the conservative priestly spirit with the progressive, prophetic spirit. In his laws and ritual, he lays down the institutions and structures which are binding for the Ezraic community. In the place of the proclaimed, passionate words of prophecy, we find the well thought-out system of a sage. And it is the same Ezekiel who, in the richness of his visions and images, lays the foundations for apocalyptic symbolism and motifs.

But it is incorrect to brand the Jewish nation in Exile as an exception. It is true that the Jews in Exile are a nation without land, but—and this is the decisive factor—they are surrounded by nations in a similar position. Exile is not just the fate of the Jews but of the whole Aramaic world. The Assyrian rulers may have been the first to use the method of sending people [*Verschleppung*] into exile, systematically uprooting subjugated tribes and nations. Nationhood was more strongly linked with land in the ancient world than it is today: religion also had its roots in the earth. Therefore, it is understandable that when nations were uprooted from their indigenous home, it must have struck deep into their very identity. The Aramaic nations were unable to put down earthly roots, but had to anchor themselves spiritually. The Jewish synagogue is only one of the national churches in the Aramaic region which is a home for the nation. The church-based nations of the Aramaic world are united in their faith.[102] God is no longer revered as the Baal of a particular place; rather, everywhere that believers assemble in "synagogues" is home. In the Aramaic region, the criterion for belonging to a particular homeland is one of faith. During the time of Exile, Jews and Persians, through conversion or by crossing borders, increase their numbers enormously from their origins as small tribal groups. Mission is the only form of conquest for a nation without land.[103] Among the Jews, mission is carried out by the groups affected by the spirit of apocalypticism. While the priests and scribes erect more and more new fences around the Torah, the apocalyptic seeds of Judaism take hold in the whole Syrian, Aramaic Orient, transforming the region inhabited by the Aramaic nations into a feverish organism. Apocalypticism is a phenomenon of the people and becomes in many of its features the common spiritual heritage of the whole Aramaic Orient.[104] Apocalyptic literature is written to awaken mind and spirit, regardless of divisions. While the canonical scriptures of individual church-nations are national, the apocalyptic writings are literally international. They encapsulate everything which makes feelings run high.

The Base Words of Apocalypticism

The elements of apocalyptic and Gnostic motifs can be extracted from the abundance of confused dark visions and speculations by examining the original linguistic elements from which they were constructed. This is because the base words [*Urworte*] of apocalyptic spirituality elucidate its central meaning much more clearly than the dark visions of the apocalypses and the extravagant speculations of gnosis. Less disguised than these finished formulations, the pure mirror of language reveals the ways and means of the soul, which is served by language and creates its symbols unintentionally from these base words.[105] The base words from one orbit [*eines Weltkreises*] prefigure all systems later to be developed and perfected. The logos of apocalypticism and gnosis is most directly articulated in Eastern Mandaean literature, because it is furthest from the source of Hellenistic influence.

The general introduction to almost all Mandaean writings begins: "In the name of that great, first, alien Life from the exalted worlds of light, that stands above all works."[106] This introduction contains the key for understanding the apocalyptic and Gnostic approach to life. The theme of self-alienation is to be heard for the first time in the context of apocalypticism. Alienness or exile [*die Fremde*] is the first great base word of apocalyticism, and it is completely new in the whole history of human speech.[107] The basic word meaning *alien* [*die Fremde*] and the topic of self-alienation permeate the whole of apocalyptic, Gnostic literature. The "alien man" of the Mandaeans corresponds to Marcion's "alien God," "the unknown God" of gnosis, the "Veiled One" of the apocalypses, and finally also to the *panton epekeina*, and the "Beyond of All" in Platonic and Neoplatonic philosophy. The key to the essence of the apocalyptic, Gnostic character is the following formula: the God of the Mandaeans, of Marcion, and of Plotinus is one and the same.[108] The common ground is God's alienation from the world, and the resulting self-alienation experienced by mankind.

To be alien means: to come from elsewhere, not to be at home in this world.[109] The here and now is the state of alienation and the un-canny. Life spent here is a life of exile and we are subject to the fate of exiles. "Exiled life," which does not know its way around here, gets lost in this strange world; it wanders aimlessly about. However, it may be that "exiled life" accommodates this all too well, forgetting its actual strangeness: it gets lost in this strange world by succumbing to it. "A life in exile" [*fremde Leben*] then makes itself at home in this strange world and becomes estranged from its origin. The suffering arising from alienation [*Fremdheit als Leiden*] is compounded by the guilt of estrangement [*Entfremdung als Schuld*]; both are implied in the two senses of *sich verirren*—to lose one's way, to err. By becoming estranged from its origins, by erring in exile in the world around us, the *self-alienation* of life has reached its climax. The way back begins with the act of recalling that "life" is a stranger in this world, and of recognizing exile for what it really is. The awakening of homesickness signals the start of our homecoming. When "a life in exile" perceives that it has erred into the unknown, it is possible not to be led astray again. It recognizes that the world is a constant turning hither and thither in suffering, and that being ruled by necessity [*Notwendigkeit*] means being exposed to suffering [*Wendung in die Not*]. A life spent in exile is conscious of the chasm between itself and the present condition of the world and therefore recognizes its superior state in the original homeland [*Heimat*]. The remoteness of exile can imply majesty. The unknown [*das Fremde*] in itself, far removed from all that is otherwise familiar, is that which is beyond, or the beyond itself.[110]

Life, which appears in its pristine state as the "great, first Life in the worlds of light," is thrown into exile in the world, where it is estranged from itself. The dramatic homecoming that follows, as ordained by the motif of salvation, is the metaphysical history of the light deprived of light, of life in the world deprived of life, of the estranged life in the estrangement of the here and now. History is the *path* of light into the world, through the world and out of the world.[111] The base word *exile* contains all the layers of meaning revealed by apocalypticism and Gnosis in the course of time, throughout the drama of history. Stating that we are estranged from ourselves is the key which enables history to be understood as a pathway. All subsequent words and motifs of apocalypticism derive from the base word *exile* and the theme of self-alienation contained in it.

Life is exiled in the world; the homeland of life is beyond the world. The beyond is *beyond* the world in its entirety. Apocalypticism introduces the dualistic feeling of God's world, a world unidentifiable with the here and now. God's world differs more and more markedly from the present world; it appears increasingly to be opposed to this world. God's world, by virtue of being defined as the absolute beyond, outside this world, reduces the world to a closed system, which dizzyingly encompasses all that is contained and lost in it, but which is still exposed as finite. The world is a power system which loses its exclusiveness when viewed from the beyond. As long as the world continues to encompass everything, and contains all [*das All*] within it, then there is nothing apart from *the* world. It would be futile to define the world more precisely by using a number or a pronoun. But if the world no longer fills the whole universe, if it is limited by something else, then a signifier of limitation is produced: *this* world. "This" world encompasses cosmic being, and the latter is opposed by that which is "entirely other," which has its home in "that" world. The base words *this* and *that* in relation to world are a further symbol of apocalypticism and are closely linked with the theme of self-alienation.[112] The differentiation between "this" and "that" world already implies a valuation. Even if in the earliest statements of apocalypticism the world is still within the sphere of God's omnipotence,[113] then God's alienation from the world progresses until the world is identified with the "fullness of evil," which God opposes as the "fullness of good."[114] The equation *cosmos* = *skotos*, world = darkness, expresses the concept of life to be found in Gnosis.

As part of this development, apocalyptic and Gnostic literature can speak of the world in the plural. The reference to "worlds" depicts the passage through the world as a "long and infinite one."[115] This plural statement refers to the labyrinth, the incalculable and confusing diversity of the world. In the "worlds" you can go astray and, while seeking the gate leading out of this world, keep arriving in other worlds, which are nonetheless still "world." This concept of a plurality of the world which multiplies and strengthens the demonic power systems that hold life in thrall is a further motif in the apocalypses and in Gnostic speculation.[116]

The spatial image of the world corresponds to the temporal concept of the aeon. Time and space represent the relative distance from the Light that life must travel in order to reach its destination: "You see, O child, through how many bodies, how many spheres of demons, through how many chains and courses of stars we must hasten in order to reach the one and only God."[117] The redeemer must pass through "worlds and generations" before he reaches the gate of Jerusalem.[118] The expression *worlds and generations* is frequently encountered in Mandaean literature.

Perhaps due to Iranian influence, the space between heaven and earth is filled with demonic powers. Because of this, the world becomes the battleground between God and the Devil. Both in Gnostic literature and in Paul's writings, the demonic powers are "the rulers of this world" and Satan is the "Prince of this World." It is not just the individual powers in the realm of the world that are demonic, but the world is demonic to its very core. The realm of this world, in which life resides, is a demonic force as such. Apocalyptic times are demonized ages.

Light and darkness are the substances from which "this" and "that" world build themselves up. That world is "a world of brilliance and light without darkness, a world of gentleness without rebellion, a world of justice without chaos and turmoil, a world of eternal life without decay and death, a world of goodness without evil . . . it is a pure world without anything bad mixed in." In opposition to that world stands the world of darkness, which is completely "full of wickedness . . . of lies and deceit . . . a world of chaos and turmoil without stability, a world of death without eternal life . . . where the good things pass away and aspirations do not come to fruition. This world is a mixture of light and darkness."[119] But the darkness prevails because the real substance of this world is darkness and the light is only a foreign intrusion: "In the brilliance of this world there is a mixture, but the brilliance of that world is brightness without any obscurity."[120] The King of Darkness is characterized in his primeval form [*vorweltlichen Sein*] in Gnostic literature as the "king of this world" and of these aeons, although "this" world only comes about from the mixture of the two substances, light and darkness.[121] Darkness is, to a considerable extent, the underlying principle of this world. All comparisons to be found in Gnostic symbolism are based on the statement world = darkness. Marcion is the most radical in his implementation of the concept of duality to be found in apocalypticism and Gnosis.[122] In Marcion's writings the God of creation is indivisible from existence in this world. Apparently Marcion makes no further mention of the creator God preexisting the world [*vorweltlichen Sein*]. The creator God, who really is the spirit of this world, stands over against the God of that world, who is the God of redemption.[123]

The *mixture* inherent in this world enables the drama of redemption, because the mixture is caused by the Fall, which is synonymous with self-estrangement. The Fall is responsible for the soul's voluntary inclination to darkness, where it becomes enmeshed.[124] In most cases the Fall appears as fate: "Why have you taken me from my place into captivity and thrown me into the stinking body?"[125] "Being thrown" [*das Geworfensein*] is one of the most powerful symbols of apocalypticism and Gnosis, and means that mankind is placed in a situation deprived of choice.[126] Not by any law does the world come into being; life is rather hit as if by an evil fate, which the creator rues: "Who has beguiled me into becoming a fool and throwing the soul into a body?"[127] Thrown into the world, the first man [*Urmensch*] is afraid to be alone, "abandoned" in this world of evil.[128] Seized by terror, man's lot is to fear that he is forgotten in the here and now of exile from the distant home: "And I cried for help and my voice did not penetrate the darkness; I looked up so that the light in which I had believed might come to my aid. Now I am oppressed in the darkness of chaos . . . rescue me from the primeval darkness so that I am not submerged in it. . . . My strength looked up from the midst of the chaos and darkness, and I waited for him with whom I am allied, that he might come and fight for me, and he did not come. . . . And when I sought the light, they gave me darkness; when I sought my strength, they gave me the substance from the beginning."[129]

The worldly powers outwit mankind:[130] "They mixed drink with their cunning and gave me to taste of their food; I forgot that I was the son of a king and served *their* king. I forgot the pearls which my parents had sent me to find. I sank into a deep sleep because of the heaviness of their nourishment."[131] The worldly powers fight with all of their might against the stranger, while they make him drunk with the "wine of ignorance."[132] The spirits and the planets of this world want to "seize and capture Adam and keep him in the Tibil. When he eats and drinks we intend to capture the world. We want to embrace it and found a community. We want to ensnare him with horns and flutes, so that he is unable to escape from us."[133] The powers of this world "want to organize a celebration. Arise, we want to have a carousal; we want to indulge in the mysteries of love, and seduce the entire world. We want to muffle the call of life and cause such dissension in the house that it will not be resolved in all eternity. We intend to kill the stranger (the redeemer). We want Adam among our followers and to see who will free him."[134] Horns and flutes are the din of the world. Man is thrown into "screaming darkness" so that he might forget the place from whence he came.[135] But the *din* of the world awakens him from his drunkenness. "When its sound came to Adam's ear, he awoke from sleep and raised his face to the place of light."[136] The din of the world, there to confuse mankind, causes him *alarm*. The uproar, which is supposed to mollify him, startles him. Amid this cacophony of sound, he *wakes up* and hears, contrary to the will of the powers of the world, the "call of life."

The redeemer "calls from without."[137] The beyond, which is not at home in this world, is heard as a *call* in the world: "He called with a celestial voice into the turmoil of the world."[138] The call is a fundamental symbol in the context of apocalypticism and Gnosis. Mandaean and Manichaean religion can be described, like Judaism, as the religions of the call. Hearing and believing are as closely linked in the writings of the New Testament as they are in Mandaean literature. Hearing corresponds to the call. The Manichaean missionary bears the title of the One Who Calls [*Rufer des Rufs*]. In Islam, too, the proclamation of a mission is the call, while the missionary is the one who calls.[139] In this way, Mandaean, Manichaean, Jewish, Christian, and Islamic religion belong together. They share the common foundation of apocalypticism. The elements which constitute the foundations of apocalypticism are the symbols of calling and hearing.

The nonworldly comes into being through the call. That which is entirely other is audible in this world, but still as that which is entirely other The call is emitted by "the stranger" [*fremden Mann*].[140] All who feel exiled from the here and now of the world and despise the powers of "this" world receive his call with joy: "Adam is seized by the love for the stranger whose speech is foreign and alien to the world."[141] The worldly powers are in turmoil: "What has the stranger done in the house which enabled him to found a party?"[142] And they protect themselves against the intruder, trying to prevent what is imminent: "We intend to kill the stranger . . . and confuse his party so that he has no share in the world. Rather, the whole house is ours."[143] The stranger must break through the whole house of the world, the many layers [*Schalen*] of the world: "in the name of that stranger who forced his way through the worlds and arrived, the one who divided the firmament and revealed himself to the world."[144] This stranger must breach the circle of the impregnable world to prepare the way for the soul's ascension.[145]

The "stranger" who is coming into the world is ultimately identical with the one to whom he comes. Not only is the redeemer described in Mandaean literature as the stranger, but so is the man to be redeemed. The world's prisoner is also given the title of stranger.[146] Adam and the Redeemer are equally the stranger. The stranger who descends ultimately redeems himself, redeems the soul he left behind in the first place, down here in the exile of the world.[147] This is why the stranger has to wander again in exile in the world, to release the spark of his own self from the prison of alienation. The stranger is, in the shapes of Adam and the Redeemer, the redeemed Redeemer.

The Apocalyptic View of History

For apocalypticism the passage through the "generations and worlds" reveals itself in the events of history. A comprehensive view of world history is an essential feature of Jewish apocalypticism in particular. This interest in the course of history is less noticeable in the Christian apocalypses and Gnostic systems, because the figure of the Savior and His second coming take center stage.[148] Research into apocalypticism and Gnosis has not, by and large, progressed beyond the cataloging stage, thus creating the impression of a tangled confusion among the apocalyptic myths and Gnostic systems. Generally, the fullness of the inventory is taken without evidence to apply equally to its essential content. The topic of self-estrangement encompasses all the elements of the apocalyptic view of history. Motifs concerning the story of the Fall and the pathway to redemption are so plentiful in apocalyptic and Gnostic literature that the original theme is often obscured. And yet the whole inventory of apocalypticism and Gnosis only serves to transpose the theme of self-estrangement: the fall into exile and the path to redemption.

In apocalypticism history is not recorded in the form of a chronicle; rather, apocalypticism attempts to gain knowledge about the future from the past and the present. Not only is the future broadly sketched out, but the significant question is *when is the end coming*? The paramount question posed in the Apocalypse is *when*?[149] The question arises from the pressing expectation of redemption, and the obvious answer is *soon*. Imminence is an essential feature of apocalyptic belief.[150] The global statement *salvation is at hand* does not satisfy those who want to know the day and the hour. So there is an attempt to give an exact numerical answer, based on calculations, or to identify signs indicating the end. Together with the perennial question *when* come whispered lamentations: how much longer will the night of this world last? The end is not just a longing; it is known to be imminent. One characteristic shared by all writers of apocalypse is that they are certain that they are about to experience the end. According to common belief, the writings of apocalyticism come from the earliest times: from Adam, Enoch, Abraham, Moses, Daniel, Ezra. These texts have been kept secret and sealed until now. But now, as the End Time is about to come, the prophecies are being revealed and the writings unsealed. That explains why the question *when* can only be asked in the context of apocalypticism, because the measure of everything lies in the divine economy. God has weighed the world on the scales and measured the hours and calibrated the times by number. The fate of the world is recorded in the heavenly books and inscribed from the very beginnings [*seit Urzeiten*] on the tablets of heaven.[151]

The science of apocalypticism can be defined as the exact numerical calculation of the end of time. It is intended to provide absolute assurance to faith and hope. The science of apocalypticism, which numerically calculates the *when* of the End Time, rests on the belief that "everything must fulfill its course out of inner necessity."[152] It is the task of the seer to reveal this necessity. An extract from world history is designed to calculate and illustrate the end: "the Almighty has revealed to you in His world the times that have already passed and those to come, from the beginning of His creation until the end."[153]

The events of the world are written on the face of the divine clock, so the point is to follow the course of world history to determine the hour of the aeon. Apocalypticism is the foundation which makes universal history possible.[154] The eschatological chronology of history continues on to the mystical numbers of the late Kabbalah, making it possible to divide world history into periods. In the Apocalypse of Daniel, the aeon of this world is divided up using the Prophecy of Seventy Weeks, a theory adumbrated in Persian eschatology.[155] Also in the Book of Daniel, history is divided into the four empires which permeate the whole of apocalyptic literature. In Daniel the four empires only span the period from the Exile in Babylon until the end of this aeon; from the viewpoint of Jewish apocalypticism this constitutes the essential period of history. In Enoch a similar period of time is divided up among the seventy shepherds, suggesting the demonic princes of the seventy different nations who represent all the nations of the world.[156] In the Apocalypse of Weeks, history is divided into ten periods,[157] and in the Apocalypse of Abraham the time of the aeon is calculated as "twelve years."[158]

The eschatological chronology assumes that the time in which everything takes place is not a mere sequence but moves toward an end. "This goal, which is the same for the individual as for the universe [*das All*], to the extent that God has created it, is the final salvation [*Heil*], and all events are the *history of salvation* [*Heilsgeschichte*]."[159] History does not complete a circle, "but a bow is spanned which rises from a beginning, overarching time until it sinks to an end, where it comes to rest and nothing further happens. Without events there is no more history, and without the progression of these events no time."[160] The number twelve, the number of the millennia in Persian eschatology, is related to the twelve signs of the zodiac. All of time is seen in this scheme as one enormous cosmic year [*Weltjahr*].[161] In apocalypticism the division into periods is always directed toward the end. It is assumed in eschatological chronology that this aeon is hastening toward its end: "The world is moving with great haste to the end."[162] And at the end, "the times hasten more rapidly than previous times; the seasons speed by more quickly than in the past; the years disappear more swiftly than they do now."[163] Apocalypticism reveals knowledge of what in time is like crisis [*das Krisenhafte der Zeit*]. Time appears as a stream, springing from the eternity of creation; after descending various gradients, it pours into the sea of eternity and redemption.

The science of apocalypticism presupposes a passive attitude toward the happenings of history. There is an absence of action. The fate of world history is predetermined and there is no sense in trying to resist it. The passive voice predominates in apocalyptic style. In the apocalypses no one "acts" but rather everything "happens." It does not say that God hears the crying, but that the crying comes unto God; not that the Messiah judges the nations, but that there is a judgment of the people. The passive style of apocalypticism, which is also prevalent in the writings of Karl Marx, is motivated by a lack of faith in mankind. The long period of suffering, the repeated disappointments, the crushing power of evil, the enormous colossus of the demonic kingdom of this world would all contribute to the despair apocalypticism felt about redemption, if redemption were at the mercy of mankind. It is only from this point that the largely misunderstood concept of "determinism" can be integrated into the thinking of the Marxist apocalypse. Marx also sees higher powers at work in history, which the individual is powerless to influence, and he dresses them up in the mythical garments of his time as "productive forces." The Kingdom of God is to become a reality without having to pass over the threshold of the human will, which is arbitrary and trapped in sin. Evil is not just a human impulse. When it manifests itself as a human impulse, this is only one form of evil, the most superficial one. Rather, it is the essence [*das Wesen*] of the world, itself a cosmic force, which is evil. Therefore, when at the End the essence [*das Wesen*] of the world passes away, evil in the form of human impulse will also pass away.

The structure of apocalypticism and Gnosis

cannot simply be described as dualistic or monistic, since the structure of these thought patterns is incompatible with modern philosophical terminology. One would have to say that the structure is both dualistic and monistic. The starting point, and at the same time the final goal, of Gnostic thinking is the union of opposites, the *coincidentia oppositorum*, and not the division of the world into two irreconcilable, opposing forces. This is achieved by a particular way of thinking and a unique concept of development. This fact distinguishes the Gnostic *Weltanschauung* from the dualism of the Platonists and equally from all Oriental dualistic systems of religion, particularly from Parsism, which starts from available oppositions. The circular pattern of basic concepts [*kreisförmige Führung der Grundgedanken*] is a fairly persistent feature of Gnosis. This serves to show how the invisible becomes visible and the visible then turns invisible again, how the evil world with its evil creator emerges from the good God and then returns to him, how light comes from darkness and becomes light again. From the spirit come soul and body; from body again comes the soul and spirit. From the eternal comes the temporal, and from the temporal the eternal again. From one comes much, and from much one. The transitions from one opposite to another are thereby ever more finely conceived: an increasing number of stages of development are inserted between the good God and the evil world and their corresponding beings in the middle. This is how the series of aeons comes about: the first comes directly from God; the last sinks into matter, giving it soul, form, and shape, but at the same time suffering because of it, until redemption and release from matter bring about the return of the fallen aeon (Sophia, the spiritual force of the world) to God. This closes the ring of development.[164]

This summary of the pattern of apocalyptic and Gnostic thought is wrong only in the assumption—and this is a significant barrier to understanding apocalypticism—that it is incompatible with modern philosophical terminology. Apocalypticism and Gnosis inaugurate a new form of thinking which, though submerged by Aristotelian and Scholastic logic, has been preserved into the present and was taken up and further developed by Hegel and Marx. The *dialectic* is both "dualistic and monistic." The "particular way of thinking" and the "unique concept of development" of apocalypticism and Gnosis is in fact the dialectical method which reconciles the opposition of thesis and antithesis into synthesis within the course of history. However, it is here that Leisegang's second error creeps in, and its presence is disturbing in what is otherwise such valuable research into these thought patterns. The logic of the dialectic, whether in apocalypticism and Gnosis or in the works of Hegel, is not circular but spiral.[165] The "bending backward" characteristic of the dialectic does not progress back to the thesis in a circular manner but broadens out into a spiral toward the synthesis.[166]

Dialectical logic is essentially historical and stands in opposition to Aristotelian logic, which is the model and basis of all rational interpretation of the world in the West. It is not without a reason that scholasticism, rationalism, and logic keep going back to Aristotle. Dialectical logic is a logic of history, giving rise to the eschatological interpretation of the world. This logic is determined by the question of the power of the negative, as posed by

apocalypticism and Gnosis. Apocalypticism and Gnosis form the basis of
Hegel's logic, which is often discussed but seldom understood. The connection between apocalyptic ontology and Hegelian logic is neither artificial
nor an afterthought. Hegel, as a young theologian, worked out his way of
thinking from the New Testament. The young Hegel's early, profound essays
are closely modeled on the text of the Gospels. Here we can trace the way in
which Hegel's dialectical mode of thinking is awakened, and how he grows
into that mode by studying sentences in the Gospels, breaking the mold of
Aristotelian, rational logic. The works of the young Hegel, *The Positivity of
the Christian Religion* and *The Spirit of Christianity and Its Fate*, lead directly
to *The Phenomenology of the Spirit* and to *Logic*, in which Hegel develops his
eschatological vision of the dialectic. Over one hundred years ago, Christian
Bauer showed the close connection between Hegelian and Gnostic metaphysics, but Hegel scholars have not paid sufficient attention to his work.[167]

The essence of history is comprised of the base words and the symbols
of apocalypticism and Gnosis, which are condensed into the fundamental
symbol of self-alienation. If the present state of the world, in which the ego
dwells, is exile, then this presumes an event which has brought this equivocal
situation about. The fact that God and the world are estranged from each
other, that the substance of mankind is torn into the ego and the nonego,
and that the ego languishes in the prison of the world—all of this only
makes sense when it is assumed that history is identical with the aeon of sin,
which is embedded between creation and redemption. Therefore, the structure of apocalypticism and Gnosis is essentially historical. When interpreted
in this way, the various figures and phenomena simply represent transitional
points in a movement which has a definite beginning and is directed toward
a definite end. The historical structure of apocalypticism and Gnosis is therefore essentially eschatological. The essence and purpose of every single form
and structure is determined by its place on the ecliptic, from the focal point
of creation to the focal point of redemption.

The features of apocalypticism and Gnosis are shaped to a considerable
extent by eschatology. Even where the "mythological" apocalypses merge
with the "philosophical" systems of Gnosis, the emphasis on eschatology
remains. Gnosis is the kindred spirit [*Geist vom Geist*] of apocalypticism. In
their narration of the history of the world the apocalyptic myths introduce
self-estrangement as a dramatic leitmotif, and it is on this very theme that
the more theoretical, ontological speculations of Gnosis are founded. The
boundaries between apocalypticism and Gnosis are, of course, fluid.

An important Gnostic source renders the dramatic, eschatological pattern of apocalypticism in the form of a programmatic questioning that holds for all of Gnosis: salvation will come on the recognition of "who we were, what we became; where we were, where we were thrown into; where we are hastening to, from what we are redeemed; what birth is, what rebirth is." Using this formula from the *Excerpta ex Theodoto*, 78, a source originating from the Eastern school of the Valentians, the whole pattern of apocalyptic mythology is transposed into the ontology of Gnosis. The first two paired themes turn on the beginning of creation; the two final themes concern the end of redemption. It is their correspondence to each other which produces the eschatological "conclusion" of the whole. Each of the four questions is posed always in a pair and thus the stages of creation-world-redemption are always distinguished. The first two paired themes inquire into the relationship between creation and the world, the last two into the relationship between the world and redemption. The complete sequence contains the entire pattern of eschatology. The questions in this ontological speculation are posed using the pronoun *we*, which elucidates the essentially anthropological thrust of the topic.[168] Already in Iranian and Jewish apocalypticism "the phases of development in world events lay down the framework for the stages of fate which the human soul has to pass through. Therefore, the great world events are mostly mentioned concurrently with what plays out as the fate of mankind."[169]

The eschatological structure can be felt through to its furthest ramifications. In the writings of Plotinus, where Gnosis has already developed into pure metaphysics and the dramatic mythological pattern of eschatological motifs has been lost, "the ontological hypostases are nothing but the steps of an existence produced by an inner dynamic leading to the universal process of self-estrangement and return [*Selbstentfernung und Rückkehr*]. Its only reality resides in the completion of this inner fate."[170] With Plotinus "existence is nothing but one's own eschatological story (at each point considered in terms of 'what we have become' [*Gewordensein*] and 'what we will become' [*Weiterwerden*], ranging from the lowest point to the transitional stage of return) and the theory emerging from this is the ontology of redemption."[171] But redemption in Gnostic terms is the removal of the distance separating us from the beginning. Distance is estrangement. The theory of self-motivated, dialectical existence comes from an apocalyptic and Gnostic source. The dialectic is the ontological form of apocalypticism and Gnosis which is passed down to Hegel and Marx.

The foundations of the dialectic are to be found in God's alienation from the world. This coincides with the division of man into psyche and pneuma. The process of redemption occurs ontologically in God's sublation [*Aufhebung*] of the world; it occurs anthropologically in the sublation of psyche by pneuma. In the apocalyptic, Gnostic dialectic, cosmos is to God as psyche is to pneuma. Psyche is the anthropological correlative of cosmos. The division [*Entzweiung*] of the human being into psyche and pneuma is familiar from Pauline anthropology.[172] Psychic man is worldly man who perishes with the world. Pneuma in the Manichaean literature of East Turkistan corresponds to the concept *grev*, which Reizenstein translates as "self," and Waldschmidt and Lenz translate as "ego."[173] Gnosis discovers the ego as self in this breach with the world. The ego as self is not synonymous with the human being. The cut separating God from the world, ego from nonego, runs straight through the core of the individual. Pneuma as self is that non-worldly spark which disrupts the ancient relationship between the world and mankind as "the whole" and the "part." In contrast to the necessity of the cosmos and the psyche, pneuma carries the "spark" of freedom, which is able to ignite the process of redemption.

In Gnosis the cosmos is seen as a world and an order devoid of meaning. For Gnosis, the unity [*Geschlossenheit*] of the ancient cosmos is conceived as a barrier or wall against which we collide in desperation. It is only this barrier, in its unity, which enables us to say that the beyond exists, which means precisely the beyond of the outermost shell enclosing the cosmos.[174] The cosmos, as portrayed in Gnosis, has not been emptied to a point of utter powerlessness; rather, the abundance of evil contained in it renders it powerful. The cosmos is ruled by the substance of darkness. It has its own spirit and, according to Marcion, even its own God. Marcion depicts an enormously empowered cosmos which dares to evolve its own "monotheism."[175] This shows that the division between God and the world, and mankind's self-estrangement, are taken to extremes in Gnosis. Gnostic mythology turns over on itself [*überschlägt sich selbst*] and rages against the origin from which it derives its revolutionary pathos. To the extent that Gnosis sees Yahweh, the God of the Old Testament, as the guarantor of this world by virtue of his creative word, the apocalyptic, revolutionary hatred of the world changes into Gnostic outrage against that God and his principle. Cain, the epitome of exiled man, who has been cursed by the creator God and who has to wander uncertainly and as a refugee on this earth, becomes the object of a Gnostic cult. Along with Cain, the other outcasts in the Old Testament are elevated, and even the serpent, regarded in Genesis as the tempter to evil, is admired in this cult. Marcion, always given to taking his conclusions to extremes, contentiously reinterprets the path of history from the Old to the New Testament when he claims that Christ descended into hell to restore salvation to Cain and Corah, Datan and Abiram, Esau and all the nations who rebelled against the creator God. By the Creator God, he means the God of the Old Testament. But Abel, Enoch, Noah, the Patriarchs, and Moses, who all walked in the ways of the God of the world and therefore, according to Marcion, disregarded the God of redemption, remain in the stagnant pool of the underworld. This is not just a piece of Gnostic eccentricity but part of the underlying sense of rebellion to be found in Gnosis, as well as in the radical pathos of revolution in general. This becomes apparent in a comparison with contemporary movements which claim for themselves the signifier "left" [*das Zeichen "links"*], despite or because of the ominously negative ring of the word *left* in all languages. Obviously, it is not for external, coincidental reasons, such as the seating arrangement in a parliament, that powerful contemporary movements choose to be called the "left" [*sich das Siegel links geben*]. Rather, these movements affirm and embrace all that the world decries when it utters the word *left*, which has such an ominous ring about it. They engage with all the questions and afflictions which are *left* by the established order of the world [*links liegen gelassen*]; that is, they side with those who are cast out and despised.

Such a rigorous negation of the cosmos is possible only because the cosmos is held in tension with its opposite pole, God. God and world are not distant but estranged and divided, and therefore hold each other in mutual tension. Just as there is nothing of God in the cosmos, so God is the nothing of the world. In the world God is the one who is "unknown," "hidden," "without a name" and "other." God's concealment is commonly explained by the fading power of perception in the context of apocalypticism and Gnosis. But these negative statements about God express a new and revolutionary attitude. The apocalyptic, Gnostic God is not *beyond* this world [*überweltlich*] but essentially *against* this world [*gegenweltlich*]. In the writings of Marcion, where Gnosis reaches its peak, the "unknown God" appears as the "new God."[176] "Unknown" means, more precisely, "unknown *until now*." Herein lies the opposition to every God hitherto acknowledged and worshiped. The enunciation [*Aussage*] of the unknown God includes the renunciation [*Absage*] of the world and is fully conscious of that renunciation. Marcion's God of creation is not only there by chance, but also known for what he is.

He is discernible [*ablesbar*] in all the works of the world and, as spirit of the world, identical to it. But the God beyond is contrary to the world and by nature unknown.[177] The negative statements about God—unrecognizable, unnameable, unrepeatable, incomprehensible, without form, without bounds, and even nonexistent—all orchestrate the apocalyptic, Gnostic proposition that God is essentially contrary to the world [*gegenweltlich*]. These negative enunciations, just like the enunciation of the new God, express the revolutionary pathos of apocalypticism and Gnosis. The negative statements about God also question any validity or claim that the world might have. The "new God" (Marcion) is the "strange God," the God who does not exist in the world. But the "nonexistent God" (Basilides) is an enormous power that embraces the world, annihilating [*nichten*] and destroying it [*vernichten*]. The God who is alien to the world and nonexistent releases the ego, the pneuma of man which feels alienated from the world; he causes the reality of the world to pass away and destroys its spell. *The God beyond*, the God of apocalypticism and Gnosis, is by nature eschatological because he challenges the world and promises new things [*das Neue verheisst*]. The original meaning of this expression becomes clear from the apocalyptic, Gnostic eschatology, and not from the static ontology of Hellenic, Hellenistic philosophy.

BOOK II

THE HISTORY OF APOCALYPTICISM

From Daniel to John

Apocalypticism and classical antiquity are based on mutually contradictory axioms. What is considered to be reality in one domain is taken to be
vanity and semblance in the other. Classical antiquity and apocalypticism
meet in the areas surrounding the Eastern Mediterranean. It is in Judea that
the confrontation arises. The Seleucid Empire of the Diadochi was pushed
back beyond the Taurus Mountains after the defeat at Magnesia. In July 168,
the encroaching Roman forces challenged Seleucid rule in the south and
forced Antiochus Epiphanes to tighten up his motley kingdom.[1] The only
possible means of bringing this about was comprehensive Hellenization. It
was this attempt that led to an uprising in Judea toward the end of 167. The
uprising was directed against Syrian rule,[2] but also against those Hellenistic,
Jewish families who were prepared to further the plans of Antiochus.[3] In this
time of persecution, the Apocalypse of Daniel, the first apocalypse to come
down to us in complete form, is unsealed. This apocalypse already exhibits
all the characteristics of apocalyptic literature, and served as a model for all
later apocalypses.[4] The belief in providence, the outline of world history, the
cosmic horizon against which world history is set, the scope and dreamlike
nature [*Phantastik*] of the visions, the concealment of the writer, the seething eschatology, the computations of the End Time, the apocalyptic science,
the symbolism of numbers and secret language, the doctrine of angels and
the hope for an afterlife—all are elements which determine the structure of
the apocalypse.[5]

Porphyry, a Neoplatonist, was the first to show the link between the Apocalypse of Daniel and the events of the Maccabee period. Modern scholarship has brought this buried knowledge to light and attempted to determine its date of composition nearly to the exact year. The literary composition of the apocalypse remains problematic because the narrative parts (Dan. 1–6) and the prophetic parts (Dan. 7–12) are written alternately in Hebrew (Dan. 1:8–12) and Aramaic (Dan. 2–7). Hölscher assumes that a Maccabean writer took the older collection of five stories (Dan. 2–6), including the introduction (1) and the prophecy (Dan. 7), slightly revised them, and placed them before his own prophecies (Dan. 8–12). There would thus be no need to look for Antiochus in the veiled figures of Nebuchadnezzar, Belshazzar, and Darius, which in any case never quite succeeded. It is clear that the narratives about earlier rulers, their arrogance and fall, were supposed to hint at what was in store for Antiochus and so strengthen the beliefs of the persecuted.[6]

Daniel's nightly vision, described in the middle of the apocalypse, introduces elements of Babylonian astral mythology into the eschatological drama. Franz Boll[7] and Gunkel[8] have confirmed the same contextual basis for the Revelation of John, while Jeremiah[9] and Eisler[10] have shown it to apply to the Apocalypse of Daniel.

The seer of the apocalypse sees into the obscurity of the decrees of fate and of the great court, since heavenly books have been opened and the constellations of the great empires of the world are emerging from the sea: firstly, the "lion," the "bear," the "panther," and finally the "eagle," symbolizing the Syrian Empire of the Seleucids. The seer sees the evil deeds of this monster pass in front of his eyes as it devours and tramples the "remnant" under its feet. The angels in the constellations of the heathen empires of the world are those in revolt against God. The events of the first rebellion against God, the rebellion of chaos against creation, are repeated in heaven [*am Himmel*]. And just as it once was before the defeat of chaos, the "Ancient One of Days," the "venerable old man," the "Lord of Judgment," appears and chooses the emperor of the world. The empire of the eagle ruling at that time is destroyed and burned in the heavenly stream of fire. In place of the transient kingdoms of animals, which disintegrate in the vicissitudes of time like the angels in their constellations, the eternal kingdom, whose star will never set, is now to arrive. Its protector is heaven's highest son, the constellation of mankind. In appearance "like a man," he stands on the conquered dragon of the pole and is always in the ascendant. The man, or the manlike figure of him who slayed the dragon at the heavenly pole, whom the seer sees in the clouds of heaven, he interprets as the son in the clouds, the "Anani." But Anani is the name of the last scion of the House of David, handed down in the genealogical list contained in the First Book of Chronicles.[11] The Targumim adds an explanation to this list in Chronicles, stating that Anani is the messianic king who will be revealed. It is surely the descendant of David, living at the time of the Seleucid rulers, whom the seer thinks will finally triumph over the monster and thus begin, in the fifth world empire, his never-ending rule over the world. Therefore, the seer's vision combines cosmic and national eschatology by suggesting that the Son of Man in the clouds, "Anani," who is to rule over the fifth empire, represents [*hindeuten*] the Anani, the descendent of the House of David. *Transcendent* eschatology and *national* messianism are already inextricably intertwined in the Apocalypse of Daniel. The "Son of David" and the "Son of Man" are identical. This identity is crucial for the contemporary messianic outlook and context into which Jesus comes. All attempts to separate the political messianic movement from the transcendent apocalypse in the eschatology of Jesus have failed.[12]

The dispute between the Maccabees and the Seleucid rulers is already overshadowed by the rise of the Roman Empire. The struggle between Rome and Judea breaks out in the moment that Pompey intervenes in the disputes over the throne of the last Hasmonean ruler and incorporates Judea into the sphere of Roman power. Nietzsche thinks that there has hitherto been no greater event than this struggle, this question, this deadly contradiction [*todfeindlichen Widerspruch*].[13] The quarrel between the Roman legions and the Jewish Zealots did not take place purely at the level of resistance, as was the case with other nations that were more successful in their blind defiance. The Zealots wanted more—they challenged the Roman Empire's dominance as a world power. This raises the struggle out of the context of the wars between the Roman Empire and the barbarians, which were being waged then and afterward on the borders represented by the Rhine and the Danube, on the banks of the Euphrates and in Britain. Two world principles clashed in this tenacious, even desperate, struggle between the Zealots and the Romans. This may not have been their first confrontation but it was the first time they were fully aware of the nature of the conflict [*Gegensatz*]: the global empire of masters against a world revolution of the oppressed.[14]

Apocalypticism is taken up by the Zealot movement. It makes apocalyptic literature its own, while apocalyptic prophecy nourishes and stokes the flames of the movement.[15] The apocalyptic literature conforms with the spiritual resistance to Rome; its last remnants are to be found in the Sibylline

Oracles.[16] *Fore ut valesceret Oriens* was a specter which weighed heavily on the ancient world, and this explains the jubilation of Rome when Augustus, from Rome, pacified the rest of the world.[17] In a world subject to the *pax Romana* the flame of the Jewish revolt is a solitary glow. From the time of Herod the fire has been glowing beneath the ashes. After his death the nation rises up in revolt; those inclined to rebellion come together in groups and demand that, along with the relaxation of taxes, the abolition of duty, and the release of prisoners, the high priest be removed.[18] This last demand having given the signal for an uprising, Archelaus allows all of his forces to be used "against the rebels." Three thousand of the rebels are slaughtered in the Temple in Jerusalem; the others withdraw to the nearby mountains.[19] But these "rebels" are those "aggressors" of whom Jesus says: "From the days of John the Baptist until now the Kingdom of Heaven has suffered violence, and the violent take it by force."[20]

This saying of Jesus clearly affirms the connection between the rebellious element [*den Stürmern*] and John. Josephus, too, knows of this connection. For, despite a few insignificant interpolations, Josephus's account of John seems to be genuine.[21] Josephus confirms the gospel account when he refers to the "miraculous attraction" of John's speaking, which caused "enormous crowds" to flock to him. Herod the Tetrarch feared that "the reputation of the man, whose advice seemed to be widely sought, would stir a revolt among the people, and so he preferred to have him duly removed." Both the Lucan[22] and the Talmudic[23] traditions agree that John lived as a hermit. Everything points to the fact that "Hanan the Hermit" in the Talmudic tradition is the same as John the Baptist; even the Lucan text seems to try to explain the name "John, the Hermit."

The synoptic tradition confirms that John preached "in the desert of Judea."[24] But away from the towns and settlements his message—repent, the Kingdom is at hand—could only be heard if "the people of Jerusalem and all Judea were going out to him and all the region along the Jordan, and they were being baptized by him in the river Jordan confessing their sins."[25] John's message of repentance spread like a powerful epidemic far and wide, among high and low.[26] All who came "were baptized by him for the repentance of sins."[27] Albert Schweitzer described the baptism of John as "an eschatological sacrament" that was to save man from judgment.[28] In the Apocalypse of Enoch, the Judgment of the World is represented as another Noah's Flood.[29] Baptism rescues us from the Judgment of the World as experienced in the flood. "The days of the Son of Man will be as in the days of Noah."[30] Just as

John baptized with water against the Judgment of the Flood, so the one who comes will baptize with *wind* (pneuma) and *fire*.[31] John cannot have foretold a baptism with the Holy Spirit (*pneuma hagion*),[32] because his disciples "had never even heard of a Holy Spirit."[33] The baptism with wind (pneuma) and fire is to save man from the Judgment of the World, just like the eschatological sacrament in baptism with water. Just as Noah's Flood is repeated in the Judgment of the World, so the deluge of fire in Sodom recurs in Babel, where the different races building the tower are dispersed in a deluge of wind.[34]

The Life of Jesus

The story of the life of Jesus has been the subject of research since the end of the eighteenth century. This research into his life has already acquired its own history. After much travail, it is now accepted that even the life of Jesus and his history are subjects for the methodology of *historical* analysis. The research begins with the anonymous Wolfenbüttel Fragment, edited by Lessing in 1778. In the short fragment entitled *Vom Zwecke Jesu und seiner Jünger* (Of the Purposes of Jesus and His Disciples), the world of Jesus is considered for the first time in a *historical* context, and his ideas are defined as *eschatological*.

Albert Schweitzer has traced the path from Reimarus to Wrede in all of its convolutions. This path is thorny, and more than once a wrong turn has been taken. Therefore, it is no surprise that Martin Kähler described all of the research into the life of Jesus as being on the wrong track [*Holzweg*]. In his antithetical juxtaposition, he rejects the "so-called historical Jesus" and adopts "the historic biblical Christ."[35] Along with the assertion "that we have no sources for the life of Jesus which a historical researcher could accept as reliable and comprehensive" comes the acceptance of Christ as he is enshrined in dogma.[36] *Because* Jesus cannot be recognized as a person in history [*historischer Jesus*], the way is left open for the figure of Christ to be interpreted from historic biblical sources [*geschichlichen Christus*]. But Martin Kähler's conclusion, which now has many adherents, seems deceptive to us. Of course, all scholarly research remains hypothetical. But its value is measured by the extent to which the available accounts can be brought into relation with one another. The sources for Jesus are no worse than those for any other figure of antiquity; perhaps they are more extensive in fact. It seems unacceptable that in classical philology, for example, Martin Kähler's conclusion could ever be applied to Socrates. The assertion that we have no sources for the life of

Socrates that we can accept as reliable and conclusive can in no way be bound to the conclusion that the Socrates of the Platonic dialogues is the historical Socrates. An antithesis between the so-called *historical* [*historisch*] Socrates and the *historic* [*geschichtlich*] Platonic Socrates is impossible. But this comparison presupposes that the manner and methods of academic research must always remain the same, whether we are dealing with texts from the Old or the New Testament, or from the Veda, the Avesta, the Koran, or the dialogues of Plato. Admirable scholarly erudition has been displayed in an attempt to blind others to the elementary nature of insights gained with immense effort from the text of both the Old and the New Testaments. Such scholarly erudition is futile, as it does not benefit academic research, and even less does it benefit belief. For, if the texts of the Old Testament are interpreted as revelation according to Jewish and Christian dogmaticism, and the texts of the New Testament as revelation according to Christian dogmaticism, there can and should be no question of proper academic research. Karl Barth's view on this in his commentary on the Epistle to the Romans was correct. How could one grasp an impression of what is "entirely other" by using academic methods? The beyond of history [*das Übergeschicht-liche*] is not to be separated from history in a way that distorts the historical foundations. Even the spirit of the world was patient enough to form the figurations of history. The beyond of history is the essence of history, which is closely interwoven with the historical foundations.

Research into the life of Jesus has turned full circle and come back to the central thesis of Reimarus. Seen in terms of Reimarus's elementary insight, academic study of the New Testament was retrogressive when it obscured his most important thesis: that Jesus is not the initiator of something new, but is to be regarded as a phenomenon within the apocalyptic movement in Israel. Jesus fits in a wider sense into the succession of eschatological itinerant preachers,[37] of whom Celsius reports that they said of themselves: "I am God or the Son of God or a divine spirit. I have come, because the world is about to come to an end and you, O mankind, will be carried away because of your injustices. But I will save you, and you will see me come again with the power of heaven."[38] Jewish messianism is only a part of the apocalyptic excitement which moved the entire Aramaic, Syrian world.[39]

"After John was arrested, Jesus came to Galilee proclaiming the good news of God and saying, 'The time is fulfilled, and the kingdom of God has come near, repent, and believe in the good news.'"[40] In this synopsis, Mark summarizes the message of Jesus as distinct from the preaching of John.

John preaches "on the baptism of repentance for the forgiveness of sins."[41] Jesus preaches "the Gospel of God's Kingdom."[42] The preaching of Jesus also contains John's command to "repent," while John's message[43] is defined by the belief that "the kingdom has come near."[44] There is, however, a marked difference in emphasis. John preaches that the Kingdom of Heaven is at hand in the form of *judgment*; Jesus preaches that the Kingdom of Heaven is at hand in the form of *promise [Verheissung]*. John rages in the first instance against "the people" as "a brood of vipers."[45] Jesus is primarily concerned "with the lost sheep of the House of Israel."[46] The introduction to Mark— "After John had been arrested, Jesus came into Galilee"[47]—clearly indicates that Jesus had worked as a follower and disciple of John before his arrival in Galilee, and may also have practiced baptism.[48] But there is a split. John "takes exception to" Jesus, probably because he notices that Jesus thinks he is the one John refers to in his preaching:[49] there comes one after me. The West reconciles the difference between John's disciples and the Christian community,[50] but in the East there is a deepening rift. The Mandaean tradition composes a dialogue between John and Jesus which reflects what eastern disciples of John saw in Jesus: "You have lied to the Jews and deceived the priests. You have robbed men of their potency and deprived women of fecundity and childbirth. In Jerusalem you liberalized the Sabbath, which was ordained by Moses. You have deceived them with horns and you have spread insults through the Shofar."[51]

Jesus also draws a sharp distinction between himself and John, such as: "amongst those born of woman, no one has arisen greater than John the Baptist, yet the least in the kingdom of heaven is greater than he."[52] The law and the prophets go only as far as John.[53] John thus belongs to the old order, in contrast to the "I am saying to you" statements of Jesus.[54]

Yet Jesus never severs the bond between himself and John, because his *consciousness of being the Messiah* is based on the prophecy of John. Therefore, John must remain as the harbinger, as the Elijah. In one saying which has come down in the scene of the Transfiguration, it is clear that the fate of Jesus is closely linked with that of John: "But I tell you that Elijah has already come, and they did not recognize him, but they did to him whatever they pleased. So also the Son of Man is about to suffer at their hands."[55]

When Jesus preaches that the Kingdom of God is at hand, his proclamation of the kingdom, as Reimarus pointed out, must be understood "according to the Jewish way of speaking."[56] Since Jesus at no point explains what the Kingdom of God is, he intends his statement concerning the kingdom to be understood in the familiar and usual way. He builds on the expectations that the people associate with God's Kingdom without changing them. *What* is coming with the Kingdom of God is known among the people. The fact *that* it is coming, perhaps will come tomorrow, or has already arrived and therefore requires one to hurry up and repent in order to enter the Kingdom—this is really the provocative element in what Jesus has to say.[57] The Kingdom of God covers a range of associations. National eschatology, Davidic messianism, the cosmic, transcendent eschatology of a Kingdom of Heaven conceived in terms of the beyond—all are tangled together here in an inextricable way. Since the Apocalypse of Daniel, the Son of Man has been identified with the Davidic Messiah king. The political expectations are reflected in the transcendental world of imagining what is to come [*transzendente Vorstellungswelt*]. It would be too narrow to conceive of the Kingdom of God as *polis* or *politeuma*, which rather suggests the idea of kingly rule, or more precisely, the realm of kingship [*Königsherrschaftsbereich*].[58] Heaven and earth are the realm of God's dominion. Heaven and earth are the kingdom to which God applies his kingship. The kingship of God is that kingdom which God gives to the House of David, as if it were a loan, so that it can exercise kingship on his behalf.[59] God's kingship assumes eschatological proportions in the form of prophecy. The apocalyptic division between "this" and "that" world, between the "present" and "future" aeon, specifies the location of the Kingdom more precisely.[60] The Kingdom of God is the Kingdom of Heaven. The apocalyptic seers pass through the Kingdom of Heaven in their visions and glimpses. They climb from one heaven to the next and return from these heavens back to the earth. When it is said that the Kingdom of Heaven is coming, it means that it is coming down from above.[61]

"Your kingdom come. Your will be done on earth, as in heaven."[62] It shall be on earth, as it now is in heaven. That can only happen when the Kingdom comes. It is not Jesus who brings the Kingdom. Such an idea is completely alien to Jesus.[63] Rather, the Kingdom brings Jesus with it. He sees "Satan falling from heaven like lightening."[64] The fall of Satan shows him that God's Kingdom is triumphant in heaven and a new heaven has come about. It is now true to say that God's Kingdom is really coming on earth as in heaven. The good news of the Gospel is the promise that the Kingdom is now also coming on earth.

Jesus understands the Kingdom as a *dynamis* to which Satan's kingdom must yield.[65] He works for the Kingdom in the capacity of an *exorcist* and testifies to the victory of God's Kingdom over Satan's kingdom. "It is by the finger of God that I drive out these demons and this proves that the Kingdom of God is surely coming to you."[66] Because Satan's kingdom in heaven has already fallen and he rages here on earth with what remains of his power, it is possible to tear from his claws those who are still "possessed" by him.[67] The era of Jesus is itself possessed, as in obsessed [*besessen*], with the power of Satan. To be sure, the possessed [*Besessene*] have existed everywhere and at all times, but not all ages have been demonized ages. The demonic often breaks through, as if an epidemic, and takes control of an area of the world. There is no doubt that, at the time of Jesus, there was a demonic outbreak which broke like a wave over the eastern area of the Mediterranean. Therefore, the message of the Kingdom of God is, in a special sense, an *evangelion*, a *message of salvation*, of healing [*Heils-botschaft*].[68] With the Kingdom of God comes the healing of a world which is threatened, plagued and possessed by devils. The Kingdom of God beams out a saving *dynamis*, a power which brings release from the claws of Satan.

Since the Kingdom of God is a real kingdom, you can enter into it. "It can be opened and shut like a gated castle. People can be prevented from entering its gates. You can be within it. You can be at table with Abraham, Isaac, and Jacob. It is like a net which can clasp and envelop and bring together all kinds of different fish. It is like a tree in whose branches the birds of the air can nest."[69] The Kingdom of God is a house you can "inherit," in the way you inherit land. You move into the Kingdom like Israel once moved into the Promised Land. Because the Kingdom of God is the Kingdom of Heaven, it is furnished with the things of heaven: the heavenly Son of Man, his throne and the Holy Spirit, the angels, the people of preceding ages, Abraham and the bosom of Abraham, the heavenly banquet. In the Kingdom of God there are differences of rank and degree; there are the lowly and the great.[70]

But the message of the Kingdom of God is particularly *good* news to the poor.[71] This is because it brings repentance [*Umkehr*] and reversal [*Umkehrung*]. In Rome each year at the feast of Saturnalia, the "topsy-turvy world" [*verkehrte Welt*] was enacted for the masses.[72] This symbolic theme is also the hope of those who preach: "The last will be first and the first last."[73] The topsy-turvy world is, from an apocalyptic viewpoint, a world which has been "purified" and "set right."[74] *This* promise that the Kingdom of God is nigh is glad tidings. The promise that the Kingdom has come is also the proclamation of the end of the kingdom of this world. Undoubtedly, the kingdom of this world is the Roman Empire. So, when someone came who stirred up the crowds with such a message, he had to be nailed to a cross by the Roman authorities.

Jesus comes at the time of Pontius Pilate, who is riling up the Jews with his rash behavior. Pontius Pilate, contrary to the hitherto restrained practices of his predecessors, orders his Roman cohorts to march with the emperor's portrait as their standard onto the Temple Mount. As a Roman, he could not have foreseen the consequences, because in so doing, he was evoking the prophecy in Daniel concerning the "atrocity of destruction."[75] The atrocity of destruction precedes the coming of God's Kingdom, which is now casting its shadow. After a brief period the Son of Man, the Davidic Messiah, must reveal himself. The Kingdom of God is quite close, so close that one can say it is here. It is possible to feel the atmospheric pressure of that which is to come. The Kingdom is *perceptibly* close.[76]

Jesus sees himself projected as the Messiah into this coming event. There has been much speculation about this consciousness of Jesus. It may have been kindled in the aftermath of baptism, which had shaken his very being. This knowledge had arguably taken shape within Jesus through John's constant, powerful preaching and prophecy about the one who is to come. Presumably, Jesus' consciousness of being the Messiah was based on his belief that he was descended from the line of David. It is generally assumed that the community only raised Jesus to a Son of David because they thought he was the Messiah. It is also possible that Jesus thought he was the Messiah because he believed that he was descended from the House of David. Paul, who otherwise records virtually nothing about the life of Jesus, mentions his descent from that ancient royal house.[77] Paul would hardly have been able to make this claim two or three decades after the death of Jesus, when many people still knew about the family background of Jesus.

Concerning the vexed issue, which is often evoked to deny the Davidic descent of Jesus, it is in fact Jesus who bolsters his claim with regard to other members of the Davidic line.[78] Jesus probably belongs to a group of impoverished relatives of that line who mixed with itinerant people. But in Jerusalem there are other members of the Davidic line who, as property owners, conform to Roman rule, as do the other members of the nobility. There is no record of the rich Davidians ever having opposed the Hasmonean rulers, or having taken part in uprisings against the House of Herod. These wealthy groups live at peace with the world and it is hardly expected that a Messiah will issue from them. The Messiah will not come "from the great sons of

Jacob" but from his "lowly children."[79] Jesus belongs to an impoverished clan of the Davidic line, and it is not surprising that people who have come down in the world treasure the memory of their descent, keeping alive the belief in the coming rule of David. The Arabs often mockingly refer to itinerant people as Sassanids.[80] This indicates that gypsy artisans and jugglers frequently entertained the genuine or deluded belief that they were descended from ancient royal houses.

Since ancient times, the wandering artisans in the Orient have been practicing prophecy and healing as an adjunct trade. While moving around, they treat people and cattle and, for that reason, are highly regarded among humble folk. If it were generally known that one of them came from a royal house, he would gain in popularity. On top of the knowledge possessed by a "healer" comes the charismatic healing power of great kings, which not only people but also animals and demons obey.[81] Precisely those people who are infirm and plagued by the evil of demons address Jesus as the son of David, because he is lord over the demons. But it would be rash to conclude that an artisan who could perform miracles and utter prophecy, while proclaiming his descent from David, would be immediately addressed as the Messiah.[82]

But when, upon the healing of the dumb and blind, the people "are beside themselves,"[83] they sense that this miracle worker is the one rumored to be *the* son of David.[84] This is also corroborated by the possessed, who are the first to address Jesus as *the* son of David. The definite article which accompanies this statement and differentiates it from all other instances mentioned by Schweitzer,[85] has a messianic ring to it. But, for the time being, Jesus conceals the fact that he thinks he is the Messiah, and he "threatens" the possessed against talking because he does not think the hour has yet come to proclaim himself openly as the Messiah. It is only in Caesarea Phillippi that he reveals himself to his disciples, also forbidding them to tell anybody that he is "the Messiah."[86] It is evident from the Gospels that Caesarea Phillipi is a turning point from a time when Jesus did not even speak to his disciples about himself as the Messiah, to a later time when he did and had to do so.[87] By virtue of this, the way in which Peter addresses him is different from the possessed: "flesh and blood have not revealed this to you, but my Father in heaven."[88] Not until Jesus believes that he has been revealed as Messiah by his Father in heaven does he reveal his secret to his disciples. Jesus says that the possessed have spoken through the power of Satan.

The life led by Jesus is only understandable when it is placed in a wider

context and the desert way of life of the itinerant artisans is taken into consideration. The Sleb, whose way of life has been recorded in detail by Werner
Pieper, present striking parallels with the life led by Jesus.[89] The Sleb are the
wanderers [*das fahrende Volk*] of the desert. Poverty is the surest form of
protection in the desert, so the Sleb, with practically nobody in Arabia to
rival them in their trade, do not have the slightest aspiration to wealth.
Because of their exceptionally peaceable nature, they have no need for riches.
Their life is comparatively carefree, whereas a Bedouin tribe is compelled to
live in fear lest a more powerful neighboring tribe rob it of its possessions.
The Sleb have a naive, carefree happiness, which marks them out from the
Bedouins, who are always distrustful.[90] They do not take part in the common
feuds among the desert tribes, but stand on the battlefield as onlookers and
afterward act as doctors by taking care of the wounded of both sides.[91] They
treat both the pursuers and those they pursue in a similar way. Robert Eisler
tries to

trace back this peculiar childlike, sublime ethic of unconditional peacefulness,
nonviolence, and reluctance to be provoked, preached by the itinerant carpenter
Jesus, to the particular experiences of these nomadic artisans. They had always made
their way successfully in life by adopting a peaceful and cooperative attitude to everybody in the struggle for survival among other armed tribes. They must, therefore,
have entertained thoughts that these other tribes could, if they only would learn to
do so, live in a law-abiding way [*nach rekhabitischer Art*]. Then they would immediately be relieved of the torment of mutual oppression and plunder, and enter the
longed-for Kingdom of eternal universal peace.[92]

As soon as a small band of followers has gathered round Jesus, he begins with
the administration of his kingdom [*Verwaltung des Reiches*]. Twelve of them
are sent out to proclaim the Kingdom to the twelve tribes of Israel;[93] then
Jesus elects seventy others whom he ordains as a form of Sanhedrin for the
New Israel, which is appointed to rule over the seventy nations of the earth.[94]
Later, Paul reincorporates this division made by Jesus into the jurisdiction of
the apostles.[95] The election of the seventy and the selection of the twelve
disciples are messianic acts of Jesus. The *metanoia* which the messengers of
Jesus are to preach is not a message of repentance intended purely to provoke
inner remorse. The disciples go throughout the land and with their *schuwu*,
their "turn around" [*kehret um*], demand an *act* which turns human life upside down [*grundlegend umstürzt*]. To give up all that you possess[96] means
selling your possessions and distributing them to the poor brethren;[97] it

means denying yourself,[98] taking up the cross, which is the sign of Cain, wandering restlessly without a home, and following Jesus as lord and master.[99] "Everyone then who hears these words of mine and *acts* on them will be like a wise man who built his house on the rock."[100] By this Jesus surely does not mean a small adventist community of prayer such as the disciples formed in the shadow of the Temple after the crucifixion. But neither can he mean a hermitage along the lines of the Essenes and the Therapeutae, because such a message could not stir up Judea and Galilee. Indeed, "the people were astounded" at the teaching of Jesus "because he preached as one having authority."[101]

His preaching is revolutionary because he demands from the people decisive action for the Kingdom of Heaven, he does not just demand it from the individual. The Promised Land is under Roman rule and has been changed into a house of slavery. This is a view which Jesus shares with John and the Zealots.[102] Contrary to the Zealots, however, Jesus teaches that one should not resist evil.[103] Therefore, he is unable to demand and plan resistance to Rome in the way the Zealots did. He demands, rather, *secessio plebis*, the exodus of the people into the wilderness.[104] The whole community [*Ökumene*] has become subject to the Romans and that means enslaved to the "Lord of *this* world." The free nation of Israel, who wishes to serve God alone, has no alternative but exodus into the wilderness, to the *aoiketos*. The time of the wilderness is the honeymoon of Israel, when the bride followed God, her divine bridegroom.[105] The tribes of Israel went into the wilderness from the house of bondage to serve God. A new exodus into the wilderness can give Israel the freedom to prepare to make herself worthy to receive the Promised Land.[106] On numerous occasions, individual Zealots have withdrawn to the wilderness. The wilderness is the way to escape the domination of this world.

Jesus repeats the two great miracles which Moses performed in the wilderness in symbolic form: feeding the people with manna and striking water from the rock.[107] The people follow Jesus into the wilderness. When he orders the disciples to give the people something to eat, they reply: "How can we feed these people with bread here in the desert?"[108] The disciples' question does not just apply to that particular moment, but is connected with the demand made by Jesus that the people follow him into the wilderness. Jesus answers such questions and similar doubts with "be not troubled."[109] This "be not troubled" of Jesus is only meaningful if the questions of the disciples and those of little faith are taken seriously as expressions of doubt and evasion. Like later messiahs, Jesus also intends to lead the people into the wilderness. Of course, he hopes to lead them out of it again and over the Jordan back into the Promised Land. Meanwhile, the nations of the world and the eternally lost children of Israel perish in the afflictions of the End Time, the last messianic wars.[110] The entry into the Kingdom and possession of the land are described by Jesus in the same words as those in Deuteronomy for the entry into and possession of Canaan by the Israelites.[111] Because the exodus into the wilderness was also a slogan used by the later messiahs, who were regarded by the early Christian community as Antichrists, this demand was effaced as far as possible in all of the Gospel accounts.[112]

This demand made by Jesus for repentance [*Umkehr*] fails, which explains the accounts describing the meager success of the disciples in their own preaching about the Kingdom. It convinces neither the rich and wealthy, who do not wish to give up everything, nor the poor and destitute, who do not wish to leave behind what little they have, "for it would have been better for us to serve the Egyptians than to die in the wilderness."[113] This reproach by the tribe in the wilderness against Moses, who intended to lead them out of slavery into the Promised Land, is ongoing and is leveled against anybody who tries to do the same. But further, Jesus distinctly announces to his disciples: "When they persecute you in one town, flee to the next; for truly I tell you, you will not have gone through all the towns of Israel before the Son of Man comes."[114] These words of Jesus are clear and are not intended to be interpreted in a woolly or evasive manner. It is equally plain, and was indeed so to Jesus himself, that this prophecy was not fulfilled: the disciples returned to Jesus and the Son of Man did not appear.

This disappointment is central to the life of Jesus; it brings his work up to that point to a close and determines his life anew from there on. If the whole history of Christendom is founded upon the delayed Second Coming [*Verzögerung der Parusie*], then the first date in Christian history can be taken to be the nonfulfillment of the prophecy of Jesus. This nonoccurring event [*nicht ereignende Ereignis*] marks the decisive, otherwise inexplicable turn of events in the work of Jesus.[115] From the moment when the disciples return to Jesus, he concentrates only on getting away from the people.[116] As long as the disciples are passing through the towns of Israel, Jesus talks almost openly to the crowds; he teaches them about the Baptist, about what will happen during the Kingdom of God and about the judgment awaiting those who do not repent.[117] Jesus visibly rejoices over those who are enlightened by God and are able to perceive what is happening.[118] But the moment the disciples return, he escapes from the people and shuns the crowds that stay close to his heels so as to wait with him for the coming of God's Kingdom and the appearance of the Son of Man.

Until the return of the disciples, Jesus turns to the multitudes to force [*herbeizwingen*] the arrival of the Kingdom. After the disappointment, he intends to bring the Kingdom about by his *suffering* and *death* on behalf of the *many*. In Caesarea Philippi, where Peter reveals to the disciples that Jesus is the Messiah, he tells them about his suffering: "And then he began to teach them that the Son of Man must undergo great suffering."[119] In the proclamation of his suffering at Caesarea Philippi, Jesus no longer speaks of the suffering of the End Time. The suffering of the many has been removed and it culminates in Jesus alone. The Messiah must suffer *for many*, so that the Kingdom may come. Jesus does not say: I must suffer. Neither does he state a general truth: he who suffers is raised up. Rather, he says: the Son of Man must suffer. The suffering of the Son of Man is for Jesus a messianic act rather than a personal test [*Selbstbewährung*]. It is embedded in the eschatological event of *kairos*: it is a suffering that redeems. The need for suffering results from God's resolve for salvation [*göttlicher Heilsratschluss*].[120] The sayings of Jesus concerning the sufferings of the Son of Man are not just random words; rather, Jesus begins "to teach" specifically about this. This new teaching of Jesus is what Peter protests against. For the disciples this teaching about the suffering Messiah and his death is perplexing. They see the Messiah as the king who is coming to judge and to rule, not to suffer. The king walks the *via gloriae* and not the *via crucis*. It is possible that Judas begins to have doubts about the new teaching of Jesus, because it proves to him that Jesus is a false Messiah; thus he hands him over to the authorities.[121]

The teaching of Jesus that the Son of Man is a suffering Messiah is closely linked with the figure of the suffering servant in Isaiah. His suffering and dying for *many* is in keeping with Isaiah's suffering servant: "because of the anguish of his soul he will bear the righteousness and sins of *many*, therefore I will give him the share of all; he has borne the iniquities of *many*."[122] The Kingdom of God cannot come before the sin [*Schuld*] that burdens the world is blotted out. Just like the suffering servant in Isaiah, Jesus will be the "expiatory sacrifice"; through his death he will bring [*herbeizwingen*] the Kingdom for all.

The preaching of Jesus is outward-looking until the disciples are sent out. When they return, the *change* [*Umkehr*] in Jesus takes place. "For the Son of Man came not to be served, but to serve and to give his life a ransom for (*lytron* = *kofer*) for many."[123] As Easter approaches, Jesus departs for Jerusalem, for the sole purpose of dying there. After the incident in Caesarea Philippi, he directs everything toward his death.[124]

The passion begins in Caesarea and with it the drama of Christian martyrdom, which separates the Kyrios Christos cult from the many other cults of late antiquity. "There is nothing in the great works of those years which can be compared to it. At that time, whoever heard or read the story of the passion which had just taken place—the last journey to Jerusalem, the anxiety of the Last Supper, the hour of agony in Gethsemane and the death on the cross—must have found all the legends and holy adventures of Mithras, Attis, and Osiris flat and empty."[125] In the Kyrios Christos cult the fate of a man becomes the symbolic and metaphysical center of creation.

Paul and the Unraveling of the Ancient World

In *ecce homo* the mystery of late antiquity is unsealed because mankind's self-awareness is born in this era. The Christian symbol is the epitome of mankind's fears of the magnitude of this event.[126] World history is the history of the spirit and the means by which mankind becomes aware of itself. The preconscious [*vorbewusste*] state of human existence corresponds to the mythological world and is, in the true meaning of the word, prehistory. In those prehistoric ages of the mythical world, human life takes on forms which have now become deeply entrenched in the community and have no individual mode of expression [*keine Individualität*]. Everything in the world of myth occurs with the strange impersonality and indifference of the dream [*Indifferenz des Traumes*]. The individual is only an echo of the whole and is separated from the members of his tribe; he counts for nothing as far as the group is concerned. The power controlling the human soul in the mythical world is *nature*. Prehistoric man of the mythical world is only an echo of nature and, seeing himself as a part of it, does not perceive himself apart from it.[127]

Nature is the sole horizon until approximately the time of the first Greek philosophers. In the oldest Ionic philosophy, nature is still the underlying principle of the world. *Re-flectio*, a turning away from nature and its contemplation, begins with the Sophists. The spirit is autonomous and incompatible with the existing order. When mankind becomes the measure of all things, then all laws become to some extent questionable. It makes little difference whether subjective man, man as a particular individual, is the measure of all things, as the Sophists believe, or whether, as Socrates teaches, man as a general being, man the subject, is the measure and judge. Aristophanes himself recognized Socrates as a cohort of the Sophists. In the Platonic thought of Socrates, mankind is shown for the first time to be in conscious opposition to the natural order of society, the community, the communal spirit of the polis.[128] When Socrates asks whether man should obey his *daimonion* rather than obey human laws, the natural social order is silently uncoupled from its reputedly divine lineage and placed within the arbitrary arena of human license.[129] This topic, once taken up by Socrates, will appear from now on in ever new formulations, until the victory of the ego breaks down the natural organic order of community, nation, state, myths, and art. All philosophy of late antiquity is concerned with the rights of the individual and man's potential for self-awareness. From that perspective, all other antitheses posed by the schools of philosophy of the period are peripheral.[130]

All things which were once valid in the mythical world become dubious and crumble in the firm grasp of the newly defined man. His attainment of self-awareness brings the loss of ancient spiritual treasures, and he, emptied of all previous content, is abandoned to a purely human future. A vast number of individuals suffering this same deprivation inhabited the Mediterranean countries at the end of classical antiquity. The central tenet of all aphoristic literature, which goes along with the history of the nations of late antiquity, is that man is superior to all forms of social order and institution, to all arrangements of ownership, honors, and professions. His value is solely to be found in his humanity.[131] This new principle becomes the system of philosophy adopted in the Stoa.[132] Seneca and Marcus Aurelius preach the spiritual autocracy of the individual. The masses, however, only understand this new spirit once it is freed from the subtle meditations of intellectuals and translated into the language of authority: you have heard that they were told in ancient times . . . . But *I* say unto you.[133]

An epochal turning inward [*Epochale Einkehr in sich selbst*] grips mankind in antiquity, as people turn away from the state and its organizations because it has nothing spiritual to offer. This creates a longing for something beyond doubt, something which would survive the collapse of the old order.[134] During the age of ancient imperialism, from the era of the Hellenistic Diadochi to the first two centuries of the Roman emperors, the social barriers finally collapse. The treasures of spiritual and intellectual achievement are rescued from the collapse of the political systems.[135] The masses have fallen on hard times under the emperor and are easily molded into the sort of spiritual community the Stoa requires. The institution of the emperor is not alone in trying to give the Imperium Romanum a center. This is attempted by all who turn away from the state, seeking a new lord who is mightier than the one who has been deposed, and more reliable than the ruler on the throne—a lord whose power reaches into the innermost soul and whose commandments encompass all aspects of life.[136]

Judeo-Christian teaching rings out into the emptiness of the Roman world. The essence of Judaism is contained in the Law.[137] The theocratic system of the Law leaves nothing, not even a trifle, to the fancy of the individual. The Law makes the distant God the spiritual center of all life. Monotheism—to which the philosophical circles of the empire had also pledged themselves, if in vague form, since the death of the ancient gods—is the absolute core of the Law.[138] So the concept of divine law comes to provide a focal point for Hellenic wisdom. Even the newly Romanized Josephus, a Jew who adores all things Roman and has no doubt about Roman victory over Palestine and the Jewish nation, believes that the catastrophe in Jerusalem is a sign to the Jewish people that the world is opening up as a stage for their greater victories.[139] He is convinced that his God, who had abandoned the shrine in Jerusalem, will take over the world and the Law of this God will subjugate the Roman Empire. The work written by Josephus against Apion testifies to his belief in the universality of the Law. This Romanized Jew hopes that the divine law of the Jews will bring world dominion and that the theocracy of the Jewish state will extend to a universal theocracy. Josephus often depicts the Pharisees, Sadducees, and Essenes as Jewish "philosophical schools." Judaism is, according to the Alexandrian Propagandists, the real philosophy from which all philosophers—Pythagoras, Socrates, and Plato—have learned. In Jewish theocracy, so they claim, the best state ideal of Plato and of all Greek utopians is being realized. Alexandrian-Jewish propaganda works the Roman Empire like a plot of ground, making it fertile for the Oriental-Christian seed.

The Jewish community of the Diaspora, which stands out from the melting pot of humanity in the empire, becomes a place of refuge for many Hellenistic Romans.[140] It is here that the Hellenistic Roman affirms his spiritual departure from all systems and constraints of the ancient world. This is why later the soul of the Hellenistic Christian wavers between involvement in the community and solitariness [*Einzelgängertum*], the ultimate consequence of the fragmentation [*Atomisierung*] of society. The Judeo-Christian community becomes the poison which constantly eats away at the pagan society of late antiquity, destroying what remains of its national, state and distinctive religious features.[141] Man's ego, having been emptied completely, is intent on releasing its final burden: the self. Even the intellectuals of Stoic or similar persuasion entrust their own ideals to a historical or mystical sage whom they worship as if a God. This removes the inadequacy felt by the individual and thereby marks the first step toward the metaphysical self-release [*Selbstentlastung*] of mankind. Seneca, on one occasion, outlines the Stoic ideal:

A man unafraid of danger, untouched by desires, overjoyed amid misfortune, composed in a storm, exalted above other mortals, on the same spiritual plain as the gods: does this not fill you with awe? Do you not say: here is something too sublime to belong to the weak body in which it lives? A divine strength has come down: a spirit which smiles so gently upon our trivial desires and fears, must be fired by a heavenly power. Sunbeams touch the earth, but remain in the place they come from. In a similar way, the great and holy man is sent to us and goes about among us, revealing to us the divine nature, but remaining true to the home he comes from. His eyes are fixed where he longs to return.[142]

But already before Seneca, Lucretius praised his teacher Epicurus in tones which represent milestones passed by the spirit of late antiquity on its journey toward Christianity: "The man who showed us the way to the highest good, freeing souls and cleansing hearts did not grow out of a mortal body. He was a God who was able to release life from darkness, pouring the light into the peace he brought."[143] And so the soul of Hellenistic mankind set out on its journey toward the heavenly savior.

Groups within Roman society are drawn to the synagogue by monotheism and by the concept of the Law. But the Hellenistic Roman who is attracted to the synagogue by the *concept* of the divine law is not prepared to take on the *practice* of the Jewish law. Those who enter the community so as to lose the last characteristics shared with their nation and their race [*völkische Gemeinsamkeiten*] have no wish to join the national community of the Jews and exchange a Roman for an Oriental nationality.[144] Even in the Jewish areas of the Diaspora, the power of individual commandments is on the wane. There are many in Alexandria who are freeing themselves from the letter of the law and wrestling with its inner meaning. When Philo warns of a merely inward understanding of the Law, he is really making way for the liberalization of Judaism which resulted from the mission of the Baptist and his disciples. For the baptism of John also implies that the Jews have degenerated into paganism. Only through baptism, which converted Gentiles receive too, does the Jew return to the Jewish community. John sees a new nation replacing the old, a new synagogue which is synonymous with the army of warriors fighting for the Kingdom of God.[145] The sacrament of baptism is a new birth for mankind.[146] John's preaching stirs up the whole Aramaic world, and in Transjordan and further east John himself is worshiped as the Son of Man, whereas Jesus is dismissed as an impostor.[147] But in the west the Alexandrian disciples of the Baptist, the Apollos group, seem to join up with the Kyrios Christus cult of the Pauline communities.[148]

The disciples of John are akin to Paul in their understanding of the message of salvation as something universal and transnational. For Paul there is no longer any difference between Jew and Greek, slave and free, because all are accepted through baptism into the ecclesia of the Messiah and have the same rights as Abraham's seed. "For just as the body is *one* and has many members, and all the members of the body, though many, are one body, so it is with Christ. For in the *one* spirit we were all baptized into *one* body—Jews or Greeks, slaves or free—and we were all made to drink of *one* Spirit."[149] Nations, classes, and sexes are just the parts of *one* body. The body is the Messiah, through whose sufferings the people come into a condition of humanity redeemed of all division [*Geschiedenheit*]. In using the metaphor of the body and its parts, Paul is reverting to the Platonic idea, commonplace in Hellenistic theories of the state, that the state is "man writ large" [*der Mensch im Großen*].[150] The body of the Messiah is mankind. It is synonymous with Adam. Because there is no word for mankind [*Menschheit*] in Greek, Paul uses the word *Adam*.

The heart of Paul's teaching is frequently defined as the "mysticism of Christ," but, to be more precise,[151] Paul's theodicy revolves around the two focal points of Adam and Christ or *protos* Adam and *eschatos* Adam. The fate of mankind is held in tension between these two poles: "because of whom, just as sin came into the world through *one man*, and death came through sin, and so death spread to all because all have sinned. For if the many died through the *one man's* trespass, many more surely have the grace of God and the free gift in the grace *of the one man*."[152] Adam is the adumbration of Christ, *typos tou mellontos, des: his anthropos Jesus Christos*.[153] The historical antithesis between psyche and pneuma is contained in the antithesis between *protos* Adam and *eschatos* Adam, who "has a natural body (*soma psychikon*), as well as a spiritual (*pneumatikon*) body. As it is written: the first man Adam 'became a living soul,' and the second Adam became a life-giving spirit. But the spiritual (*pneumatikon*) body is not the first; rather, the natural body (*psychikon*) is first, then the spiritual body. The first man is of the earth and earthly, the second man is the Lord of Heaven. Whatever is of the earth is earthly, and whatever is of the heavens is heavenly. And just as we have borne the image of the earthly, we shall also bear the image of the heavenly."[154] The Targum addition to the Septuagint translation of Genesis contains the critical sentence, *egeneto ho (protos) anthropos (Adam) eis psychen zosan* [The (first) man (Adam) became a living creature]. The *protos* Adam is the Adam *rischon* of rabbinical theology, which also includes the idea of *eschatos* Adam, though admittedly without the characteristic Pauline typology.[155]

Philo himself divided up the twofold account of man's creation in Genesis so that the first refers to the creation of the original man [*Urmenschen*] "in the image of God" and is synonymous with *logos*,[156] while the second narrates just the creation of Adam "from the dust of the ground."[157] Similarly, Paul's reference point in the first account of man's creation is Christ, "who is the image of the invisible God, the firstborn of all creation."[158] Only the second account refers to the creation of Adam. Christ is identical with Adam Kadmon; the king of the End Time is the original king [*Urkönig*] of paradise. The anointed one of God is identical with the original father [*Urvater*] and original king, Adam, who still encompasses the whole of mankind undivided: man and woman, nations and classes. In Paul, who goes beyond Philo, the role of the first created Adam, Adam Kadmon, is essentially eschatological. Adam and Christ, *protos* Adam and *eschatos* Adam, are moments, fixed points in history, which for Paul is essentially eschatology. And eschatology is the *history of salvation*.

The dialectic of Paul's history of salvation is both *quantitative in terms of world history* (Hegel) and *qualitative in existential terms* (Kierkegaard). The objective course of history "as a whole" [*im Grossen*] is not, as with Hegel, of no consequence for the private existence of the individual, but rather is decisive for his salvation and damnation. And the fate of the individual is not, as with Kierkegaard, independent of the course of history, but stands in the middle of the historical process in which salvation unfolds. The merging [*das Ineins*] of universal history with the individual's ethical existence occurs in the union of man with mankind, in Adam.

In the same way as Isaiah's servant of God is synonymous with suffering Israel, so Paul identifies the suffering Messiah with suffering humanity.[159] The suffering of the Messiah encompasses the suffering of humanity and serves as expiation for the Fall of Adam. The Fall of Adam is synonymous in turn with the sinfulness of mankind. The nation of Kyrios Christos represents humanity. The sacrament of baptism which John requires of the Jews, and through which he founds a new community of Israel, is extended by Paul to include all of humanity. The individual repeats the death of the suffering Messiah in baptism, and through baptism the resurrection of the dead Messiah is also reenacted: "Do you not know that all of us who have been baptized into Christ Jesus were baptized into his death? Therefore, we have been buried with him in death by baptism into death, so that, just as Christ was raised from the dead by the glory of the Father, so we too might walk in newness of life."[160] All of the lines of Paul's historical view converge in the doctrine of the resurrection: "For if the dead are not raised, then Christ has not been raised. If Christ has not been raised your faith is futile and you are still in your sins. Then those who have died in Christ have perished. If for this life only we have hoped in Christ, we are of all men most to be pitied."[161] But for Paul it is the death of Adam which makes the resurrection of Christ necessary. "But in fact Christ has been raised from the dead, the first fruits of those who have died. For since death came through a human being, the resurrection of the dead has also come through a human being; for as in Adam all die, so all will be made alive in Christ."[162] The Pauline doctrine of *protos* and *eschatos* Adam is based on the idea of the original man whose fate symbolizes the destiny of mankind. By bringing this symbol to the center of Christianity through baptism and the communal meal, Paul lays the foundations for a cult church of the Christian nation, which will be the newly founded community of mankind.

In theological studies of Paul, it is usually his theology that is rigorously examined and subjected to dogmatic analysis. The most pertinent historical question is suppressed and obscured by these peripheral historical issues: what does the birth of this literature say about the spiritual state of a considerable, and probably predominant, part of the Imperium Romanum?[163]

The people who come together in the Pauline community have severed all of their natural, organic allegiances to nature, art, worship, and the state, and thus their feelings of emptiness and alienation from the world and separation [*Entzweiung*] with secularism have reached fever pitch. These Hellenistic individuals, among whom there must be numerous Hellenistic Jews like Philo, join the mystical community of the Church. In contrast to the old, organic allegiances, the Christian community is an inorganic, subsequent [*nachträglich*] togetherness of individuals based on "pneuma."[164] In the

Christian community the man of late antiquity blots out his own ego in favor of the superego [*Über-ich*], which, coming from beyond, descends to the people. This superego is one and the same in each member of the community, so that the community represents a collective of the spirit [*das pneumatische Wir*]. The spiritual center of man is the superego of the beyond [*das jenseitige Über-Ich*]: "It is not I who live, but Christ who lives in me."[165]

The superego of Christ is seen by the masses as opposing Caesar [*Anti-Cäsar*]. It outshines and devalues the Caesarian superego [*cäsarisches Über-Ich*].[166] The mankind of late antiquity, having been reduced to the existence of a colorless mass, begins for a while to revere its lost self in the divine emperor.[167] But the Caesars are no less people of the masses than their subjects are. What Nero has in common with Christianity is his loathing of the world and its people. He gives vent to this in deeds which often seem grotesque and gruesome, though their underlying tragedy cannot be overlooked. This emperor would have liked nothing better than to see the corrupt world burn before his own eyes. Such a vision is not an unfamiliar one in Christian fantasy.[168] The contempt that Caesar feels for the masses and the hatred of the masses for the Caesarian god-emperor, who still represents nation, state, religion, and art in his person alone, are one and the same. Basically, they are just individual features of the contempt and hatred which the era feels for itself.[169] In the Imperium Romanum this contempt paves the way for the Christian denial of the world, for the appointment of a ruler who is not of this world. The fulfillment of the hopes of the masses is postponed to the world beyond. For nobody wants to exchange forever the substance of their being for a corporate identity [*Sammel-Ichs*], equally devoid of substance, whose feasting and circuses are no less degrading for the individual than are its brutalities.[170] Therefore, the true god-king becomes a *protest* against this world, against the world of the empire and its emperor-saviors [*Kaiser-Retter*]. Once the masses place all their hopes in a single man who is supposed to heal the sickness of the world, the dreams of man [*das Träumen des Menschen*], who has thus given himself over, wander restlessly, and—since the fantasies of a "political" savior remain unfulfilled—men finally end up in the belief in the "true" savior from above [*Heiland aus dem Jenseits*].[171]

The History of Early Christianity

The secret history [*innere Geschichte*] of Christianity issues from the nonoccurring event of the Parousia and consists of attempts to understand this nonoccurrence in terms of a Christian design. The first event to delay the Parousia occurs when Jesus sends his disciples out to storm the cities of Israel: "You will not go over the cities of Israel until the Son of Man appears."[172] But because the Son of Man does not appear, Jesus believes that he alone as God's servant has to atone by suffering on behalf of the many, for the guilt of the many, and that this removes the last barrier to the arrival of God's Kingdom.[173]

The death of Christ is decisive for both the unity at the core of early Christianity and for the antithesis between the original community and the Pauline church. The death and resurrection of Jesus are for the original community [*Urgemeinde*], as for Jesus himself, stages in a series of messianic occurrences. The original community gathers around those close to Jesus and waits in ceaseless prayer for the Parousia. The risen Christ speaks in visions to the disciples "of God's Kingdom."[174] The community paints the Kingdom and the hopes for it in the colors of the popular version of the apocalypse, which Jesus had done to a much lesser degree. The small community, scarcely larger than a conventicle, comes together as an economic collective. Those who have property subject themselves to the new order and the elders are strict in their treatment of financial misappropriations arising from any weakness of faith. When the members of the early Christian community give up fields, houses, and all of their possessions, it happens in the secure hope that they will soon receive "houses, fields and eternal life, a hundredfold."[175] The communism of the early community is rooted first and foremost in the tribal practices [*Stammesverfassung*] of Jesus' relatives, who, like other itinerant artisan families, held things in common. In this sense, the Gospel, the good news, surely serves as another source of income. Celsus writes about Syrian prophets who prophesy that the end of the world is imminent.[176] These prophets claim to be judges of the world to come, who will return at the head of the heavenly hosts. They will protect and spare the villages and towns of those who show them favor; the others they will visit with eternal fire and severe judgment. Jesus and his disciples, as well as the first Christian community, also fit into this account:

Whenever you enter a town and its people welcome you, eat what is set before you; cure the sick who are there, and say to them, "The kingdom of God has come near to you." But whenever you enter a town and they do not welcome you, go out into the streets and say, "Even the dust of your town that clings to our feet, we wipe off in protest against you. Yet know this: the kingdom of God has come near." I tell you, on that day it will be more tolerable for Sodom than for that town.[177]

The community of the disciples fits into the communal family unit [*Familienkommunismus*] of Jesus' relatives and then broadens out to the social economy [*Gemeinwirtschaft*] of the early Christian community. There is a clear connection between enthusiasm for the Kingdom and communism.

By adopting a life of communism, the early Christian community seeks to anticipate the divine economy of God's Kingdom. The Epistle of James attests to this thinking, and there is no reason to suppose that Jesus differed. The Epistle of James is the oldest extant Christian document. There is no evidence against the authorship of James, the brother of Jesus; on the contrary, only the assumption that it was written before the Council of the Apostles makes it possible to interpret the epistle without distorting the facts.[178]

The early community [*Urgemeinde*] also knows that friendship with the world means enmity to God.[179] In the early community, poor and rich are synonymous with good and evil.[180] Their expectation of the Kingdom is guided by prophecies and the apocalyptic depiction of it. It has been frequently pointed out that there is "no sign of any program of social reform" in the teaching of Jesus.[181] But it is clear that whoever feels called to comply with the Law and the prophets will also set out to implement the social program of prophecy. The Good News brought by the apostles has the power to engage the lower orders in the Imperium Romanum, since the Gospel proclaims an imminent revolution [*Umwälzung*], when nothing will remain as it is: "And see the last shall be the first, and the first, last."[182] On this point, the priests of Zeus and Jupiter, Osiris and Sepharis have nothing to say.

The early community waits for the coming [*Hereinbrechen*] of God's Kingdom, and the longer this event does not occur, the more desperate their situation becomes. Paul overcomes this impasse by teaching that the new aeon has dawned despite the continued delay of the Parousia. But the protracted delay disturbs even the Pauline communities. When people in the community die, this undermines faith. This is because the glory of the messianic age is reserved for the last generation and does not apply to those who have died, although they were already in the new aeon by virtue of baptism. Yet Paul lays this doubt to rest by granting an "order" of resurrection: the departed Christians will also rise at the Parousia, and only they, for all the other dead must wait until the last *tagma* of the resurrection. The resurrection at the end of time thus proceeds in stages.[183]

In the Kyrios Christos cult the regime of the King recedes into the background and the King himself takes center stage. The political and social aspirations which link Jewish apocalypticism to the coming of the Messiah are overshadowed by the mystical, symbolic union of humanity as the Body of Christ. While Philip still preaches "the good news about the kingdom of God and the name of Jesus Christ,"[184] Paul declares that he knows nothing except Jesus Christ.[185] This shifts the emphasis and opens the way from apocalypticism to Gnosis.

Paul marks the exact turning point from Christian apocalypticism to Christian Gnosis; eschatology and mysticism meet in him.[186] In contrast to Greek and medieval mysticism, the union of the natural [*Irdischem*] and the supernatural [*Überirdischem*] does not take place in the heart of the individual, but rather "this" and "that" world interlock as independent power systems, as "kingdoms." The moment when "this" world touches "that" world, when they interlock, is the *kairos*. Paul defines the time between the death of Jesus and the Parousia of Christ as the *kairos*, which is characterized by the crossing over of the still natural and the already supernatural states of the world. With the death and resurrection of Jesus, the turning point [*Wende*] is reached: the fashion [*das Wesen*] of this world will pass away. But the fashion of this world is the Law. For that reason, the Gentiles who believe in Christ should not be bound by the Law. It is not that the Gentiles need not keep to the Law, but rather that they must not do so, at the cost of their salvation. This same premise, on the other hand, compels the Christians from Israel to continue to conform to the Law. As it is the task of Christ on his return finally to dispose of this world, a world which is already passing away, the believer should not act on his own authority to bring about [*vorgreifen*] the eschatological events and suspend the old order of things in which he found himself on joining the Christian community:[187] "Let each of you remain in the condition in which you were called."[188]

However, just as quickly as Paul moves on from the communality of the early Christian community in Jerusalem, so is his eschatological mysticism superseded. Jesus' news that the end of the world is nigh, which still resounds in Mark and Paul, is already far *behind* John and Marcion. The End of the World has receded into the distance and "being in Christ" is the foundation on which the design of the Christian world is based. The subject matter of John is neither the eschatology of Jesus nor Paul's eschatological mysticism about the turning point of the *kairos*; rather, it is the mystery of the universe [*das Geheimnis des Weltalls*], on which the watermark of Christ is indelibly engraved. Early Christian art represents Jesus and his disciples wearing a *tribon* and holding the staff of the itinerant Cynic preacher. The disciples are now principally portrayed as pupils of a philosopher, *mathetai*, and no longer as royal messengers, *apostoloi*.[189]

The distinct physiognomy of the Christian community becomes increasingly blurred, as more people from the upper strata of society join religious groups of Christians and rich people become patrons of communities with whom they have dealings [*Klientelgemeinden*]. As those seeking salvation leave the Oriental-Hellenistic mystery cults and join the Christians down in the catacombs to celebrate the agape, it is not surprising that the Christian community comes to resemble those cults more closely. In the time of Severus, statues of Abraham, Moses, and Jesus are set up alongside those of Orpheus, Pythagoras, and Plato in the *lararium* of the emperor and of many nobles. They are all objects of hero worship.[190] But in the Christian mysteries the word, the logos, replaces nature. This overcoming of the religion of nature from within, which also holds the Hellenistic mystery cults under its spell, shows that the Kyrios Christos cult does not come about by chance. It is a necessary part of the spiritual movement which is attempting to break free from the fetters of nature. In this new development, of course, the rebellious tone of former promises is subdued and adapted to the ears of new listeners. Paul's admonition that each should remain in the state in which he was born facilitates this change. Whenever the rich or fashionable join the Christian Church, the question *quis dives salvetur?* (Clement of Alexandria)—can a rich man be saved?—becomes significant. The question is answered to the effect that, given the omnipotence of God, everything is possible. Warnings are uttered against those poor who presumptuously believe themselves to be the sole inheritors of the Kingdom of Heaven: "Because it is foolish to assume automatically that the poor are blessed, as so many of them live in a dissolute manner."[191]

The hiatus between the Resurrection and the Parousia is so great that a situation of constant expectation [*steten Harrens*], characteristic of the Jewish Apocalypse, is mirrored in Christianity. The Revelation to John is evidence of this change. In the early Church it certainly was already treated with suspicion as being "Jewish," and Luther placed it on a par with the Fourth Book of Ezra. In his early work, Eberhardt Vischer, supported by Harnack, made a brilliant defense of the theory that "the Revelation to John is a Christian revision of a Jewish Apocalypse." As Harnack said, Fischer's theory really seemed to be the "egg of Columbus."[192] At a stroke, problems were solved which had forced research into a cul-de-sac for decades, if not centuries. Recent research on the subject of the Revelation by Charles, Loisy, and Lohmeyer is based on Vischer's discoveries.

The Revelation to John thus fits into the series of noncanonical apocalypses, which all involve Christian interpolations around a Jewish core. There is an obvious reason for this: apocalypses arise in times of persecution, when people are on the lookout for signs of divine judgment and the devout are encouraged to wait patiently. However, if they are to retain their validity in the community, apocalypses have to be adapted to each new situation, and this inevitably leads to interpolations. There is no question that an apocalypse like the Testament of the Twelve Patriarchs is a piece of Jewish writing which was later reworked by a Christian editor. This has generally been acknowledged to be the method behind the writing of almost all apocalypses. The position of the Revelation to John within the canon of the New Testament may prevent us from drawing similar conclusions about it.

The Jewish Apocalypse, which forms the basis of the Revelation to John, is framed by the Christian epistles (1–4) and a final warning (22:6 ff.), in which the words of the prophet and the words of Jesus are strung together. Added to the Apocalypse itself is the vision of the Christian Messiah symbolized by the Lamb. It runs alongside "the Jewish Messiah of the original text containing the narrative of his birth and his coming to destroy the world; he is merely God's agent coming to set in motion the wine press of God's wrath."[193] Therefore two concepts of the Messiah come together in the Apocalypse: the militant Jewish Messiah, who comes to sit in judgment over the power of the world and whose birth is still awaited, and the Messiah in the figure of the Lamb, who has already come.[194]

The heart of the Apocalypse is the prophecy of the Messiah's birth (11:15–12:17). Israel is "a woman clothed with the sun, with the moon under her feet, and on her head a crown of twelve stars. She was pregnant and was crying out in birth pangs, in the agony of giving birth."[195] It is not possible that this narrative is about Christ's birth, since for the Christian prophet this event would have to be in the past. Describing the battle against the dragon, a Christian apocalypse would also have mentioned the crucifixion. In line with the vision of the Apocalypse, a Jewish tradition, recorded in the Talmud, relates that the Messiah was born in Bethlehem on the same day the temple was destroyed but was shortly afterward taken from his mother by a tempest.[196] "The Revelation to John expects the Messiah to be born at the beginning of the oppression, directly after the destruction of Jerusalem, when the Holy City and the outer court of the temple are being trampled under foot by the heathen. Likewise, the Talmud assumes that the Messiah was to be brought into the world when the power of the Gentiles appeared to be at its height and the destruction of the Holy of Holies marked the zenith of wickedness."[197] The historical background of the time can clearly be gleaned from the Christian interpolations. Just as the Jewish source text originated from the period of Jewish persecution under Titus, so the Christian interpolations in the Apocalypse are "a harsh reflection of the bloody persecution which threatened to destroy the existence of the Christian cult in Asia Minor at the time of Domitian."[198] The twentieth chapter of the Revelation, which, except for two interpolations,[199] belongs to the original Jewish document, is the Magna Carta of chiliasm. All chiliastic rebellion and yearning are fed by this chapter from the Book of Revelation.[200] In it, all the apocalyptic hatred against the Imperium Romanum and against "Babylon, the great mother of whores and of earth's abominations,"[201] flares up once again.

The roaring of the Apocalypse finds resonance in the Christian community. Even the Gospels testify to the appearance of other Messiahs.[202] The Montanist prophets do not stop with the proclamation of an imminent end, but cause the faithful to gather in Pepuza, where the heavenly Jerusalem is supposed to descend. Each time it is predicted that the Parousia is about to happen there is turmoil and public uproar in the community. Hippolytus gives an account of these occurrences in his commentary on Daniel.[203] These are not dubious itinerant preachers stirring up fanaticism but elders of the Church, who carry the whole community, or a large part of it, with them.[204] The people leave their fields and trades, they abandon their property and go into the wilderness or wander in the mountains waiting for the Parousia. In Syria the *strategos* pursues these people almost as if they were bandits. There is always great disappointment. The elder of the church in Pontus reaffirms his prophecy with the words: "If things do not happen as I said, then do not believe in the scriptures any longer but each of you should do as he pleases."[205] The author of the Second Letter to the Thessalonians addresses this confusion. He appeals for calm and asks the brethren "to be not shaken in mind or alarmed, either by spirit or by word or by letter, as though from us, to the effect that the day of the Lord is already here."[206] For the conditions for the Parousia have not yet appeared. The day of the Lord cannot come "unless the rebellion comes first and the lawless one is revealed, the one destined for destruction. He opposes and exalts himself above every so-called god or object of worship."[207] The author of the letter explicitly opposes those people who give up their trade: "For we hear that some of you are living in idleness, mere busybodies, not doing any work."²⁰⁸ The Gentile opponents may well have been the first to probe the sore point of the nonoccurring event. The Second Letter of Peter states "that in the last days scoffers will come scoffing and indulging their own lusts and saying: 'Where is the promise of his coming?' For ever since our ancestors died, all things continue as they were from the beginning of creation!"²⁰⁹ Doubt creeps up also in the ranks of the community.²¹⁰ The First Epistle of Clement loudly denounces the doubters: "Unhappy are the doubters, those who are in conflict with their soul and say: we heard this back in the days of our fathers and look how we have become old and none of those things have happened to us."²¹¹

From the second to the fourth century, eschatological hopes continue to fade away. The sources document this process only in fragments.²¹² Christian theology comes under the sway of speculative Gnosis. In exactly the same way as early Christianity develops in the climate of Jewish apocalypticism, Christian theology develops in a Gnostic environment. The nearness of the *coming* Christ changes into the nearness of the *present* redeemer [*anwesender Erlöser*]. Redemption [*Erlösung*] now means the release [*Lösung*] of pneuma from the prison of matter. The path to salvation is signposted by mysteries and sacred rites. In place of the early Christian expectation of the Kingdom comes the destiny of the soul. The events of the End Time fade into parables depicting the journey of the soul. Ascension into heaven, once conceived as a future event, becomes the ascent of the soul through the aeons.²¹³

Gnosis is already the watchword of Clementine theology, which seeks to merge the strange syncretism of Greek mysticism, the Oriental magical arts, and the evangelical tradition.²¹⁴ The knowing *Gnosis* replaces the Pauline *pistis* and thereby diminishes the importance of eschatology. The radical sayings [*der Stürmerspruch*] of Jesus are interpreted as a call to gain the Kingdom through a life of constant action and prayer.²¹⁵ For Clement the biblical life is one with Platonic ideals; his concept of the Kingdom is determined as much by the New Testament as by the Greek theory of the state. For instance, the heavenly banquet is not painted in the colors used in the New Testament parables but more closely resembles a Greek symposium. Heavenly Jerusalem merges with the Elysian Fields and the Platonic State.²¹⁶ This prepares the ground for Origen, whose importance for Christian metaphysics cannot be overestimated.

Origen sets the pattern for Christian theology. The whole of early

Christian theology comes under his spell. Ambrose learns of him through the Capadocian writings and, by way of Augustine, Origen's legacy anonymously trickles down to the Middle Ages. This heritage shines through in various ways in the works of the medieval mystics, such as Eckhart and Joachim. The age of Pietism and the Enlightenment mirrors the borderline situation of Origen's time, when the joint heritage of ancient, traditional forms and apocalyptic, Christian elements disintegrates, now standing opposed to each other. At that point Origen's concept of *apokatastasis* reemerges and his theodicy of history appears anew in Lessing. Therefore, Origen is to be found, but not seen, everywhere [*unsichtbar allgegenwärtig*] in the Christian context, although the Orthodox Church proclaimed him a heretic.

It is not easy to pinpoint the main motif in Origen because his writings are a hotbed of arguments among philologists and because it has not been possible to reconstruct a coherent framework for the Gnostic-philosophical and religious-ascetic elements of his work. Koch, following de Faye, stresses solely the intellectual and philosophical aspects; in so doing, he emphasizes what is central to Lessing rather than to Origen.[217] Völker, on the other hand, gives priority to the ascetic, monastic ideal and plays down the rational dialectic in Origen.[218]

The central theme of Origen can be identified as the *mystery of the logos*. God is pure spirit. But this spirit is not at rest; rather, it is always creating and is relentlessly active. It does not disclose itself in the world, but in the mystery of the supernatural logos. The logos fills the earthly realm, baptizing, scorching it with its fire, and changing it into spirit.[219] The soul is only the allegory [*Gleichnis*] of the logos, only the open window which the enlightening beams of the logos penetrate. The logos is incarnated in all stages and steps of the world. It is a man for all mankind, an angel for all angels, and, for the soul, it becomes the living stairway to heaven, the cosmic way of truth, as the soul climbs up to God.[220] The soul is neither spirit nor body, it is the transitional stage between the two. Because of its neutral position, it is the place of man's choice between living according to the flesh or the spirit. If the soul chooses the spiritual way of life, then it walks in the "spirit"; if it chooses the material life then it walks in the "flesh."[221] The soul is imperfect by itself, coming into its own only in the spirit. In the spirit the soul shares in God's nature and it is this sharing that determines what it finally is. Only the soul governed by reason shares in the life of God, and therefore man is simultaneously spirit-soul [*Geist-Seele*], the "inner man" who shares in God's nature, and also body-soul [*Leib-Seele*], the "outer man" created by God.[222] The life of the spirit is lived out as the ascent of the soul, which in its upward movement cancels out the primordial Fall. Corporeal matter comes into being as a consequence of the Fall.[223] Although the body becomes the prison of the soul, it is not the case that spirit and matter embody the antithetical principle of good and evil.[224] Matter is also God's creation. The world as a place of punishment and a consequence of sin, and the world as God's creation, destined for God, are connected by Origen's idea of punishment as *paideusis*.

The cornerstones of Origen's theodicy of history are *pronoia* and *paideusis*: providence and education."[225] When providence is understood as an educative process, God's purpose can be fulfilled without hurting [*kränken*] man's sense of freedom. Punishment means cleansing and is therefore only an episode within the economy of salvation, whose purpose is to disclose the logos.[226] All punishment is limited, transitory; nothing of creation gets lost, everything created ultimately returns to its origin. The leitmotif of *apokatastasis* dominates Origen's eschatology: "If the will of God is done in heaven as on earth, then the earth will not remain as it is, and we will all become as if in heaven."[227] As Origen explains, in the Pauline phrase *from him and through him and in him*, "from him" means that the first creation and everything that is takes its origin from God; "through him" means that everything that has been created is directed and guided by him, to whom it owes its being; and "in him" means that those already educated and bettered are grounded in his perfection.[228] In the end, God's presence encompasses all through the logos. The mystery of the logos in Origen is *eschatological pan-theism*.

This outlines the main features of Origen's Christianity. It is not a gift [*eine Gabe*] but a task [*eine Aufgabe*]; it signifies not redemption but an uphill struggle [*Weg aufwärts*]. Therefore, incarnation cannot be at its center. Its starting point is God, who is like a teacher and educator. Origen constantly uses the image of the teacher and father who disciplines and nurtures his child. God's nurturing begins immediately after the Fall and continues right to the end. The coming of Christ as the logos is only one among the many measures [*Massregeln*] which are given us by providence.[229]

It marks—like everything God does for the sake of mankind's education—a step forward, may be a very important step, but only one of many. God is like the good housekeeper who knows what his creatures need and how to accommodate his treatment [*Handlungen*] to the individual's needs. He knows eras and moments and directs the process step by step toward its goal. This educational process [*Pädagogie*] began, as mentioned earlier, immediately after the Fall and is continued through a series of worlds. The goal lies ahead and God wants man to keep striving. The logos-become-man is able to help in a particular way but even his presence does not represent the final stage. Redemption lies in the gradual education of the human race.[230]

God's education is administered by creation, philosophy, the Jewish people, Christ, the life of the Church and any future development.[231] And yet it is too narrow to describe Origen's overall view as "educational idealism,"[232] because the "spiritual ascent" of the soul is not an intellectual process but one that reaches deep into man's corporeality and his personal life.[233] Origen is also a precursor of Eastern monasticism.[234]

Eschatological mysticism reaches its climax in Origen. Eschatology moves away from the vision of the end of the world [*weltliches Endspektakel*] and turns inward to become a great drama of the soul. Just as Plotinus can be seen as the pagan successor [*heidnische Ausläufer*] of Gnosis, so Origen is the Christian successor of Gnosis, which has become pure metaphysics. The dramatic, mythological motifs of eschatology fall away, and in the ontological hypostases, being [*das Sein*] is represented as a movement whose inner dynamics trigger the universal process of self-distancing and return. It is only when undergoing this fateful process that being is real. Being is its own eschatological history and its lesson is the ontology of redemption.[235]

The great change which Origen describes first affects the *apocalypses*. Generally speaking, how the apocalypses are valued is an excellent yardstick for measuring the strength and scope of apocalyptic expectations.[236] The Jewish apocalypses enjoy very wide circulation well after the period of the early Christian communities. Enoch, the Fourth Book of Ezra and Baruch are felt to embody the atmosphere of the Christian community. The Apocalypse of Enoch is recognized in the New Testament as prophetic scripture and is quoted as an authority in the Epistle of Jude.[237] For Barnabas, who has no knowledge of the New Testament canon, Enoch and the Fourth Book of Ezra are part of holy scripture. Even Tertullian wants to see the Apocalypse of Enoch recognized as part of the canon of scripture. The ancient Abyssinian Church still retains it in its modern canon, which indicates the value originally attached to it.

Later on, however, the apocalypses became suspect and were excised as heretical literature. The Canon Muratori only recognizes the apocalypses of John and Peter. However, these are not to be read out in public. Moreover, despite being included in the Canon Muratori, the two apocalypses remain controversial. The Apocalypse of Peter has gradually fallen into oblivion and only fragments are now extant. Much heated argument surrounds the Apocalypse of John, which can retain its place in the canon of the New Testament only because it carries the name of Jesus' favorite disciple. It is still regarded with suspicion and is not recognized as canonical in the Syrian Church.[238] The dispute concerning the Apocalypse of John is evidence of the Christian Church's disassociating itself from apocalypticism. To do so is to lose all insight into the connection between the teaching of Jesus and Pauline theology on the one hand, and apocalypticism on the other, which means losing the key to understanding early Christianity.[239]

Chiliastic sections of text have been removed from the more ancient Christian scriptures. Even if chiliasm finds a number of supporters in the Christian Church—such as Cerinth, Papias, Irenaeus, Hippolytus, Lactantius, Tertullian, Methodius of Olympus, Apollonarius of Macedonia—it still has to lead an underground existence. Chiliasm was mainly supported by the lower social orders. In the Egyptian Church, whose Christian community mainly consists of the non-Hellenized, lower strata of the Fellachian Copts, who produced their own literature in the vernacular, there is violent resistance to the Gnostic tendencies of the Alexandrian theologians. The Egyptian Christian communities, led by Nepos, resist any attempt to reinterpret the promises in the style of Origen and aim for an interpretation which is more "Jewish in character."[240] Irrespective of this, the spirit of Origen prevails and his pneumatic exegesis of the biblical texts puts an end to the apocalyptic eschatology of the New Testament: "Those who have a profound understanding of the gospel . . . are not particularly concerned with the end of the world in general, whether it will come at once or creep up on us, but their thoughts are on one thing only: that the end of every one of us will come without his knowing, since the day and hour of his death remains hidden from him."[241] This is the first instance of the motif of *individual eschatology* which has dominated the Christian Church ever since Augustine.

Origen describes chiliasm as the "the spirit of those who call themselves Christians but interpret the scriptures in a rather Jewish manner and do not find anything in them worthy of the name of divine revelation."[242] Eusebius of Caesarea is in fact only drawing the logical conclusion when in his history of the Church he keeps trying to brand chiliasm as a "false Jewish doctrine" and denounces its adherents as heretics. He is simply reflecting the generally held view of the Church that chiliasm is "a doctrine of the flesh" belonging to Judaism. Finally, at the Council of Ephesus in 431, chiliasm is condemned as "error and illusion."[243]

There are occasions in the Church when even the plea for the Kingdom in the Lord's Prayer is altered: *Your Kingdom come* is replaced by *Your Spirit come.* The spirit is sufficient for the Church, rendering apocalypticism dispensable.[244] The Parousia not only becomes superfluous but Christians eventually pray for the *end to be delayed*, "for we do not wish to live it, and by praying for the delay of these things, we are promoting the continuation of Rome."[245] This change is already noticeable in the First Letter to Timothy. He is not advised to pray for the dawn of God's Kingdom but to offer quite a different prayer, "for kings and all who are in high positions that they may lead a quiet and peaceable life in all godliness and dignity."[246] Far from representing a revolutionary faction, the Christian Church is overtly placatory to the empire [*reichsfreundlich*] well before its recognition by the Imperium. The Church no longer feels it is a community in exile, and for Eusebius the empire and the congregation of believers are synonymous. Once Christianity has been raised to the status of the religion of the empire, any hope for God's Kingdom is snuffed out. Ever since Constantine, even the Roman Empire has been referred to as "holy" ["*heilig*" *gesprochen*]. This state of affairs, in evidence since the days of Constantine, becomes an ideal in Augustine's City of God, is effectually established by the policy of Charlemagne, and ends in the Christian Europe of the Western Holy Roman Empire.

From Augustine to Joachim

By the third century A.D. the end of the world has receded into the distance and the Christian community has finally been transformed into a church. The great theological systems come together into a dogmatics which is the new principle of interpreting the world. Theological speculation, to be sure, presupposes belief in the permanence of the doctrine to be established.[247] The change from community to church does not take place within the Christian community exclusively. In the third century the pagan cults in the West combine to form a church as well. A new form of Hellenism emerges in a national church similar to the Jewish synagogue and the Christian Church. The incursion [*Einbruch*] of the *Aramaic church idea* into Rome is marked by Decius, who, at the time of the first millennium celebrations of Rome, requires a testimony of faith from his subjects.[248] Membership of the Roman Imperium is now defined by a declaration of faith, as is the case with the Aramaic nations. The enemy of the Christian Church is not actually the ancient religion, which Christianity scarcely encountered, but paganism, which is a new and powerful church derived from the same spirit as the Christian cult church.[249]

In the third century, two cult churches coexist, one consisting of the Christian community and the other of the many pagan communities in which the same divine principle is worshiped under a thousand different names. This pagan cult church attacks the Christian Church. All the great persecutions of Christians, later to be paralleled exactly by the persecutions of the pagans, issue from the pagan church. The Roman state is involved only because the pagan cult church is also both nation and fatherland.[250] The savior of the pagan cult church is the emperor, the messiah of all syncretists.[251] The Roman state turns itself into a church and its ruler into a caliph, who rules not over an area but rather over all believers.[252] Even in the Roman state of the third century, having orthodox faith is a necessary requirement for true citizenship.

Toward the close of the third century, Diocletian raises Mithras to the status of imperial god among the other deities.[253] The priests of the syncretic cult churches are no different, at least spiritually, from the Christian priests. Ever since the commentary written by Poseidonius about Plato's *Timaeus*, this Platonic text has been the bible of syncretism.[254] Numenius simply transfers to Plato the office of the Christian Son of God. The figures of divinity from the Platonic *Timaeus* are transformed into fantastic Gnostic beings. Occidental speculation is steeped in the dark pools of Oriental mysticism.[255] By interpreting the *Timaeus* in a kabbalistic manner, Numenius lays the foundations for Neoplatonism, which aspires to become more than just a school of philosophy. Proclus is a true father of the Church, who receives clarifications of dark, textual passages in his dreams and who would like to see all texts destroyed except the Chaldean Oracles and Plato's *Timaeus*, which he considers canonical.[256] His hymns testify to the contrition of a genuine hermit. Fear of sin, struggles with temptation, the deep remorse caused by his own wickedness—all vividly recall the state of mind of many Christian hermits.[257] Hierocles compares the new Pythagorean Magus, Apollonius of Tyana, with Christ,[258] and his breviary of morals for believers in the new Pythagorean community is little different from the Christian equivalent.[259] Without undergoing any process of conversion, Bishop Synesios changes from being an adherent of Neoplatonism to a prince of the Church [*Kirchenfürst*]. Moreover, he retains his theology, changing only the names.[260]

Asklepiades writes a comprehensive study on the similarity of all theologies.[261] There are pagan gospels and saintly lives alongside Christian ones. And there is hardly any difference in these writings, all of which begin and end with a prayer.[262] Like Paul, Porphyry defines belief, truth, love, and hope as the four elements of godliness.[263] Origen is to the Christian Church what Plotinus is to the pagan church. Koch argues plausibly that Origen and Plotinus were students of Ammonius Saccas.[264] The contours of Greek philosophy and Gnostic speculation come together in Plotinus and from then on run in unison in Neoplatonism.

Around the year 300, the greatest successor of Plotinus, Iamblichus, draws up for the pagan cult church a system of orthodox theology and priestly hierarchy that follows a strict ritual. Personal religious experience declines in favor of a mystical church with meticulous ceremonial performances of religious devotion, the enactment of rites associated with magical powers, and a priesthood.[265] An orthodox fanaticism pervades this teaching and there is already an intimation of the new age, as characterized by Julian's endeavors . Julian tries to establish the pagan church for all eternity. It is wrong to view his attempt as an isolated undertaking. Julian only carried out the program of Iamblichus,[266] whom he places on a level with Plato and so accepts into the canon.[267] Many of the inscriptions in honor of Julian can more or less only be translated as saying: there is only one God and Julian is his prophet.[268] The only reason why the Roman Catholic Church is able to grow into the organism of the Roman Empire is because the pagan Roman Empire of the third century is itself a church.

Ever since the third century, the state has been completely embedded, in the congregation of believers, in the Church. The Christian community embraces this world as well as the world beyond, the devout along with the good angels and spirits. In such a community the state is only a scale model of the visible part of the *corpus mysticum*. The *civitas dei* is neither an ancient polis nor a modern state;[269] for the polis and the state have their center of gravity in the here and now, in a particular geographical location. The *civitas dei* is neither in a fixed location nor tied to the people of a particular area; it may best be compared to the Islamic community. "The mystic community of Islam extends from this world to the other world; it reaches out beyond the grave and embraces dead Muslims of earlier generations, even the righteous who lived before Islam. All of them are in the company which the Muslim joins; they help him and he can even add to their bliss by bestowing on them his own merits."[270] This is the foundation on which the Augustinian City of God is built.

In the twenty-two books of the *City of God* Augustine lays the spiritual foundations for the Holy Roman Empire in the Middle Ages, which stretches from Constantine into the age of the German emperors. The eschatological hope for the Kingdom, which since the Apocalypse of John has been able to express itself only as chiliasm, loses its final thrust and is constricted by Augustine to the doctrine of the Church.[271] Unlike the previous Church Fathers, Augustine does not fight chiliasm but reinterprets it in such a way that it loses its eschatological vigor. Augustinian chiliasm bears the marks [*Antlitz*] of the Church, which is only possible because he *reverses* its general direction. The chiliastic kingdom is generally thought to be in the future, but it is precisely the futurity of this thousand-year empire that Augustine reverses; in his opinion the future orientation of chiliasm fails to grasp the implications of the Revelation to John. For "the Church is already the Kingdom of Christ and the Kingdom of Heaven."[272] The kingdom of the Apocalypse, which lasts a thousand years, is the period when the Church reigns. The Kingdom of God is prefigured and realized in the Church: "But while the devil is bound, the saints reign with Christ during the same thousand years, understood in the same way, that is, of the time of His first coming."[273] With this, the hope for a thousand-year kingdom is finally driven out [*verdrängt*] of the Church, and from now on becomes a sectarian issue. Instead of the concept of *universal* eschatology, *individual* eschatology emerges. The destiny of the soul is central and the End Time is eclipsed [*verdrängt*] from the last day of human life. Ever since Augustine, *individual* eschatology has dominated both the Catholic and Protestant denominations of the Christian Church. Universal eschatology, which bears within it the expectation of the Kingdom, from now on appears within the Christian sphere of influence as *heresy*.[274]

Augustine's *civitas dei* is the foundation of the medieval state. In the Christian age there is no separate state and church, but in the *corpus christianum* the state is always embedded in the bosom of the Church. The state is essentially oriented toward God: theonomic.[275] But a world state which is not directed toward God is subject to demons. The antithesis between divine and demonic reality is the central motif of Augustine's *de civitate dei*. The *civitas dei* is opposed to the *civitas terrene*, which is synonymous with the *civitas diaboli*.[276] Augustine usually avoids the expression *civitas diaboli* because of its strong associations with the Manichean dualism of God and the devil.

The antithesis between the Kingdom of God and the kingdom of the world becomes the guiding principle of history for Augustine and the *medieval philosophy of history*.[277] Even Augustine looks beyond the Imperium Romanum. Rome will not be followed by a new world but by the End. The entire historical framework of the Middle Ages, as he perceived it, is suspended within this vertical projection. All the visitations by the Germanic tribes are just seen as the punishment of God, who is to purge and change the empire for the better. Rome will stand as long as the world stands.[278] Famine, plague, earthquakes, comets, and doom, but especially social and political upheaval, are always interpreted apocalyptically in the West. The devastating treks of migrating peoples and the Normans, the collapse of the old Roman Empire, the threat of Saracen rule are all easily interpreted as those "wars and rebellions" which the Gospels announce as signs of the End. Around the year 1000 the general state of excitement intensifies, stopping the pulse of medieval life.[279] And yet, the apocalyptic tremors caused by the migration of peoples around the year 1000 are not part of the expectations of the Kingdom of God;[280] thus they are still accommodated within the interpretive model of the medieval system. It also incorporates the abundant apocalyptic, mystical, and apocryphal legends and narratives in which the imminent End is welcomed as it draws ever closer. "Sagas of the Antichrist, circumstances surrounding the Second Coming, and the situation to be encountered in the other world are all discussed in these *summa theologica*, and, to no lesser extent, fully articulated elements of myths find their way into general historiography."[281] However, the division of world history into periods gives rise to an element which points beyond the medieval system and which announces, though still concealed, a new method of interpreting the world. For in a *summa theologica* there is no place for a directed, purposeful conception of history. Otto of Freising's *Chronicle* ends in an eschatology which has lain dormant [*latent*] throughout his work: the third age of mankind [*das Greisenalter*] has come, the age of weariness, which is symbolized in Daniel by the colossus with the feet of clay. According to Otto of Freising, the marked polarization of the antitheses indicates the imminence of the End.[282]

Literature [*Dichtung*] is the intermediary between historiography and folktale. The early scholarly anti-Christian literature, from Adso's *libellus de antichristo* onward, gains its popularity through drama, and in the thirteenth century through the literature of the Wandering Scholars. "Through Walther, Reimar of Zweter, Conrad of Würzburg, through the great writings of Frau Ava and Heinrich of Neustadt, additional eschatological mythology pours out of the Church into art and popular consumption."²⁸³ All political and religious events are immediately seen to reflect the apoca- lypse: they appear as the chiliastic dream of a last empire [*chiliastischer Endreichstraum*], which inspires Charlemagne, Barbarossa, and Frederick II, or takes the form of the chiliastic papacy in the tales of the angelic popes. This murky leavening agent becomes clearer in the work of Joachim of Fiore.²⁸⁴

Joachim's theology certainly formulates all the Christian promises and expectations, but these are transferred to a *new age* and announced in a way which makes a new historical claim, one that positions itself alongside, and in the course of its development, counter to the claim made by the Roman Church.²⁸⁵ This is because, in Joachim's theology of history, the status of the Church is followed by a new, changed status for the human community: the age of the Holy Spirit. By setting the starting date for the new world age of the Holy Spirit in the year 1200, Joachim is attempting to gain independence from the medieval *corpus christianum*. Shattering Augustine's dual image of history, which determines medieval metaphysics, Joachim introduces a third, antithetical factor to the religion of the Old and New Testaments: *ecclesia spiritualis*.

In so doing Joachim sets his sights firmly on the essence of the modern age [*Wesen der Neuzeit*], which he christens as the Millennium of Revolution. Joachim's new calendar of history [*Zeitrechnung*] and his division of history into periods have to be understood as the context for all subsequent, apoca- lyptic waves of the modern age [*Neuzeit*]. Joachim inevitably equates the first wave with the entire millennium of apocalyptic flooding, but places the law of the modern age at its very inception.²⁸⁶ The tiresome dispute over the beginning of the modern age pales into insignificance alongside Joachim's achievement. In fact, the model of antiquity–Middle Ages–modern age is nothing but a secular extension of Joachim's prophecy of the three ages of the Father, the Son, and the Holy Spirit. Every revolutionary eschatology since Joachim has suggested that with it, beyond the prehistory represented by antiquity and the Middle Ages, something definitive is beginning, some- thing which brings fulfillment: the third empire, the age of the Holy Spirit.

BOOK III

THE THEOLOGICAL ESCHATOLOGY OF EUROPE

The Law of the Modern Age

The history of modern eschatology enables us, if our focus remains riveted on the key events, to discern a regular rhythm. A summary of eschatology can be given in the apocalyptic phrase *God's Kingdom on earth*. The formulation of God's Kingdom on earth is ambiguous and the emphasis lies either on the beginning or the end. First, it is the idea of the coming, future Kingdom of God which bursts the established horizons of a cycle of life. A self-contained, mature system, which has found its own point of equilibrium, established itself absolute and contained all disruptive forces, is then burst open by the prophecy of God's Kingdom as the *ecclesia spiritualis*. But the inner light of an *ecclesia spiritualis* burns down the walls of external institutions. The inner light becomes a devouring flame and is transformed into a world on fire. This is how the final stage of the apocalyptic formula comes front and center. The proclamation of God's Kingdom presses toward its realization. This rhythm of proclamation and realization, of *"ecclesia spiritualis"* and "on earth," permeates eschatological events.

Each of the apocalyptic waves of the modern age [*Neuzeit*] is a variation on this theme, emphasizing one aspect of it. Each new eschatology shatters an established horizon and becomes perceptible when it hits a strident note, since its language assumes an argumentative tone quite alien to prerevolutionary humanity. With each new apocalyptic wave a new syntax is created, and the breakdown of meaning in language makes people from the old age appear deranged to those of the new, and vice versa. "To those in olden days it was said, but I am saying to you . . ." this is the ever-recurrent situation in apocalyptic times—times which are truly out of joint. The old man is a dead body to the new man, a has-been, as the Russians call the émigrés, while the new man is deranged in the eyes of the old. It is in these terms that Thomas Aquinas regarded Joachim and his disciples.[1]

Joachim's theology of history shatters the foundations of medieval theocracy. The slogan *ecclesia spiritualis* destroys the equation that has applied since Augustine and on which medieval theocracy is founded: Church = Kingdom of God. Joachim and the Spirituals proclaim God's Kingdom as the *ecclesia spiritualis*, as a spiritual kingdom. Joachim's theology of history is taken to its conclusion by Thomas Müntzer's theology of revolution. Müntzer and the Anabaptists want to bring about the *ecclesia spiritualis* on earth. Inevitably, the problem of violence arises in Müntzer's work, and his theology justifies the use of force in a good cause. The theology of revolution is the theology of violence.

The breakdown in Münster concludes the chapter of the Anabaptist revolution, which takes place in the shadow of medieval theocracy. Meanwhile the Christian foundations of the medieval world are crumbling. Not until the Enlightenment will a new system of comparable weight be created, one that finds a new center in rationalism. In the age of rationalism the "church of reason" is synonymous with the Kingdom of God. It is not by chance that the goddess of reason and her church celebrate their triumphs in Catholic France. Dostoyevsky, in his political writings, discovers the link between rationalism and Catholicism. The age of Enlightenment derives its historical claim from the Catholic Church. Medievalism and the Enlightenment are the two static spheres of life in Europe. The Medieval Church and the church of the Enlightenment establish themselves as absolute and are based on the equation, the church *is* the Kingdom of God.

The blessed cultural age of eternity represented by the Enlightenment is shaken by the earthquake in Lisbon. Depths open up which the system of reason is unable to fathom. The problem of evil sparks the dialectic of German Idealism, which has effects beyond the age of rationalism. Lessing is the first of many who do not see the Kingdom of God realized in the world of rationalism but prophesy that it is yet to come. Joachim's configuration is restored and Lessing, too, reaches back to Joachim's prophecy of an everlasting gospel. The *Education of the Human Race* is the first manifesto of *philosophical chiliasm*, which determines the eschatology of German Idealism from Kant to Hegel. In his *Philosophy of World History*, Hegel moves within Joachim's orbit. The "Kingdom of God" in Hegel's philosophy of religion is synonymous with the "kingdom of the mind" [*intellectuellen Reich*] (*ecclesia spiritualis*) in his *History of Philosophy*. And Hegel's philosophy of history is taken to its logical conclusions by the philosophy of revolution in Marxism. The Hegelians of the left want to realize the Kingdom of God, the Hegelian "kingdom of the mind," on earth. Marx aims to revolutionize the world along the lines of Hegelian reason. According to Engels, the proletariat is the heir of German Idealism.

Groups of utopian socialists, directly linked to the Anabaptists, join Marxism (Weitling). Inevitably, the problem of force arises in Marx's works and he justifies its use in revolution; the philosophy of revolution is the philosophy of force (Sorel). The tides which flow in the course of revolution are not trivial and random but rhythmical and inevitable. Ideas and events which transform the nature of man and the features of humanity cannot be compressed into moments but must be seen through: they complete their course within a historical economy which comprises seemingly disparate centuries.[2] Since the spirit of eschatology grows more transparent to itself each time, the tidal flow quickens its pace. The temporal course of philosophical eschatology flows more rapidly than does that of theological eschatology.

As a comparison with Jewish eschatology of the same period demonstrates, the steady rhythm of eschatology was not a singular development exclusive to Christian Europe. The Zohar, the key text in Jewish eschatological mysticism, was unsealed at this time, when the movement of Spirituals was reaching the height of its prominence in Petrus Olivi. The eschatology of the Zohar, like that of the Spanish Kabbalah, runs along lines which are closely akin [*isotop*] to those of Joachim and the Spirituals. Moreover, there are historical links which cannot be dismissed. Just as the eschatology of Joachim and the Spirituals is radicalized by Müntzer and the Anabaptists, so too the eschatology of the Zohar and the Spanish Kabbalah is radicalized by the Lurian Kabbalah. Like the Anabaptists and Müntzer, the disciples of Luria also seek to use force, admittedly through the magical power of prayer, to bring the Kingdom of God into being. The messianic wave of Sabbatai Zvi is most closely linked to the Lurianic enthusiasm for the End. Münster, where the most intense focus of the Anabaptist movement was, also has its parallels in Safed, the city of the kabbalists. It was in Safed that the sacred community associated with redemption, by both the Zohar and medieval Jewish eschatology, was meant to arise.

The history of European eschatology being history's most intimate unfolding [*das innerste Geschehen der Geschichte*], it is orchestrated by the history of the European revolution, which is the external version of the innermost core [*das Aussen dieses Innen*]. A history of European revolution is identical, however, with the history of the loss of Europe's Christian-Catholic essence. Around 1800, Novalis, in his work *Christendom and Europe*, seeks to equate these two realms of humanity, Christendom and Europe. Endeavoring to do so in 1800 can only be called romantic, but in the beginnings of Europe, in the West before Joachim, there was unity between Catholic Christendom and the European population.

The medieval Church is characterized by the Ptolemaic worldview. The world, as it is, is an image of its archetype, and by elevating its proper nature to a higher plane, the imperfect image of this world approximates its archetype. The earth, according to Ptolemaic theory, is beneath the heavens, and everything which happens on it is an image of the archetype, a symbol. Ptolemaic man, who still believes the world to be the image of its own archetype, seeks fulfillment in rising toward the idea. The Church as the body of Christ acts as an accomplice of Christ. The medieval Church is a *charismatic* form of Christianity; at the heart of medieval religion is the Mass, where heaven and earth become one.[3] The history of European revolutions is the history of resistance to the Ptolemaic Kyrios Christos cult of medieval Christianity. The word *revolution* is found in the writings of Copernicus and Galilee, the fathers of the modern worldview. Because of them, mankind living in the modern age experiences his historical existence as *revolution*. In the main work of Copernicus, dating from 1543, and even earlier in Dante, revolution means the rotation of heavenly bodies and heavenly worlds. The generation following Dante is the first to apply the concept of rotating heavenly bodies to events in the small Italian city-states. The perennial changes in the constitution of these small states appear to stage the drama of the world. Ever since Galileo and his contemporaries Rohan and Hobbes defined man as a speck of dust on the planet and ejected him from the center of the cosmos, we dare to refer to the pronounced upheavals of the great empires as revolutions.[4]

In the Copernican view of the world there is an earth but no heaven.[5] The earth mirrors no heaven, and the reality of the world is gained by *Copernican* man, not by having the world emulate a superior archetype, but by revolutionizing the world in terms of an ideal that lies in the future. The Ptolemaic world is ruled by the Platonic concept of *eros*, which attracts the lower sphere to the upper sphere. The Copernican world is ruled by the *spirit*, which invariably presses ahead. The ethics of Copernican man is an ethics of the future. As heaven above has lost its moral significance [*Wertgehalt*], the

Ptolemaic worldview

moral will [*Wertwille*] is focused on the future. Because the Copernican realm has been emptied of its meaning, fulfillment for Copernican man lies in time and hence in history.

The transition from the Ptolemaic to the Copernican conception of the world does not happen all at once and does not really begin with Copernicus. Its beginnings stretch back to Joachim of Fiore, who tears down the partitions separating heaven and earth by stipulating a specific date in the near future on which man will realize his ultimate goal [*Erfüllung*]. The Platonic relationship of image and archetype, which Origen and Augustine set up between earthly history and heavenly guidance, is transformed for Joachim into a powerful chain of events within history: the Kingdom of Heaven becomes the final realm of the spirit. In Joachim's theology of history, Christ, having acted as a stabilizing force [*ruhender Pol*] in Christianity, is drawn into a Trinitarian, historical process. While Christ is the absolute center for the medieval Catholic Church, dividing time into B.C. and A.D., he becomes a powerful agency [*Potenz*] in the historical process first in Joachim's theology and then in the modern theology of history. With the rejection of the papacy and the charismatic church by Hussites and reformers, the unity of Christendom, the bulwark and last valuable possession of the Catholic Church, collapses. Yet Lutheran Christianity is closely linked to Catholicism because Paul is the foundation of both. This is why there can still be a reformed Church, because the Pauline heritage of the Reformation equates the Church with Christ. While Luther rediscovers in the "word of God" the new center around which the reformed community can gather, this word of God, holy and charismatic to Luther, is a mere shred of paper to Müntzer, a successor to Joachim. With that, the last ties of Christian unity are severed and the way is open for the spiritual religion of Sebastian Frank and Jakob Böhme. Prometheus arises in Christ's shadow. The mythological point at which Prometheus appears is always in the present time for German Idealism and has become a frequent idée fixe.[7] Schelling explicitly invokes Prometheus as the symbol of philosophy. "Is it not evident that the tendency to transpose the infinite into the finite, and vice versa, is dominant in all philosophical discussion and exploration? Such thoughts are eternal . . . a gift of the Gods to mankind, a divine gift to man which Prometheus brought down to earth along with the purest fire of heaven."[8] Marx celebrates Prometheus as "a saint in the philosophical calendar."[9]

But in the kingdom of Prometheus, Antichrist becomes a title of honor. In the final sentences of *Belief and Knowledge* Hegel transforms the death of

God into a "speculative Good Friday." The feeling that *God Himself is dead*, this endless pain on which modern religion is founded, is construed by Hegel as a moment containing the ultimate idea, a moment of absolute freedom.[10] Feuerbach points out quite correctly that "until now philosophy has fallen into the period of Christianity's decline, the period of its negation, which at the same time is meant to be its affirmation. Hegelian philosophy concealed this negation of Christianity in posing a contradiction between idea and thought."[11] Feuerbach, moreover, derives his understanding from Luther. In a special treatise on the *Essence of Faith According to Luther*, Feuerbach shows the identity of Luther's concept of subjective faith and his *Essence of Christianity*.[12] Finally, Bruno Bauer proves to his contemporaries that even Hegel was an atheist and Antichrist.[13] In the circle of the Berlin freethinkers, Antichrist is a title of honor, which Karl Marx also acquired. Bruno Bauer, in discovering the real genealogy of Christendom, refers back to the young Hegel and anticipates Nietzsche's *Genealogy of Morals*. His theory claims that Christianity was born from the collapse of political freedom in the Roman world.[14] Marx introduces his critique of Hegel's philosophy of law in the following words: "As far as Germany is concerned the critique of religion has essentially come to an end, and the critique of religion is a requirement of all criticism."[15] Nietzsche sees himself confronting the ebbing waters of the Christian religion. All possibilities of the Christian life, both the most serious and the most casual, have been explored. It is time for the birth of something new. If Heine wittily dismisses baptism as an entry ticket to European culture, then the good European, after Nietzsche, shakes off the last vestiges of Christianity. This also spells the end for the history of European apocalypticism, for the *corpus christianum* has come undone, and that includes Protestantism.

Joachim's Prophecy and Hegelian Philosophy

Joachim's theology, which Ernst Benz admirably expounds in connection with the history of the Spirituals, is founded on the Apocalypse of John. Since Tyconius, a predecessor of Augustine, the Apocalypse of John has not been central to Christian theology, which goes to show that Joachim's theology leaves behind Augustine's doctrine of history.[16] The Apocalypse is revealed to John as the scripture of salvation, which unfolds in riddles, images, and visions and lasts from the beginning until the end of the world. The individuals and figures, and the various symbols of the Apocalypse, point to particular people, groups, and events in the history of salvation. It is the task of the exegete to find the right key to these figures and symbols so that he can unlock the mystery of the scripture, and in so doing unravel and reveal the history of salvation.[17] Joachim's theology is essentially directed toward the history of salvation, and all of his speculations are fundamentally historical ones. The ages of salvation are separated from each other and yet interrelated, like the Old and New Testaments. The course, goal, and culmination of the history of salvation can be gleaned from its progression in past periods: in the time of the Old Testament, from Abraham to Christ, and in the time of the New Testament, which embraces the history of the Christian Church up to the time of Joachim. All important events have, as far as their function and sequence are concerned, a correlative in the ages of salvation. This results in a system of correspondences [*Gleichzeitigkeiten*],[18] because certain people and events play the same role and have the same historical function in different periods of salvation, separated by centuries.[19] Joachim's theology draws the Old and New Testaments into a net of relationships governed by a definite order and sequence.

The Trinitarian nature of God is explained in Joachim's theology in a purely historical way so that one of the three divine persons is prominent in each of the three ages. Like Hegel, Joachim sees the three persons of the Trinity as the three world periods of history. It is within the context of these three periods that the unity of the three persons in the Trinity emerges. The first period of the world is the age of God the Father, the second of the Son, and the third of the Holy Spirit. Like the persons of the Trinity, the three periods of the world also stand in a progressive relation [*Steigerung*] to one another.[20] The essence of the dialectic develops out of this Trinitarian view of history formulated by Joachim. The Hegelian trilogy [*Dreitakt*], thesis-antithesis-synthesis, can only be understood in terms of Joachim's rhythm of the ages of Father, Son, and Holy Spirit. That is why Hegel insists, even in the *Philosophy of World History*, on the intimate connection between the Trinity and the dialectical understanding of history.[21] Hegel elucidates the essence of his philosophy of history in sentences which perfectly mirror Joachim's writing. The nature and progression of history have their origin in the nature of the triune God. "God is only perceived as spirit in that he is known as the triune. This principle is the pivot on which the history of the world turns. History builds up to this point and moves on from this point. In this religion all enigmas are solved; all mysteries are revealed. Christians know from God what he is, as long as they know that he is three in one [*dreieinig*]. He who does not know this knows nothing of Christianity."[22]

In his theology Joachim gives a dialectical interpretation of the concept of the mystical Christian bride; he sees the union of Christ and his bride, the Church, as the metaphysical archetype of sexual union. The charismatic church of the second age needs a son who is to be the bearer of her promises: "Mother Church, crying out in labor, keeps saying in her prayers the same words that her archetype Rachel said to her husband: Give me children, otherwise I must die."[23] The second age thus does not bear any significance in itself, but presses toward fulfillment in a new age. The idea of development determines the progression, sublation [*Aufhebung*] (Hegel), and sequence of the individual epochs of the world and times of salvation [*Heilszeiten*]:

The Holy Scriptures point us to three world orders (*status*): to the first when we were under the law; to the second in which we are under grace, and to the third whose imminent arrival we already await, and in which we will enjoy an even greater degree of grace. This is because, as John said, God gave us grace to receive grace, that is, faith to receive love, and both in like measure. The first status is that of science, the second that of partial wisdom, the third that of absolute knowledge [*Fülle der Erkenntnis*]. The first is in the servitude of slavery, the second in the servitude of sons, the third in freedom. The first in fear, the second in faith, the third in love. The first is the status of bondsmen, the second of freemen, the third of friends. The first of boys, the second of men, and the third of the old. The first in the light of the stars, the second in the red light of dawn, the third in the bright light of day. . . . The first status refers to the Father, the second to the Son, and the third to the Holy Spirit.[24]

Hegel constructs world history from the same principles of love and freedom, anticipating an end which brings fulfillment. Hegel shows "that the world history is nothing other than the realization of the spirit and the development of the concept of freedom."[25] In the course of history, the spirit develops out of bondage into freedom. The Orient only knows that one is free, the Greek and Roman world that a number are free, the Germanic world that all are free. The history of the Orient is the childhood of world history, the time of the Greeks and Romans is the age of youth and adulthood, and the Germanic world, primarily his own age, is what Hegel knew as the "mature age of the spirit" [*das Greisenalter*].[26]

The transition from the old to the new order is accomplished by way of sublation as defined by Hegel. The new order grows out of the old, and remains in the lap and protection of the old until it bursts the frame of the old and is able to assume a particular form. "When such fruit emerges, is the established order to feel pain because it sees that what has been raised to an imperfect state is now followed by universal perfection? . . . Never, never, never may it come to pass that the succession of Peter should be eaten up with envy because the *ordo spiritualis* is about to come to perfection."[27] The goal of history is the kingdom of the spirit, and the church of the spirit is the future, complete and mature social order. Joachim's theology invalidates the claim made by the Roman Church, which takes itself to be the only valid manifestation of the Christian spirit until the end of the world.[28] Within the process of history, which is moving toward its goal, the institution of the papacy is subject to the same law of sublation (Hegel) as all other historical institutions.

Joachim depicts the displacement of the papal Church by the *ecclesia spiritualis* as a withering away. He often describes this displacement by the church of the spirit as a passing over [*Übergehen*], a *transire*.[29] Joachim's *transire* coincides with Hegel's concept of sublation [*Aufhebung*]. *Transire* and sublation are ambiguous, depending on whether they mean entering into a new form of historical existence or passing into death. Therefore, *transire* (Joachim) and sublation (Hegel) encompass two separate stages [*Momente*]. First, the transformation of the social order (therefore, *transire* can become synonymous with *mutare vitam*);[30] second, and already implied [*mitgesetzt*] in the pattern of change, is the fact that the new order will represent a higher, more spiritual, and purer stage than its predecessor.[31]

An element in Joachim's theology that is equally "Hegelian,"—or, to be more precise, what is essentially "Joachimite" in Hegel's philosophy—is the equation of the history of the spirit with the course of world history. While the first stage [*Status*] only contains *scientia*, insight into the way human life is ordered, the second stage has *sapientia ex parte*, a limited knowledge of the divine mystery, and the third stage has *plenitudo intellectus*, the fullness of spiritual knowledge. In the third stage all mysteries are revealed and one sees divine things, no longer in riddles, through the reflection of a dark word, but as they really are, face to face.

In his *Phenomenology of Spirit* Hegel outlines the developmental history of the spirit's manifestation. In the stages of knowledge, the systematic, logical steps are inseparable from the way they relate to history, because they permeate one another.[32] Both Hegel and Joachim equate the history of the spirit with the course of world history; this is possible because they both share the same concept of the spirit. They identify the spirit, not with the logical principle ordering the world of forms, but with the principle that realizes the history of salvation. *Intelligentia spiritualis* does not mean a timeless act of union with God, as occurs in mysticism in the twinkling of an eye [*Augen-Blick*]. Given their *historical* interpretation of the idea of spirit, Hegel and Joachim see *intelligentia spiritualis* rather as the future goal of the historical process, the fulfillment of all that lies in the future—they see it, that is, in eschatological terms.

For Hegel the history of the spirit is the core [*das Innerste*] of world history. Movement is essential for the spirit, and so is history. Hegel's work not only contains a philosophy of history and a history of philosophy; rather, the basis of the whole work is historical to a degree that no philosophy previously was, and can only be compared with Joachim's theology of history. The goal of the dialectical movement of the spirit is "absolute knowledge," *plenitudo intellectus*. "Absolute knowledge" is attained by way of "recollecting" all preceding manifestations of the spirit. This "tour" of earlier manifestations [*gewesene Wesen*] of the spirit, of the history of the spirit, is not a detour but is the only possible way to absolute knowledge. History is the process of salvation. History is not external to the spirit; rather, the spirit is at bottom only the movement of self-development. The dialectic of becoming [*Werdens*] does not run to infinity, but strives for the Eschaton, where it finds fulfillment. To the extent that the spirit reaches its *end*, that it reveals its *full* form, the history of the spirit is *complete* [*voll-endet*].[33]

In his *Lectures on the History of Philosophy*, Hegel expounds the construction of the *Phenomenology of the Spirit*.[34] The first age of the spirit stretches from Thales to Proclus. It reaches its climax with Proclus in the ancient reconciliation [*Versöhnung*] of the finite and the infinite, the earthly and the divine world. The second age stretches from the beginning of the Christian era to the beginning of the modern era. In this age the same reconciliation of earthly and divine occurs, but on a higher level within the Christian Church, so it can finally be perfected in the third age of *plenitudo intellectus*, in the Christian philosophy which stretches from Descartes to Hegel. The systems of philosophy in this final age enable *knowledge* of reconciliation [*Versöhnung*], which had formerly been an act of *faith* [*geglaubt*], to be grasped in intellectual terms.[35] At the very end comes Hegel's absolute system, in which the real world has become "spiritual" in a Christian sense. Hegel's history of the spirit concludes not provisionally, at some random point, but is final and consciously "finalized": "The world spirit has come this far. The final philosophy is the result of all earlier philosophies; nothing is lost. All principles are preserved."[36]

The theme of Hegel's philosophy is the unity of divine and human nature guaranteed by the incarnation of God. This is because all the stages of the spirit are only the ways in which God forever becomes man. In the Kingdom of God the earthly and the heavenly are finally reconciled. God's Kingdom is a reality where God reigns as the one and absolute spirit. The "kingdom of God" from the *Philosophy of Religion* is identical with the "kingdom of the mind" [*intellectuellen Reich*] from the *History of Philosophy* and the "kingdom of the spirit" [*Geisterreich*] from the *Phenomenology*.[37] The kingdom of the spirit finally enables " state power, religion, and the principles of philosophy to become one [*zusammenfallen*], bringing the reconciliation of reality with the spirit of the state, with religious conscience, and likewise with philosophical knowledge."[38]

Joachim's exegesis explains the metaphysical fate of Christ and his resurrection in terms of world history. The whole of Christ's life, his human and divine existence, is an archetype of the fate of the world. The suffering, death, and resurrection of Christ are lived out in his body, in the *corpus christianum*. The Roman Catholic Church of the second age is beleaguered [*heimgesucht*] and withers away, but out of the decaying body of *corpus christianum* is born the *ordo spiritualis*, in which the *corpus christianum* rises to a new spiritual form in the *ecclesia spiritualis* of the third age. Decay and reformation are understood by Joachim to be related in terms of a historical dialectic. The concept of the Reformation, *redire ad formam illam*, does not aim to transfer the early Christian forms directly to the contemporary church. For *redire ad formam illiam* is only a *similitudo*. It is about the analogy of an earlier stage of history taken to a higher historical plane. Fulfillment lies in the future, not in the past. The original form of the Gospel is only an initial stage and an imperfect likeness of the coming realization of the splendor [*Herrlichkeit*] of the spirit.[39]

Similarly the Reformation for Hegel begins the "period of the spirit."[40] Hegel, too, understands decay and Reformation to be related to each other in terms of a historical dialectic. The Reformation has emerged from the ruins of the Church. Hegel depicts the relationship of the medieval Catholic Church to the reformed Church of the modern age in terms strongly reminiscent of Joachim. The principle of spiritual freedom is unfolded in the Church of the modern age.

The basic teaching of Luther is the teaching of freedom. . . . The process of salvation only comes about in heart and spirit. This teaching does away with all externals, the many different types and divisions of the spirit's bondage. . . . As the individual has become aware of being filled with the divine spirit, all ties with external forms are removed. Now there is no difference between priest and laity; no one class exclusively monopolizes the body of truth as it does with respect to all the spiritual and temporal treasures of the Church. It is the heart, the innermost consciousness and conscience, the spiritual sensitivity of mankind which can, and is, expected to lead us into an awareness of the truth. This subjectivity is the possession of every man.[41]

The period of the Middle Ages was the Kingdom of the Son. God is not yet complete in the Son but only in the spirit. As Son he has been set apart from himself, and there is a difference in being [*ein Anderssein*], which must be sublated [*aufgehoben*] only in the spirit, in the return of God to himself. Just as the relationship with the Son is essentially an external one, the Middle Ages placed an emphasis on externals. However, the Reformation marks the beginning of the kingdom of the spirit where God is truly known as spirit. This unfurls the final, new banner around which the nations gather, the flag of the free spirit which contains the truth and, only in so doing, remains true to itself. This is the flag which we bear and under which we serve. The only reason that time has existed until now is to achieve this purpose, to establish it in such a way that it grows into the true form of freedom, freedom for the whole community.[42]

The Owl of Minerva begins its flight at twilight. Hegel was thinking of dusk in his famous sentence, but it also applies to dawn. The same historical perspective opens up at the beginning and end of the modern age, as at the beginning and end of the last epoch of the Christian Church in Europe, in which the Christian logos is revealed in the form of the spirit. Admittedly, at the beginning such a perspective is one of pro-spective prophecy [*vorschauende Prophetie*]; at the end, it is retro-spective prophecy [*zurückschauende Prophetie*]—in other words, the philosophy of history.

Hegel assigns philosophy the task of reflecting [*nach-denken*] on events and realities, but prophecy must think through events and realities in advance [*vor-denken*]. That is the reason why for many Joachim appears as an enthusiast [*Schwärmer*]. Perhaps, wrote Lessing in the *Education of the Human Race,* even

certain enthusiasts of the thirteenth and fourteenth centuries had caught hold of a beam of light from this new eternal gospel and their only mistake was to announce its arrival as imminent. Perhaps their view of a world divided into three ages was not such an empty whim, and certainly they had the best of intentions when they taught that the New Covenant would inevitably become outmoded in the same way as the old one. They always held on to the same economy of the same God. It was—to put it in my own words—the same plan of the universal education of the human race. Except they were too precipitant; they thought that at one stroke, without enlightenment or preparation, they could make their contemporaries, who had hardly grown out of childhood, into mature men worthy of their third age. That was what made them into enthusiasts. The enthusiast often has correct glimpses of the future but cannot wait for this future. He wants this future to be accelerated and wants to be able to bring it about. In doing so, he is expecting something to come about in the moment of his lifetime which takes nature millennia to achieve.[43]

If one calls Joachim an enthusiast, it must be borne in mind that, unlike many others who inspired people in the Catholic Church, he does not rave [*schwärmt*] about a heaven to be found beyond. Nor does he extol a new way of life based on personal experience, like many in heretical movements; rather, he sees the fulfillment of his idea in the future, in an age of the world yet to come. But perhaps Joachim is not an enthusiast at all, because he recognizes the law of the new world age, which he knowingly inaugurates and which Hegel knowingly concludes. It is true to say that Lessing begins the final phase of spiritual Christianity. The *break with* the Christian logos and the *break from* the *corpus christianum* of the European world announces itself in German Idealism up to Nietzsche.

Hegel is aware of coming at the end of the last Christian world age in the same way that Joachim sees himself at its beginning. Joachim knows he is at the *turning point*, when the new world age is already beginning to unfold of its own accord, while the old age is still in full swing and asserting its exclusive historical claim. The two world ages collide and the resulting situation of *coartatio* is fundamental to Joachim's understanding of his own age. Basing his speculations on the generations, Joachim comes to the conclusion that around the year 1200 the institution of the Catholic Church will come to an end, and that the *ecclesia spiritualis* will arise around 1260. His main works date from 1190 to 1200. So he considers himself to be positioned at the time of the greatest tension in the history of salvation, positioned in the *kairos*, in which the new spiritual world is dawning and he himself is called to aid the breakthrough of the *ecclesia spiritualis*. Joachim recognizes that he is witnessing the struggle between two world ages and this motivates all he does and says.[44]

He is living under the sway of the medieval Christian Church just as Hegel lives within the system of bourgeois society. Joachim ensures that all of his writings be subject to the judgment of the Church and he agrees in advance to any emendations it may make. To be open to the truth and yet dependent on the Church is a contradiction that Joachim can easily reconcile, it seems. In a similar fashion Hegel is able to combine being "priest of the Absolute" with acting as an official of the Prussian state.[45] The scheme of history which Joachim and Hegel design allows them to blend in smoothly with the prevailing order, and this prevents any revolutionary elements from erupting. Yet the conservatism of this viewpoint is relative; its revolutionary character is *absolute*. For Joachim and Hegel understand the process of world history as a progressive movement and, consequently, as a permanent negation of the existing order (Friedrich Engels).[46] The young generation of the Spirituals and the Hegelian left, who regard themselves as the fulfillment of Joachim's promised *ordo spiritualis* and aim to transform reality according to the guidelines of Hegelian reason, draw the revolutionary consequences from Joachim's and Hegel's historical perspectives. They are already at variance with the system of the existing Church structure and bourgeois society. The Church separates the Spirituals from the rest of the medieval world and blatantly persecutes them as heretics. Similarly, the Hegelian left is ejected from society. Feuerbach has to relinquish his unsalaried position as a lecturer [*Privatdozentur*] at Erlangen because of his *Gedanken über Tod und Unsterblichkeit* [*Thoughts on Death and Immortality*] and to lecture unpaid in a village without a church. Ruge loses his lectureship at Halle in his constant dispute with the police; his attempt to found a free academy in Dresden fails. To avoid going to prison for the second time, he escapes to Paris and then to Switzerland before finally arriving in England. Bruno Bauer is deprived of his lectureship because of his radical theological ideas. Karl Marx's plan to qualify [*habilitieren*] as a lecturer of philosophy in Bonn comes to nothing. Pursued by the governments on the continent of Europe, Marx seeks refuge in a series of countries; his final place of exile is England.[47]

The Spirituals as Successors to Joachim

The confusion surrounding Joachim arises essentially from the fundamental ambiguity of *transire*, an ambiguity which is shared with the Hegelian concept of sublation [*Aufhebung*]. At first, the Catholic Church attempts to accommodate the teachings of Joachim into the system of medieval Christianity. Joachim's theology is not heretical as long as its ambiguous promise of transforming [*Aufhebung*] (*transire*) the Roman Catholic Church into the coming spiritual church is confined to the future, and provided he subjects himself to the authority of the Catholic Church, while at the same time accommodating himself into the system of medieval theocracy.

But the revolutionary elements in Joachim's theology of history have a historical impact and the medieval church thus has to declare him a heretic.

This is because the sublation of the Roman Catholic Church in the world age of the spirit points beyond its present organization toward a new concept of humanity, a new potential for community, which Joachim makes sufficiently clear in his few treatises. It is a free community of the church of the Holy Spirit without a pope, sacraments, canonical scriptures, dogma, or priesthood. The typology of history as developed by Joachim serves no other purpose than to prove that each form and expression of Christian spirituality fulfills and perfects the revelation and promises given at the beginning of the Christian religion.[48] Christian spirituality is to Joachim, as to Hegel, the true elucidation of the idea implicit in the original Christian promise.

In depicting the *ecclesia spiritualis* as sublating all external aspects of the institution—the sacraments, its scriptures and hierarchy—Joachim takes an ax to the roots of the medieval Church. *Ecclesia spiritualis* is not some transcendent *civitas platonica*; rather, Joachim projects the church of the spirit as the historical authority of the age to come. In so doing Joachim steers the younger generation away from attempting to reform the Church from within, and toward realizing the transformation [*Aufhebung*] of the Roman Catholic Church into the church of the spirit.[49] Based on his speculations about generations, Joachim calculates the time of the *ecclesia spiritualis* to fall on the next generation, thus enabling a group within the next generation to see itself as the forerunner of the church of the spirit and to model its awareness of history on the schema Joachim drew up for this church. Moreover, he provides a future group with the opportunity to supplant the claims of the Roman Church with their own claims, based on theology and the logic of history, and he gives them reasons for denying the Church its right of existence in history. Joachim creates the weapons which the future Spirituals can use in their struggle against the Catholic Church.[50]

Joachim envisions the great battle of the *ordo spiritualis* against the powers that be at the end of the second empire, as the age of the third empire [*des dritten Reiches*] is in preparation under the motto of Christ and Antichrist. Joachim thus makes it possible for a future group acting as messengers of the spiritual church to brand the Roman Church, which rejects this claim, as the Antichrist[51]—a blazing epithet [*flammendes Kennwort*] that the Spirituals pass on to Dante and the Hussites pass on to Luther and Müntzer.

Joachim's theology takes historical effect through the Spirituals of the Franciscan order, whose eminent historiographer is Ernst Benz.[52] The work of its founder, the self-proclaimed mission of the order [*Selbstanspruch*], and the historical reasons for its reformatory effects on the Church at large all presuppose a latent tension and expectation of the end. Joachim's prophecy strikes the underlying eschatological atmosphere of the Franciscans like lightning and shapes the Spirituals' concepts of the kingdom of the spirit, the age of the spirit, and the church of the spirit.[53] The impact [*Einbruch*] of his prophecy on Franciscan piety is responsible for the revolutionary element of the order. The Spirituals are revolutionary in as much as they see themselves and the great events of their time as the fulfillment of Joachim's prophecy and act according to its principles in a way which precipitates the coming age.[54]

In 1241 Joachim's writings are taken to Pisa, where a group of Franciscans become the missionary force for his prophecy, secretly spreading his thoughts far and wide. Before long traces of Joachim's ideas are to be found among laypeople. This dissemination among laypeople is made possible by the third order of Franciscans, and it is likely that the Anabaptists emerged directly from these groups of Franciscan tertiaries.[55] Laypeople and monks influenced by Joachim form proper conventicles, which spread from Pisa over the whole of Italy, France, and Catalonia. Those who join these communities are predominantly intellectuals. Somewhere in the south of France, "many lawyers, judges, doctors, and other educated people meet in the chamber of Frater Hugo to hear about Joachim's teaching."[56] His propaganda, distributed by the Spirituals, also reaches large numbers of the bourgeoisie. The origins of the Beguines are to be found in Joachim's conventicles; his theology of history forms the spiritual basis of the Beguines.[57] In the Beguine communities Olivi's devotional book of the Apocalypse, the best-known document in Spiritual circles, is regarded by them as canonical. Passages from this text are translated into the vernacular and revered like the Gospels.

The conflict between the Dominicans and the Franciscans, fought on the ground of Joachim's historical theology, escalates into a fight over the leadership of the Church in the End Time. For a start, the Spirituals compete for leadership of the Church itself, and with the pope's support they defend its freedom against the Hohenstaufen dynasty.[58] From the reign of Frederick II, this empire emerges as a political force making messianic and apocalyptic claims, which push the papacy reluctantly into a revolutionary position. However, it cannot quite be described as a "papal revolution" because the papacy remains suspicious of the "left wing" within its own ranks.[59] It is not until the death of the Hohenstaufen emperor that a critical turning point is reached for the Spirituals, because only now are the Spiritual forces free to mount a final challenge against the Catholic Church.

The very first document from the circle of Spirituals has a barb directed against medieval theocracy. Gerard sums up the writings of Joachim under the title *The Eternal Gospel*, to which he adds an introduction. The phrase *eternal gospel* contains all the leitmotifs of Joachim's theology of history. The eternal gospel "is the gospel which issues from the Gospel of Christ. As it is said: the letter kills but the spirit gives life."[60] The eternal gospel is therefore not the Gospel of Christ, which is the same as the New Testament canonized by the Church, but is a new one. It is likely that what Joachim meant by the eternal gospel was not anything written down. He calculates the age of the eternal gospel to fall within the next generations. Only a few years, says Gerard of himself, separate him from this time of fulfillment [*Zeit der Vollendung*]. But the central message of the new age is the proclamation of the eternal gospel. Thus, Gerard arrives at the following equation: Joachim's writings *are* the eternal gospel. This means in turn that *intelligentia spiritualis* is synonymous with the historical typological exegesis, as practiced by Joachim.[61] The *intelligentia spiritualis* is therefore that historical purpose [*jener historische Sinn*], which was still being invoked by Hegel to prove the divine nature of existence.

It falls to the second generation of Spirituals to formulate the historical theology of the church of the spirit. Peter Olivi puts this in a nutshell in a letter to the sons of the king of Anjou and sets out the law of the dialectic for history and nature: "He who contemplates the universe is struck in many remarkable ways by the hierarchical law of Christ, which he solemnly announced to the whole world: when the seed falls into the earth and dies, then it remains alone, but when it dies, it brings forth much fruit."[62] The dialectic is realized in the stages of suffering, death, and resurrection. "This underlies the flux and course of all natural change and movement: the death of one leads to the birth of another, and all material entity passes through formlessness [*das Formlose*] into form. What is even more remarkable is that its lack of form [*Unförmigkeit*] is at the same time the origin and foundation of forms."[63] God *comes into being* through history, through antithesis and negation, through *corruptio*, through suffering and formlessness [*Formlosigkeit*].

The dialectic of materialization [*Verwirklichung*] through antithesis and negation determines God's works in creation. "It is the foundation and prelude of creation that God may create his works out of nothing and that the created works in existence serve obediently the mighty word of the highest God, so that at his slightest behest they are transformed from each thing into every other."[64]

This law of the dialectic, the materialization of God out of the present state, not only applies to the realm of nature, but is also revealed with particular clarity in God's work of salvation: in history. "And so the root of all grace, and of the church in and beyond the heavens, is to be found at the very center of *humilitas* and, so to speak, at the center of nothingness; and that is where they grow."[65] The divine dialectic of history is manifested in the death and resurrection of Christ. The law according to which all life comes into being through death, through the removal of the old form, also applies to human life. "This is affirmed throughout our lives in a number of ways, in as much that the seeds and fruits from which we live do not receive life unless they first die. Do we not receive this freedom on leaving our mother's womb, a prisonlike grave? Do we not finally emerge from this into the light as if we rose from the grave and were released from the confines of a dungeon and a gloomy prison?"[66] Finally, Olivi applies the dialectic of history to the history of salvation within the Christian Church, whose fulfillment he visualizes in terms of the seven stages depicted by Joachim. The early history [*Urgeschichte*] of the Christian Church is proof enough of the universality of the dialectic of history.

According to this wondrous law, the Church was conceived in the womb of the synagogue, was born in labor, and came into being. In accordance with this law and plan, the people of Israel went out of the fiery furnace and the harsh bondage of Egypt, divided the Red Sea by the strong hand of God and passed through with dry feet. In the same way the whole host of the elect will rise swiftly out of the exile of this world and the tyrannical power of Satan, going through the pathway of earthly death as if through the middle of the Red Sea into the heavenly realms.[67]

Olivi, inspired by Joachim, interprets his own age as the time in which the sixth seal will be opened and the vessel of the sixth angel will be poured out.[68]

Olivi's letter, which proceeds fully under the spell of Joachim, anticipates in miniature the main images and figures of the *Postilla super Apocalypsim* [Devotional Book of the Apocalypse], which applies concrete names only to the figures of the End Time.[69] The main problem addressed in Olivi's devotional book of the Apocalypse is the transformation [*Aufhebung*] of the Roman Church of the second age into the church of the spirit in the third age, which is supposed to be happening *now*. What in Joachim's prophecy is a future claim for the *ordo spiritualis* becomes a political program given the concrete situation of the Spirituals.[70] The Franciscan church of the spirit seeks the same authority for its assigned world age as the Roman Church claims for itself in the second age.[71] The men of the spirit "who have full insight into the scriptures are worthy to be raised above the supremacy of the Church and to receive the direct unyielding and insuperable power like an iron rod. Using it, they can crush the vices of the nations and receive the fullness of heavenly wisdom, so as to direct the church and contemplate heavenly things."[72] In the new age the Roman Church no longer has any spiritual power or jurisdiction over the faithful. Papal apostolic succession has been superseded and transferred to the *ordo spiritualis*.[73] "The prestige afforded to the synagogue and its priests, if they had believed in Christ, was transferred to the early Church and its pastors. Therefore, the prestige afforded to the final form of the Church (meaning the Roman Church) in the fifth stage will be transferred, because of her adultery, to the elect in the sixth stage (meaning the Franciscan church of the spirit)."[74] Now that the age of the spirit has dawned, the Roman Church is the church of Antichrist because, out of slothfulness of the flesh, it resists its transformation into the church of the spirit.[75]

As far as the sects are concerned, dialectical historical theology is reduced to the simple equation, Church of Rome = Antichrist.[76] In his *Brief an Alle* [Letter to Everybody] Dolcino develops the most important aspects of his view of history, which also takes the form of apocalyptic interpretation largely influenced by Joachim's ideas. Running through Dolcino's division of the epochs is the theme of decline.[77] The institution of a new age of salvation [*neuen Heilszeit*] with a new dispensation [*Heilsordnung*] is decreed each time the established order declines. Just as the Franciscans regarded themselves as a force for the renewal of evangelical life at a time of overall decline, the apostolic brethren see themselves as a force for renewal in the last epoch of the history of salvation after the decline of the Franciscans. The theory of decline is applied to the Franciscan orders, and indeed the whole history of the Church is subjected to it. The age of Constantine is clearly depicted as the time of the Church's greatest apostasy, because it was then permissible to acquire and possess money and property of all kinds. The "rich and venerable Church" of the second age is from its beginning the "evil Church."[78]

In Dolcino's writings the theology of history is visibly linked to a utopian society. The apostolic brethren abandon the path of monastic propaganda and take to armed rebellion. That is why they and Dolcino have to look to the peasants for support. The number of peasant revolts and wars increases in the last centuries of the Middle Ages. It is Dolcino's ideas which lay the groundwork for the peasants' uprising at Valsesia. This unrest is followed, toward the end of the fourteenth century, by the disturbances of the Jacquerie in France, which are quickly and thoroughly put down. And finally, throughout the whole of the fifteenth century, Germany seethes with peasant unrest.[79]

The large peasant uprisings in the Middle Ages are legitimized by the concept of natural law linked to Christian freedom, equality, and the original state of paradise [*Urstandsgesetz*].[80] The Christian idea of natural law is mainly interpreted in an egalitarian and communistic way; in instances where it is necessary to legitimize force, reference is always made to the Old Testament or the Book of Revelation. For this reason the ruling powers want to diminish the Ten Commandments to the status of "the civil code of the Jews" [*der Juden Sachsenspiegel* (Luther)], and the Book of Revelation appears to them as "as a ragbag of delusions," while the peasant group within chiliasm follows the precepts of Moses and John.[81] The alliance between the peasant community and chiliasm characterizes the late Middle Ages and is particularly evident in Hussism. The idea of the Kingdom of God is clearly relocated to the utopia of a Kingdom of God on earth, "a new ideal world whose contours are increasingly well delineated and which illuminates them."[82]

Sectarianism sees itself as continuing the role of the early Church community (*sequor*); it is only when the Church introduces heresy laws that sectarianism becomes separate from the Christian society (*secare*). The Church is largely conservative and relatively worldly [*weltbejahend*], intent on controlling the masses and embracing society as a whole, whereas the sects are comparatively small groups eager to bring a greater intensity into Christian life.[83] The Church is there to get good service from the state and the ruling classes. Because of this it is integrated within the general system of government. The sects are indifferent, tolerant, or hostile in their attitudes to the world, the state, and society, and therefore seek the support of the lower classes or those groups who are in opposition to the state and society.[84] And yet, the concrete particularity [*irdische Partikularität*] of the sects conceals their absolute universality. For the dissolution of Christendom into such small communities of people leaving the degenerate Church can be reconciled by the sects themselves with the concept of Christ's reign over the world only on the following assumption: that the great mass apostasy prophesied by the Book of Revelation and the reduction of Christendom to the faithful few are in fact now happening.[85] This fundamental motif of sectarianism becomes apparent, however, only in the ecstatic high points of heresy, such as in the Anabaptist movement.[86] The sects are no longer religious orders; people hate the orders and do not want authority figures but the freedom and equality which characterized early Christianity.[87] The Church, which embraces the whole of Christendom [*die allgemeine Christenheit*], confines the intensity of Christian life to the monasteries. Monasticism conceals the different factions within the Church at large, which come into their own only in sectarianism. The Franciscan movement is on the borderline between the religious orders and the sects. When founding his new religious order, Francis seems to have been no different from his predecessors; it is only by degree that the brothers' estrangement from the world, by virtue of their complete poverty, stands apart from the intentions of earlier foundations. Nonetheless, Francis's unmistakable intention in forming his order is to restore true Christianity, the religion of Jesus, and indeed this is how his intention is understood by his contemporaries.[88] In the tertiary orders, the boundaries between being a monk and a layperson are blurred. "Simplification of life and the religious organization, a passion for the original Church and literal understanding of holy scripture, following exactly the word and teachings of Christ and the complete and almost mechanical repetition of the life of the apostles: that is the common ground from which the various sects arise, though the differences can be extraordinarily large."[89] The aims of the sects are an amalgam of religious and social dimensions, some explicit and conscious, others largely uncertain and in disguise. The battle over Tabor features ancient Slav customs and militant communism [*Kriegskommunismus*] mixed with Joachimism, which finds its way to Bohemia via the Beghards, Dolcinists, and Italian chiliasts. Joachimite influences make themselves plainly felt in the Anabaptist movement, which reinvigorates the Franciscan Reformation.[90] Therefore, the separation which Trœltsch makes between the Anabaptist movement and mysticism is completely erroneous and defies all historical evidence. All Anabaptist movements draw on mysticism. Everywhere in Anabaptism the emphasis is on the "spirit," as opposed to the letter. All the Spiritualists, even those like Denck and Franck, who lost their faith in the Anabaptist movement, in spite of that felt the strongest inner kinship with the latter.[91] The thesis of Albrecht Ritschl, despite the objections raised by Troeltsch and Holl, is quite correct, "that the Anabaptists evolved directly from the groups of the Franciscan tertiary order, particularly the

Observants."[92] Luther's Reformation certainly has a bearing on the sudden emergence of the sects and the Anabaptists in particular. But, and this is an oversight on Holl's part,[93] the Reformation only functions as a catalyst for the sectarian movement of its time. The Reformation brings Christian life into the sphere of bourgeois society, endowing the state legal system with tremendous authority over the conduct of Christian life.[94] But Anabaptism seeks to transform Christian life in a way which runs counter to the intentions of Luther or Zwingli. The motives and goals, the means and individual rules of the Anabaptism are completely in line with the medieval ideal of perfection. The baptism of adults is the tie binding the community of saints; and this is how the single innovation falls in line with the religiosity of Franciscan Christianity.[95] While the Reformation has no affiliations with mysticism, mystical theology does find a home in Anabaptism.[96] The Anabaptists come from the strata of society which have been the sphere of activity of the mendicant order for three hundred years. The extent to which the traditions and intentions of the Anabaptists correlate with the rule of the Franciscan tertiary orders as well as with the first rule of Francis of Assisi makes it impossible to miss their genetic link. In all matters, there is a striking similarity between the Franciscans and the Anabaptists.[97] But the idea of the absolute life of the monastery broadens out to encompass the whole of society, and since Anabaptism is unable to put this into practice, it remains in a state of unredeemed Catholicism. Thus, Anabaptism is nothing else but the renewal of the storm of the Franciscan Spirituals.[98]

Thomas Müntzer: The Theology of Revolution

What in the spiritual mysticism of the Middle Ages was known as inner light becomes in Müntzer's theology "a consuming flame which turns outwards." As a result, the spiritualization of the world is at the same time a secularization of the spirit; the materialization of the spirit means losing it to the world.[99] Hopes which hitherto had only been fostered internally suddenly turn outward, giving the historical process great impetus. There is still some difference of opinion about Müntzer, arguably because his cause still inspires fear. Without doubt the best account is Ernst Bloch's, who, by virtue of his own affinity, grasps what is essential about Müntzer.[100] Ernst Bloch also forced Holl, the great Lutheran historian, to take Müntzer "more seriously than is usually the case in the history of the Church."[101]

Even if traces of immaturity and a monomaniacal pathos characterize

Müntzer, his desire is firmly geared toward the absolute.[102] Even if Müntzer demands the extraordinary, he does not just hit up against illusions. He may not be as gifted at grasping and executing practical realities as at indulging in flights of fancy and adeptly raking about among the depths of the people [*in den Tiefen des Volkes wühlen*], but this lies in the fact that he is surrounded by half-measures.[103] What is decisive is that he does not confine his influence to a small community, an upright sect, but addresses all the contemporary revolutionary factions. For good reason, the princes demand that he be handed over: his work is a powerful mixture of social revolution and chiliasm. Orgiastic energies and ecstasies are bound to the world in Anabaptist chiliasm. The courage that pushes beyond world becomes explosive in the world; the impossible gives birth to the possible, the unconditional to what is actually happening.[104] Wherever a sectarian movement of visionaries and mystics springs up, Müntzer is present.[105] Hussite influences are stirring among the spiritual crowds in the textile town of Zwickau, where Müntzer meets Niklas Storch in 1520. The latter's chiliastic, Taborite sayings and teaching of the spiritual word leave a lasting impression on Müntzer. In Prague, where he strongly believes there to be an element of Hussism, he puts a memorable poster up on the wall in German, Czech, and Latin. Its message shows what surviving book invoices confirm: that in those years he is studying Eusebius, Jerome, and Augustine. Among the books left behind on his death is Tauler's *Sermones*, which, along with the *Theologia Germanica*, he particularly admires. Clearly, he is familiar with the works of Joachim: "I have great esteem for the testimony of Abbot Joachim."[106]

Müntzer's theology is ultimately an eye-to-eye confrontation with Luther. This is a match not only between them, but through them also a decision between two principles: the *Reformation* and *revolution*.[107]

It is often overlooked that Luther's Reformation concerns the *Church* and is not aimed at mysticism and lay religion outside the Church. The Church is the place where man as a sinner encounters God's revelation. According to the Ptolemaic system, heaven as God's abode is above the earth, and so everything that happens on earth acquires symbolic meaning. The community sees itself as the "body of Christ," as fellow workers [*Mittäterin*] in what Christ does. The Church in the Ptolemaic age is the charismatic church, which encapsulates the contemporaneity of the heavenly and the earthly. This contemporaneity means that the Church conforms to the word of scripture, and that what is below and what is above see eye to eye.[108] The transition from the Ptolemaic to the Copernican view of the world is not sudden and certainly did not begin with Copernicus, but rather has its origins deep in the Middle Ages. Nevertheless, the period of the Middle Ages generally clings to the assumption that the visible heaven above the earth is where God lives. The modern age dismisses this as an illusion and admits that this perspective is wrongheaded. Whereas the unity of earth and heaven seems secure in the massive architectural towers of the Romance cultures, a ripple of anxiety is felt in the Gothic towers, nervously shooting upward, about the impending loss of heaven.[109] In the transition from the Ptolemaic to the Copernican worldview, the West is shaken by a demonic fever because the loss of heaven, a fact now known by all, results in constant attempts to build bridges to the other side and magically restore the link between heaven and earth, which metaphysics had severed.

For this reason Copernican Christianity, which acknowledges the situation of an earth without a heaven, attacks the sacrament of the charismatic, Ptolemaic Church, which assumes the unity of heaven and earth repeatedly afforded by the Mass. On the Copernican earth, the Mass is magic and the work of Satan.[110] Within the Ptolemaic world the natural moral order is the work of man, as illuminated by the proximity of heaven and seeing itself as a response to God's command. But under an empty heaven man's efforts are totally insignificant as far as salvation is concerned. In the Copernican world salvation can only be the work of grace, to which man cannot contribute anything. Man's fulfillment of the law becomes pointless [*gegenstandslos*]; in fact, it inevitably turns into a mere attempt to seek justice by good works [*Werkgerechtigkeit*] and their magic as soon as any claim of merit is associated with works.[111] In the case of Plato, whose philosophy of eros assumes this Ptolemaic unity of heaven and earth, justice is to be found in public, political life. However, for Kant, the philosopher of the Copernican earth, it is a matter for the individual endowed with practical reason.[112] Thus, in Ptolemaic Catholicism, "rebirth" also obtains the sanctification of material life, a tangible accommodation of empirical life to divine law. In the Protestantism of Copernican Christianity, by contrast, rebirth acquires no positive earthly meaning to reshape this life. He who is reborn, who is chosen, remains throughout his life at once righteous and a sinner. He is a sinner insofar as he is visible, and righteous insofar as he is invisible. Even though righteousness and sinfulness come together in a single "I," they are as widely separated from one another as earth is from heaven and redemption is from reconciliation. Between righteousness and sinfulness there is the cross.[113]

The dissenting voice of the Reformation challenges the assumption made by the Ptolemaic, charismatic Church of Catholicism that sinful man has the power to become righteous and to act upon the divine sphere from his human sphere. Therefore, the Reformation rejects the *theologia naturalis* of Scholasticism as well as Catholic ethics, which ascribe a relevant religious value to the moral works of man.[114] Protestantism, particularly Lutheranism, is contemptuous of the workaday life, of the entire wicked world, which is completely cut off from heaven, in a way that the medieval Church never was, based as it was on the assumptions of the Ptolemaic worldview. Consequently, Protestantism detaches life from all Christian guidance and any possible reference to man's vindication,[115] "In his kingdom, in which Christ is King and Lord, he does not teach us how we should till, plough, sow, harvest, keep house, amass money, carry on wars, and rule over lands and people. In his earthly kingdom the emperor can do as he pleases."[116]

As the Copernican world no longer has a heaven above it, nature and grace, which Catholicism placed in a hierarchy, are separated in Lutheranism and seen as two distinct, continually alternating points of view. Luther shifts this double moral standard [*doppelte Moral*] ultimately onto the Bible itself, dividing it between the New and Old Testaments in such a way that the rift cannot be closed, not between nature and grace, the Law and the Gospel, Christ and his office, and not even within God.[117] The complete emancipation of this relinquished world finally makes possible a secular world in which all spirituality [*aller Geist*] is subordinated to, and defenseless against, worldly power. Protestantism oscillates between the theology of the cross and an enthusiasm for the world which can almost be called petit bourgeois. It is more pessimistic than Catholicism because it recognizes that in the Copernican world, without a heaven, man's good works cannot achieve salvation. And yet, it is more optimistic because life on earth is liberated from the demand that it emulate its archetype.[118] Thus, Luther reveals himself to be the theological version of Machiavelli, and the state is empowered by the move with which its theological Machiavelli dismisses faith from all active responsibility within society.[119]

The Reformation effects an enormous reduction in the dogma concerning the hierarchical relations between earth and heaven.[120] In Protestantism, dogma is newly grounded in the subjectivity of faith. The freedom of the Christian, the *pro me* of Luther, fits in with the awakening of the ego, which constitutively transforms the foundation of human structures. Grace is no longer a substance which is poured out in the sacrament, but rather the loving free will of God is manifested in faith.[121] This means that any bestowal of grace by means of hierarchy and the sacrament is made redundant, and in this respect Luther approaches the tendencies of lay mysticism practiced by the Spirituals. Absent from Lutheranism is only the administration of the sacrament by the priesthood, and its central place is taken by the sacrament of the word, which alone discloses the free will of God.[122] In Lutheranism all faith refers to the holy scripture, which alone conveys the will of God. The word is the sacrament of the Lutheran Church; through it the Lutheran Church restores the objectivity and independence of the subject as institution [*Anstalt vom Subjekt*]. Lutheranism founds a new church on the Copernican earth devoid of heaven.[123] But as a church not even Lutheranism can do without the political and policing forces that keep external Christendom on the straight and narrow. That is why church organizations exist in each state. These suppress the tendencies of the Spirituals, not unknown to the young Luther, by means of inquisition, and punish dogmatic heresies by expulsion, life imprisonment, and death.[124]

The freedom of the individual Christian unfetters the soul and accompanies the birth of the ego. And the freedom of the individual Christian bears the mark that enables him to break the power and force of the Church, which bestows the objective sacrament. It is understandable that many Christian communities spring up in the wake of the Reformation; they are resolved to take this freedom seriously by founding the community of Christians on the principle of freedom, without state or hierarchical control. A visible external manifestation of this community is adult baptism which indicates the need for a community of *born again* free Christians. However, adult baptism is only the stigma [*Zeichen*] of this group; their real longing is for the apostolic community.[125] Therefore, these people, focused on the apostolic community, inevitably find themselves in opposition to Lutheranism.

The seething mass of desires associated with the Anabaptists culminates in Thomas Müntzer, who confronts Luther eye to eye and professes: "At last I can give my honest opinion: I am preaching a kind of Christian faith which disagrees with Luther's, but it is to be found uniformly in all the hearts of the elect on earth. And even a native Turk would have the rudiments of the same belief. That is the movement of the Holy Spirit."[126] In his Prague proclamation Luther comes dangerously close to becoming a seller of indulgences [*Ablaßkrämer*]; as Thomas Müntzer declares: "He did not hear the ordinances of God, as implanted in all his creatures, from any learned person. I only heard from them the naked word [*bloße Schrift*] which as murderers and thieves they stole from the Bible, never having heard it themselves from the mouth of God."[127] The scribes have the humble letters in their mouths while their heart is well over a hundred thousand miles away. But if the word is like the sacrament, then the soul is poor and its mystery dwells not within but outside it. In truth, "the human heart is the paper or parchment where the finger of God inscribes his unchanging will and eternal wisdom. This scripture can be read by anybody if he exercises his reason."[128] "That is why all the prophets speak in the way: this is the word of the Lord. They do not say: this is what the Lord said,—as if it had happened in the past; rather, they speak with regard to the here and now."[129]

Even if Luther's name is not mentioned in the *Protestation* (Protestation) and in the *Gedichteten Glauben* [*Writings on Faith*], despite the fact that they are clearly directed at him, the *Ausgedrückte Entblößung des falschen Glaubens* [*Manifestations of False Belief*] exposes the gulf between Luther and Müntzer. Müntzer "hammers home" his message in it.[130] Scripture bears *witness*, whereas the scribes say it brings *faith*. Following a more perverse line than the scribes in the time of Christ, the new scribes make "a mockery of the Spirit of Christ and are so bold as to venture forth exclaiming and writing: regardless of the spirit [*Geist hin, Geist her*], I commend my writing, it is my work."[131] Therefore,

the poor, wretched people are deceived beyond measure. With all the words and works they make out that the poor man cannot learn to read because he is more worried about feeding himself. And in their preaching they openly exhort him to allow himself to be oppressed and exploited by tyrants. When will he then learn to read the scriptures? Here, dear Thomas, you are deluded [*schwärmst*]. The scribes are supposed to read fine books and the peasants to listen to them because faith comes through listening.[132]

In furious "defense, after much provocation, and in response to that unspiritual, easy-living man of the flesh from Wittenberg, who completely and pitifully defiles poor Christendom by the perverse manner in which he plunders holy scripture," Müntzer sums up his opinion of the Lutheran Church of the word:[133] "You will now be duped with a new kind of logic, with the deception of the word of God."[134] The new scribes, of whom Luther is only the most ambitious, are acting in exactly the same way as the Pharisees did long ago, "extolling the holy scriptures, covering all the books in ink and endlessly gabbling 'believe, believe'—while denying the advent of faith, mocking the Spirit of God and actually believing nothing about anything."[135]

Luther's countercharge, that Müntzer's "intention was to start a rebellion,"[136] as his letter to the mine workers shows, is something that Müntzer takes up and launches the theology of revolution. For Luther says one thing but he

stays silent about the most modest of all, as I am clearly proving to the princes that a whole community has the power of the sword and also holds the key to change the present order; and that the princes are not lords but servants of the sword. They should not do as they please; they should act justly. For, according to ancient custom, the people must stand to one side when one is judged justly by the law of God—why? If the authorities seek to reverse the verdict, Christians should deny it and reject it. It is the greatest atrocity on earth that nobody cares for the needs of the deprived; the powerful do as they please.[137]

Luther seeks to

be like Christ in a purely fabricated sense of goodness and says in the book concerning the purchase of goods that the princes should safely prowl among thieves and robbers. Look, our overlords and princes are themselves the breeding ground of extortion, and theft of all kinds; they take possession of all creation, the fish in the water, the birds of the air, all that grows in the soil; everything has to belong to them. Then they spread God's commandment among the poor, saying, God has commanded that you shall not steal. But it is of no use to them at all because the princes cause the people, the poor ploughman, the craftsman, and all who live in that way to toil and to be ground down to nothing. If he then commits the slightest act of theft, he must hang. To that the lying doctor says, Amen. The lords are responsible for the fact that the poor man becomes their enemy. They do not wish to remove the causes of their rebellion. How can this be good in the long run? Therefore, as I say: I must rebel, and intend to do so.[138]

By drawing a line between the Old and New Testaments, between the Law and the Gospel, Luther cuts Christ down the middle. Faith, however, is not founded on "half" of Christ, but on the "whole" of Christ. "Whoever will not have the bitter Christ, will die of eating honey."[139] With flattering amiability Luther defends the ungodly, using the words of Christ. Luther "despises the law of the Father, and is a hypocrite by exploiting the most precious gift of Christ's mercy. He invalidates the gravity of the Father's Law with the patient suffering of the Son. He scorns the distinctive nature of the Holy Spirit and defiles one part of the godhead with the other. This continues as long as there is no judgment on earth and Christ alone is patient, so that the godless Christians torment their brethren."[140] Finally, Müntzer draws Luther's attention to his alliance with the princes:

You take and steal the name of God's Son and seek the reward of your princes. . . . But you know very well whom you are supposed to be slandering! The poor monks and priests and merchants cannot defend themselves. This is probably why you have to scold them. But is nobody to judge these godless rulers, although they have already tread on Christ?[141] ... The fact that you have stood before the kingdom in Worms is thanks to the German nobles whose mouths you have smeared and fed with honey. It was no surprise that with your sermons you gave Bohemian gifts: monasteries and religious foundations which you are now promising the princes. If you had wavered at Worms you would have been stabbed by the nobility rather than allowed to go free.[142] ... If you want to dance, monk, all the godless are paying court to you.[143]

In his defense and answer to Luther, Müntzer rages with deep disappointment and bitterness against him, who had first accepted the help of all the spiritual and revolutionary factions and given them hope; only when he could no longer carry the burden on his shoulders did he come down on the stronger side of the princes. When, at the outset of the Peasants' War, the rebels turn to Luther, his language is opaque and casts aspersions on both sides, but he sees Christian suffering as the exclusive lot of the peasants.[144] The peasants, however, resort to force, and it becomes clear to Luther "that it was a vain and deceitful affair which they had drawn up in the twelve articles in the name of the Gospel."[145]

Luther's pamphlet *Against the Thieving and Murderous Gangs of Peasants* particularly addresses "the arch devil who rules in Mühlhausen and commits nothing but theft, murder, and bloodshed."[146] Luther's pamphlet is the answer to Müntzer's defense. To Müntzer's "therefore I say: I must rebel, and intend to do so!"[147] Luther replies that

a rebellious person who can be shown to be such is certainly an outlaw, both in the eyes of God and the emperor: and that the first person able and willing to kill such a person does well and justly. Anybody is both chief judge and executioner to such a person who makes himself a rebel to the people ... because rebellion is not a simple case of murder, but a conflagration which ignites a country and devastates it ... the greatest of all disasters. For this reason, whoever smashes, strangles, and stabs, secretly or publicly, should consider that there is nothing more poisonous, harmful, and of the devil than a rebellious person.[148]

Luther takes up Müntzer's reproach that he scorned the law of God the Father, and invalidated the gravity of the Father's Law by emphasizing the patience of the Son:

It is of no help to the peasants either that you claim from Genesis 1 and 2 that all things have been freely made and are held in common and that we are all equal through baptism. Moses is not contained in and does not apply to the New Testament. But our Lord Christ is to be found there, and he subjects both our body and possessions to the emperor and to worldly justice. As he says: give to Caesar what is Caesar's. Similarly, Paul when addressing all baptized Christians says: all are subject to authority. And Peter: be subject to all human authorities. We owe it to Christ to live, as our Father in heaven commands us . . . because baptism does not liberate our bodies and our possessions but our souls.[149]

As the peasants "continue to be in uproar," Luther has to "instruct the worldly authorities how they should conduct themselves with a good conscience in this matter."[150] The authorities should smite them [*dreinschlagen*] in good conscience.

Neither patience nor mercy are appropriate. It is time for the sword and anger and not for mercy. . . . We live in such strange times now that a prince can win heaven by bloodshed, better than others can by prayer.[151] . . . Therefore, dear sirs, hasten hither, save somebody, render help to others. Have mercy on the poor people. Let him who can stab, strike, and throttle. If you die through this, good for you. You could not suffer a more blissful death. May each God-fearing Christian say Amen to that. For I know this is a prayer which is just and good, and pleasing to God.[152]

In Müntzer's theology the soul disassociates itself from all the dross of the external world, overrides all earthly powers, attaches no value to any sacramental institution, and has the most profound and intimate understanding of grace as its own abyss, as the advent of faith. The more violently Müntzer rejects all external institutions, the more pressing becomes the issue of the criteria applicable to the real spirit, beyond the sacraments and scriptures. How can the soul be certain of God "in an objective sense" when God was not an "object" mediated by sacrament or scripture?

It is clearly very stupid, begins a letter from Müntzer, that "for everybody to think that God should hasten to their aid when nobody is in a hurry to suffer. Because where there is no poverty of spirit, the rule of Christ can never dawn."[153] For faith to enter the soul, it is necessary for "the ear to be swept clean from the sound of cares and desires. For just as the field is unable to bear much wheat without the ploughshare, a person is unable to say he is a Christian without first taking up his cross and making himself ready to attend to God's work and word." We encounter the word through "patient endurance"; "a man who has not undergone trial who seeks to boast with God's words will do no more than waste his breath."[154]

Dilution of the word is the first sign of this. "Everybody jabbers freely about faith. You cannot believe what these wanton upstarts say because they preach things which they have not practiced themselves and poison the holy scripture for the Holy Spirit."[155] "Before man can be sure of salvation, there come so many turbulent waters, with their awful roar, that he loses the will to live, because the storm waves of this wild sea consume many who think that they have already won the battle. Therefore, we should not flee from these storm waves but break through them like experienced sailors. The Lord will not give anybody his holy testament unless he has studied it with a sense of wonder."[156] This lofty sense of wonder bears fruit, creating a pathway in the depths of the soul. "He who does not have this pathway knows nothing at all about faith."[157]

The pathway leads from wonder through faith into tedium, the torment of spiritual emptiness [*innere Öde*] of the soul. This journey through the torment of hell is like encroaching waters, which whirl up from the depths to engulf the ego. "When man, tossed and moving in the wild sea, becomes aware of his origin, he must act like a fish which has followed the dirty water downward. It then turns round, swims, climbs back up through the water so that it can reach the place from which it originated. That is what I call tedium [*Langweil*]."[158] This stage of tedium or emptiness is what both the individual and the community have to go through in order to be renewed. "It is also necessary for people to be severely punished for slovenly wantonness, for passing their time voluptuously, so that they lack the courage to engage in serious contemplations about their faith. Therefore, very few of them have any experience of the first stirrings of the spirit. Because of this they mock the experience of tedium [*Langweil*], which however is the only way we find the work of God."[159]

Truly, the advent of faith is accompanied by the most intense birth pangs, the deepest disbelief: "Moses was not prepared to believe the promise of the living God. First, he needed to come to terms with his disbelief, before he could automatically [*ungedichtet*] rely on God and know that the devil was not deceiving him. Moses could have thought God was a devil if he had not recognized the deceitfulness of man and the purity [*Einfalt*] of God in the order implanted in God and his creatures."[160] If a man studies the scriptures,

he will find that all the fathers, patriarchs, prophets, and particularly the apostles find it quite difficult to believe.[161] . . . It is hard to say, therefore, how distressing, irksome, and abhorrent it is when people without faith seek to preach the Christian faith to others, a faith which they have neither discovered nor experienced for themselves, and do not even know what it feels like to be a believer. They imagine, or allow themselves to think, that faith is easily arrived at, and almost all of them prattle boastfully about it. . . . So the intoxicated world devises a frivolous promise, a poisonous faith much worse than the faith of the Turks, the heathen and the Jews.[162]

Everybody can clearly see how lack of faith [*Unglaub*] is to be found among those who are chosen. The fathers of old persisted in their fear of God, "until, in the form of that small grain of mustard seed, their disbelief was overcome by faith. Such faith can only be found with much trembling and tribulation."[163]

It is not by chance that the advent of faith described by Thomas Müntzer calls to mind Kierkegaard's analyses of the religious life. All of his analyses have one focus: to wrench man away from all objectivities and to set him on his own feet [*ihn ganz auf sich selbst zu stellen*]. Thus, man is placed before nothingness and because of that finds himself confronted for the first time with the decision of whether to fall into despair or to venture into the leap of faith. Personal confession [*Aneignung*] of the Christian faith amounts to a repetition of the Lutheran criticisms of Catholic objectivity. "If you remove the personal confession from the Christian faith, what has Luther achieved? But open up his writings and you will feel the strong pulse beat of personal confession in every line. . . . Did not the papacy have objectivity, objective provisions, and the objective, the objective, the objective in excess? What did it lack? Personal confession, spirituality."[164] Kierkegaard transposes Luther's *pro me*, going beyond Luther, who still keeps the objectivity of the written word in "personal confession" and "subjectivity."[165] God can only be revealed in man when man accepts him through his own subjective spirituality. God is truth, but truth is subjective. "If man does not have faith, there is neither a God nor is God to be found for him. This is irrespective of the fact that when God is perceived to be eternal, he is eternal."[166] God only exists in subjectivity.

Having established spirituality as the main criterion, Kierkegaard breaks down the objectivity of historical Christianity. His measure for evaluating secular Christendom, as found in church and state on the one hand and theology and philosophy on the other, is the degree to which it distances itself from the original spirit of Christianity.[167] Religious *feeling* (Feuerbach) is increased to a *passion*, which does away with eighteen hundred years as if they had not existed, and is spiritually [*innerlich*] contemporaneous with the original Church. The highest expression of spirituality in any existing subject is passion. Passion corresponds to truth as a paradox. The fact that truth has become paradoxical is grounded precisely in its relationship to an existing subject.[168]

In terms of spirituality, the question necessarily arises as to what is the criterion of *truth*, and Kierkegaard emphasizes this very problem in the text of his writings by using spaced letters:

When we inquire into truth objectively, we think objectively of truth as an object in itself, to which the subject of cognition can relate. We do not reflect upon the relationship, but on the fact that it is the truth, the real thing to which it relates. If the thing to which it relates is pure truth, the real thing, then the subject exists in truth. When we inquire subjectively into truth, we subjectively reflect upon the relationship of the individual. If it is only the *how* of this relationship which exists in truth, then the individual exists in truth even if he were related to untruth in this way.[169]

It can happen that one person prays "in truth" to God, although he worships an idol; another prays "in untruth" to the true God and therefore "in truth" worships an idol. The decision is only to be found in subjectivity, whereas the will implied in objectivity is untruth. What is crucial is the *passion* of eternity, not what it contains, because what it contains is just itself. Therefore the subjective *how* and subjectivity are truth. Truth is interior [*innerlich*] and not exterior [*äusserlich*]; it is the *how* and not the *what*.[170]

As truth is dependent on subjectivity, the moment of objective uncertainty still remains in the personal confession of faith made from passionate spirituality. This stage of "objective uncertainty" is synonymous with the stage of "disbelief" found in Thomas Müntzer. In objective terms man is only left with uncertainty, but it is precisely this which makes the infinite passion of spirituality more intense, and truth consists exactly in this wager, when we choose in our infinite passion what in objective terms remains uncertain. Faith is a category of despair. This contradiction changes passion into despair. Faith is precisely the contradiction between infinite passion of spirituality and objective uncertainty.[171]

Christianity, which according to Kierkegaard seeks to proclaim the essential eternal truth, in fact presents itself as this paradox. It cannot be put any clearer that subjectivity is truth and that objectivity is abhorrent. "And yet the Christian message must ultimately end with its witness because, looking at things from a Christian viewpoint, the truth does not lie in the subject (as Socrates understood it), but it is a revelation which must be proclaimed."[172] Significantly, Kierkegaard does not appear as a witness to the truth because that is permitted only to the apostles, not to a genius.[173] But even the apostle is able to witness the truth only in his community. Kierkegaard's spirituality is always restricted to the individual's existence. In his particular Christian context, as a religious writer, Kierkegaard's religious life is always being overtaken, constrained, and devalued by his aesthetic life. Therefore, his faith, which is ultimately achieved by the genius of his own existence, appears ambiguous, as a kind of personal hygiene, which leaves one wondering whether the person who suffers should "take tablets" or "believe."[174]

There is a great gap between Kierkegaard and Müntzer on the fundamental issue of spirituality. Kierkegaard cocoons himself, on the grounds of spirituality, in his own subjectivity, whereas Müntzer establishes spirituality as the grounds of belief for the whole community of God and thus sublates [*aufhebt*] the *religious* life of the individual (Kierkegaard) into the social life of the masses (Marx). The religious reality of the passion of spiritual action [*inneren Handelns*] (Kierkegaard) is woven in Müntzer's work into *social* intercourse as lived out in society (Marx). While at the end of the bourgeois world criticism disintegrates into a critique of bourgeois *Christianity* (Kierkegaard) and bourgeois *capitalism* (Marx),[175] Müntzer's critique of Christendom is aimed simultaneously, and in equal measure, at its religious and worldly nature. It is not possible, Müntzer writes to the miners, "to tell you anything about God, while they lord it over you."[176] "With the advent of faith we all, earthly people made of flesh, must become gods . . . so that our earthly life soars into heaven."[177]

The Collapse of Christian Eschatology

The work of Thomas Müntzer does not end with the battle of Frankenhausen; rather, it is in Münster, "in the aftermath of the spiritual act of the Peasants' War,"[178] that all of Müntzer's preaching comes together. In Münster the chiliastic revolution suddenly ignites. The Anabaptist movement bursts into life in Zurich, where Zwingli's Reformation is quickly dwarfed, and it spreads unbelievably fast in all directions, since it gathers to itself everything left unfulfilled and disappointed by the Reformation. It moves out from its center in Zurich and intersects with Müntzer in southern Germany, and it is certainly due to this strong impulse that Waldshut and the Moravians gravitate to chiliasm on an accelerated track.[179] The Anabaptist communities cover the whole of central Europe,[180] and Catholic and Protestant potentates everywhere manifestly unite to root them out by fire and sword, as the Anabaptists shake the foundations of a feudal society which is already disintegrating from within. The Habsburg inquisition crushes the Moravian headquarters of Anabaptism, and what remains of them scatters to Hungary. Driven on from there, their descendants move to the Ukraine, where the Moravian community has affiliations with Russian sects. In the nineteenth century, legislation for compulsory conscription is introduced, driving them to the United States, "where the Brethrens' farms still prosper on the Missouri, and their colonies, isolated from the world and almost like museums, are a true Icaria of Christian Socialism."[181]

Other branches of the Anabaptists take refuge in Holland. These splinter groups quickly merge into the new sect of the Melchiorites, who choose to use force.[182] It is from there that the Anabaptists suddenly erupt in Münster. In ferment they come from Holland, and soon afterward from all parts of the empire, pouring into the heavenly Jerusalem. But the heavenly Jerusalem falls, suffering the same fate as the real Jerusalem when it was besieged by Titus. This marks the disappearance of the militant arm of the Anabaptist movement, while the more peaceful, tolerant sector, which had been infiltrated by chiliasm, remains active for a little longer under David Joris. The movement, however, finally ends in the "renewal" introduced by Meno Simons.[183] The Anabaptist revolution makes "its empty peace with the world, no differently than early Christianity did to a greater extent; even the separate forms of Protestant or Catholic settlement are surprisingly repeated."[184]

The final waves of the movement hit the coast of England and pour into Calvinistic Protestantism.[185] Puritanism finds itself interspersed with Anabaptism already under Cromwell, and such tendencies are even stronger in the American colonies. Puritanism is receptive to Anabaptist influences by virtue of its self-discipline and emphasis on the Ten Commandments. Therefore, the Proclamation of Human Rights and even the proclamation of freedom of conscience, allowing one to profess a form of spirituality outside the established confessions, can come about in the course of and protected by a brand of Calvinism which is open to radical ideas. Lutheranism, on the other hand, keeps its distance, and remains aloof from the fundamental principles of a democratic constitution within society.[186] Harrison's regiments are the rallying point for the Anabaptists in the Cromwellian army.[187] In the Parliament of the Saints (Barebone's Parliament) Harrison's supporters try to do away with the legislature and Court of Justice, so as to rid the people of all worldliness and prepare them for the second coming of Christ. Furthermore, all private wealth and earthly authority is to be destroyed in face of the coming Kingdom of God.[188] The Parliament of the Saints dissolves into a moderate Cromwellian majority and a chiliastic minority headed by Harrison.[189] The leaders of the Levellers[190] and Diggers,[191] who influence Robert Owen[192] and thus eventually forge direct links with the modern socialist movement, finally enter into an alliance with the Quakers. After the rebellion is put down with much bloodshed, Harrison, the founder of the Millenary Petition or Fifth Monarchist sect, dies in the firm belief that he will soon return at Christ's right hand when God's Kingdom is established. So the revolutionary Anabaptist movement disappears from England and, nominally, also from Europe as far as influence and any external historical reality is concerned. The hour of *homo spiritualis* has passed, and *homo economicus* takes up the reins of bourgeois society.

The Lutheran Reformation places all emphasis on individual eschatology because it abandons society to the world. There is sharp condemnation of the Anabaptist tendencies of chiliasm in the Augsburg declaration. It is expressly dismissed as a Jewish doctrine, as was chiliasm in the early Church at the Council of Ephesus; the Kingdom of Christ is taught to be a purely spiritual matter.[193]

It is only later in Pietism that expectations of the Kingdom make themselves heard again in a weak and timid way. Pietism introduces the ideal of the sect into the domain of the Protestant church. Obviously, it does not achieve the world-historical culmination [*welthistorische Aufgipfelung*] of medieval Anabaptist spirituality, which is needed to spell the end of worldly rule and usher in the hour of God's Kingdom. Pietism, particularly in Germany, wastes away, limited to an existence linked to church and theological groups.[194] When the Protestant church is founded on the revelation of God's word, which it identifies as the text of scripture, chiliastic tendencies receive a fresh impetus. Scripture is regarded not just as the sum of God's wisdom, but also as the theology of history, a view which promotes its interpretation along the lines of historical imminence found in apocalypticism. Cocceius in his *Dissertatio theologica de Regno Dei* [Theological Treatise on the Kingdom of God] was the founder of this biblical theology in the Netherlands,[195] in the midst of attempts to renew Protestant spirituality by Gisbert Voet, Brakel, and Witzius.[196] The Kingdom of God is no longer to be seen in terms of Lutheran inwardness [*Innerlichkeit*], but is understood as the movement of God within the temporal confines of this world. The biblical documents are read as depicting a history of God's Kingdom divided into stages, revealing the image of the grace of God. But the Kingdom of God is also within [*inwendig*], and its real home is the human spirit.[197] Cocceius links two motifs: the biblical one, according to which in the Old Testament God made his covenant of grace with man, and the rational one, according to which the relationship between God and man was naturally centered on

God's Kingdom from the beginning.[198] The first motif is more prominent in Pietism; the second is particularly noticeable in the theology of the Enlightenment.[199]

The "spiritualized chiliasm" [*vergeistigte Chiliasmus*] of Cocceius, which timidly confines itself to proving the fulfillment of prophecies in the past and in the present yet is reluctant to foretell the future, soon makes way for less cautious figures. "When, in the wake of Brakel and Labadie, chiliasm takes hold in Germany under the leadership of Theodor Undereyck, it emerges in a more radical form alongside the moderate ecclesiastical branch continued by Campegius Vitringa and Friedrich Adolf Lampe. Heinrich Horche, a restless agitator, proclaims the impending day of Judgment on the basis of visions, and finds a kindred spirit in Samuel Koenig, the leader of the Pietistic movement in Bern."[200] J. W. Petersen and his wife make the "discovery of chiliasm" in 1685 and noisily disseminate it in countless tracts. Even Francke turns toward the teachings for a time, while Spener and the Pietistic Movement in Halle remain cautiously restrained. Spener no longer has any expectation of seeing the day of Judgment, which Horb, his brother-in-law, has raised to an article of faith.[201]

In the Württemberg branch of Pietism, the most influential exponent of which is Johann Albrecht Bengel, a historical theology of the empire arises.[202] Bengel sees

the books of the Bible not just as books containing sayings and exemplars, nor as scattered remnants of the ancient world which do not amount to a meaningful whole, but as a beautiful and coherent system, as incomparable news about the divine economy embodied in the human race from the beginning to the end of all things, throughout all ages. Although each book in the Bible is an entity of its own and each writer has his own style, there is a spirit which pervades all of it: one idea permeates the whole work.[203]

Holy scripture presents "a double monument: on the one hand we find knowledge about God, the creator, redeemer, comforter; about the angels, mankind, sin, grace and so on, and this knowledge is essential. Then we learn about the nature of the divine economy in its education of the human race and in the promises given, fulfilled, or to be fulfilled in Christ, in his reign over the nations from first ages until the last."[204] The Kingdom of God is founded in God, and encompasses the visible and invisible world and many eternities; it is the spiritual bond of all of God's works, deeds, and revelations. Unlike orthodox Lutheranism, Bengel understands the Revelation of John as the document [*Urkunde*] of God's Kingdom. "This book, with its uniquely rich contents and its incomparable terseness and tension, is as all-encompassing as the Kingdom of God itself. Truly, this book contains the most important mysteries, the very particular circumstances of God's Kingdom and the adversities through which it has to battle its way."[205]

Mathematics and holy scripture merge in Bengel in a way reminiscent of the cantatas and passions of Johann Sebastian Bach, who fulfills the longings of the Protestant Baroque in his music just as Bengel does in his apocalyptic writings.[206] Admittedly, the eschatology of the Baroque is ambiguous because a large part of its eschatological compositions [*Dichtungen*] are personal confessions of a humanity whose vague desire for eternity is conceived in the forms of an arid faith.[207] Moscherosch's satire *The Last Judgment* is a bitter farce that exploits the situation of the Judgment of the World as a comic circumstance of unexpected psychological relevance. Likewise, the chiliasm of Bengel has a clandestine link with the Enlightenment, "not only through his mathematical mastery of history and revelation, but also through certain common doctrines which are derived from the pietistic Gnosis of Jakob Böhme and Weigel."[208] The idea of the "age of the spirit" [*Säkulum des Geistes*] can be interpreted either as the Enlightenment concept of the "kingdom of reason" or as the chiliastic concept of the "millenium" [*tausendjähriges Reich*]. Adam Kadmon from the Kabbalah, who returns as the comic law-abiding archetypal man in the writings of Jakob Böhme, is made into a secular figure in the pietistic mysticism of the Enlightenment. This is achieved by deducing from the natural "inhabitation" [*Einwohnung*] in the individual soul of this divine law as "Christ" or the "Virgin Sophia" that there is a spiritual equality shared by all human beings and, consequently, all external religious creeds are equal.[209] Peter Poiret certainly shares this conclusion, and the anticlerical polemic of Dippel and Gottfried Arnold is based on him. Johann Christian Edelmann finally manages in his *Innocent Truths* clearly to equate Sophia's inhabitation with the "innate ideas" of rationalism.[210]

BOOK IV

THE PHILOSOPHICAL ESCHATOLOGY OF EUROPE

The Structure of Philosophical Eschatology

Since the collapse of the theocracy of the Middle Ages, since the Renaissance and Reformation, history has moved to the Copernican earth, over which no divine heaven any longer is spread.[1] It is on this earth without a heaven that the Anabaptist Kingdom of Heaven is established. Belief in the transcendent has been shaken and alchemy spreads throughout this realm. While the analogy between the Catholic *officium divinum* and the chemical *magisterium* is striking, their difference remains evident. For, in the Christian world the actual work of redemption is achieved by the transcendent God or his mediator.[2] In alchemy, where the bridges to the beyond have been burned, man himself has to perform the redemptive act. Therefore, he attributes suffering, and consequently the very condition of requiring redemption, to the *anima mundi* which is constrained by matter, to the spirit of the world [*Weltseele*] which has been breathed into matter.[3] In Catholicism, man's deeds are for the glorification of the redeeming God as a response to the word of redemption. The Protestant man refrains from performing any act for the glory of God because he can no longer assume that earth and heaven are one in the Ptolemaic sense; he entrusts redemption to pure grace. The works of alchemy are positively based on a Copernican earth deprived of heaven and represent the endeavors of man to redeem the dormant spirit of the world that awaits redemption. The Catholic earns the fruits of grace *ex opere operato*; the Protestant, because he is standing on the Copernican earth with no prospect of heaven to which he can devote his actions, allows grace to be given to him freely, as pure grace. The alchemist, in contrast, creates for himself *ex opere operantis* a remedy to life which either replaces the means of grace provided by the Church or completes God's act of redemption.

Thus, at the turn of the Ptolemaic Middle Ages to the new Copernican age, Paracelsus sees man as the prime mover [*Operator*], who on "God's behalf" brings an imperfect world to perfection. But "the alchemists' formula of *deo concendente* is only too easily turned into *deo accendente*. The bond with the transcendent is reduced to an accidental, ephemeral relationship which eventually enables the process of self-redemption to operate fully autonomously";[4] this is how the successors of Paracelsus proceeded. His concept of the world is built on the foundation of Joachim's eschatology. He awaits the return of the apostolic community: this will bring a new people and a new law. Paracelsus believes in a cosmic rebirth which will transform the old order into something completely new.[5] There can be no doubt that his expectations of salvation are linked to Joachim's theology of history, for in several places he speaks of Joachim's three ages of the world: the ages of the Father, the Son, and the future kingdom of the Holy Spirit, as visualized in the eschatology of the Franciscan Spirituals. He also prophesies the appearance of Elijah, while his followers even identify him with the person of Elijah. Elijah, the artist or *reparator omnium* who will reveal all the hidden secrets of the cosmos,[6] is the great heir and herald of the tradition of alchemy. It is in this context that the Rosicrucians speak of the figure of Elijah as the harbinger of the new age, which in the seventeenth and eighteenth centuries sustains the expectations of the Pietists. The pietistic doctrine of rebirth is linked to the ideas of Paracelsus. The title of one of Dippel's writings sheds immediate light on these connections: *Retirade der lutherischen Orthodoxie hinter eine von einigen Leibnizischen Ingenieurs aufgeworfene Schanze* [*Retreat of Lutheran Orthodoxy Behind One of Several Entrenchments Thrown Together by Leibniz's Engineers*].

Leibniz stands at the turning point between the alchemists' view of the world [*Weltschau*] and the worldview [*Weltanschauung*] belonging to the natural sciences. On the one hand, Leibniz has, "since his student days in Nürnberg, remained indebted to the alchemist-Rosicrucian tradition to a much greater extent than it would appear from his historical and philosophical views";[7] on the other hand, Leibniz helped inaugurate the age of the modern natural sciences, which are founded on the "Copernican turn" and are recognized by Kant in his introduction to the *Critique of Pure Reason*. Whereas in the Middle Ages cognition is dependent on objects, the axiom of modern, scientific metaphysics is that objects depend on the cognition of the subject.[8] People in the Copernican age no longer see the world as produced independently of the subject's own cognition, as if created by God; rather, they understand the world as their own product.[9] This turn does not begin with Kant, but is part of the fundamental change from the Ptolemaic-medieval conception of the world to the Copernican-modern one; Kant merely gives a clear account of its repercussions for metaphysics. Another product of that same turn is Vico's philosophy of history, which suggests that the history of mankind differs from natural history in that we have made the one but not the other.[10] A direct line extends from Descartes' *cogito ergo sum* to Hobbes, Spinoza, and Leibniz, whose decisive and much varied theme is the axiom that the object of cognition can be known by the subject precisely because and only to the extent that it has been produced by the subject.[11] "The methods of mathematics and geometry, the methods of construction, the production of objects from the formal requirements of objectivity itself, and later the methods of mathematical physics become the beacons and criteria of philosophy, all leading to the knowledge of the world as a totality."[12] This explains why all philosophical developments of the modern age have been in constant interaction with the developments of the natural sciences; they, in turn, have been in constant interaction with the rationalizing force of technology.

The *mos geometricus* is the claim for the world to be fully comprehensible, culminating in the ideal of a *mathesis universalis*, which has been offered by astronomy as a "theory of everything" [*Weltformel*].[13] "Knowledge," all by itself, breeds new categories of being: the universal laws, according to which science seeks to explain phenomena, are eternal and timeless *in mente divina*. It is consistent with a *mechanismus metaphysicus* that God has chosen the best world.[14] The finite world unfurls the ideas which it contained in embryonic form until they coincide with God's ideas. So the "law" of progress blends with the other laws of the natural sciences, without its postulate character being recognized as such.[15] The law of progress is sustained by an optimistic outlook. Each individual phenomenon [*das Einzelne*] has to overcome its limitations. Each individual [*der Einzelne*] must achieve perfection, but, as this life is not long enough, it is "necessary" to believe in immortality. Both those who are certain of salvation through Luther and those certain of development through Leibniz can say with serene composure: death, where is your sting?[16] An optimistic outlook is also associated with the moral destiny of the soul, as discussed in the theodicies. The series of theodicies, which give the best account of the century's endeavors from Leibniz to Nicholai in theology and philosophy, Pietism and literature, seek to "vindicate the honor" of what is good and "refute" what is evil.[17]

But in the theodicy of Leibniz there is a more profound intimation of a new philosophy of history, in the center of which is God's Kingdom and which is passed on to German Idealism by Lessing.[18] Even Hegel sees his "philosophy of world history" as "the true theodicy, the justification of God in history."[19] Leibniz and German Idealism, contrary to dogmatic rationalism, grasp as their task the irrationality of things as they are.[20] Just as in mathematics, whose task it is to demonstrate that everything which is given has ultimately been produced, so in the metaphysics of theodicy facticity is resolved into necessity. This fundamental tendency of Leibniz's philosophy is taken up again in the philosophy of Maimon as the resolution of the thing itself and the concept of "intelligible chance." Maimon has a significant influence on Fichte and, through him, on the later development of German Idealism.[21]

In the theodicy, providence is seen as "development according to the law of reason," and is synonymous with the "education of the human race" in which "punishment" is meaningful only as a passageway. Thus, the configuration of Origen's theology is restored. Just as Christian concepts blend with those of antiquity in Origen's work, so too in the seventeenth century is Christian apocalyptic eschatology merged with the static, scientific conception of the world, which in turn draws on the heritage of the antiquity. Origen's apocatastasis is born from this encounter between Christianity and the antiquity. It acts as a mediator between the eternal return of the antiquity and the Christian anticipation of the Eschaton. The doctrine of the "restoration of all things" inspires not only the mystical elements within Pietism but the pietistic Enlightenment, too. Pietism and the Enlightenment both put their faith in the final abolition of evil.[22] Along with most followers of mystical Pietism, Petersen and Arnold, who were students of Böhme, spread this particular doctrine, which takes such a hold of people's minds that it gradually displaces any chiliastic expectations of an imminent return and becomes the real ground of inquiry into eschatology during the pietistic Enlightenment.[23] Oetinger accepts without reservation this doctrine of the "restoration of all things," but he wants it to be treated esoterically, that is, by a select group of initiates.[24] Oetinger transmits it to Phillipp M. Hahn and it thus moves into the broad circle of Pietism in Württemberg. Oetinger's detailed explanation of the self-destructive nature of evil clearly anticipates the eschatology of German Idealism and of Schelling in particular. Eberhard, in his *Apologia pro Socrates*, takes up the doctrine of apocatastasis, and the circle is closed when it passes via Gottsched and Klopstock into the

Enlightenment.²⁵ The doctrine of the restoration of all things, which renders
the idea of eternal damnation contradictory, continues to be refuted by those
whose philosophy is in line with the optimism of the Enlightenment. It is not
until Lessing, drawing on Leibniz, takes up the full implications of the issue
once more that the mold [*das Schema*] of the Enlightenment is broken.

Driven by optimism, the law of Progress also bears to a considerable
extent on history, which is very closely linked to the idea of progress. From
this optimism emerges the proper science of history, which makes accessible
an abundance of material and provides those living at the time of the
Enlightenment with a life history of humanity, so they can posit themselves
at its end.²⁶ Voltaire was the first to organize historical data according to the
principle of immanent reason; in so doing, he inaugurated the concept of
cultural history. The model of cultural history, as conceived by the
Enlightenment, is the simple line of ascent divided according to the three
spiritual powers of "universal" man: sensuality, imagination, and reason.
Reason, by virtue of overcoming the previous stages, becomes the final goal
of history, which is held to be identical with the epoch of the
Enlightenment.²⁷

The system of the Enlightenment is really characterized by the sudden
fusion of an extremely historical (teleological) and an extremely unhistorical
(axiological) moment, as was the case in the Middle Ages. It combines an
absolute distance from the last things with a naive accommodation of them,
as was the case in chiliasm. Semler's scorn of the Revelation of John leads to
Corrodis's *Kritische Geschichte des Chiliasmus* [*Critical History of Chiliasm*],
which describes the "history of the sickness of the human soul."²⁸ The *Critical
History of Chiliasm* is written from the Enlightenment standpoint of a cul-
turally optimistic [*kulturselig*], deistic eternity of time. Reimarus finally
destroys the last remaining fragments of Christian, biblical eschatology
when he uses textual criticism to turn the "miracle" of the resurrection into
the disciples' "deception."

Rationalism, like medieval Scholasticism, claims to represent the universal method for acquiring knowledge about every conceivable form of
existence, but in doing so it faces the crucial question of how rational systems
of thought relate to irrational phenomena of life.²⁹ Every rational system
must come up against the barrier of the *irrational*.³⁰ So, for example, the
Enlightenment idea of history as a straightforward progression is under-
mined by the possibility of regression and devolution. A symptom of this is
the Lisbon earthquake, which profoundly shakes the whole world of the

Enlightenment: it becomes clear at one stroke that the system based on rationalism has come up against an unexpected, insuperable barrier. If the foundation of the new worldview is not to falter, a new model of development must be found which accommodates both progress and devolution.[31] This opens up a new mode of eschatology and marks the arrival of the historical dialectics of Idealism.

It is vitally important for the history of German Idealism that the eschatology of early Christianity, even if clandestine and apocryphal, continue in Pietism alongside the Enlightenment, so that knowledge of the radical nature of evil is preserved. Where the weight of the irrational side of being is overlooked, there arises, according to German Idealism, the philosophical "dogmatism" of the Enlightenment, which naively equates the forms of its abstract concepts with the structures of reality.[32] By shattering the illusions of the philosophical *dogmatism* of the Enlightenment, the philosophy of German Idealism soon encounters the limits imposed by facts [*die Schranke der Gegebenheit*]. If German Idealism is to encompass the world in its entirety, it has to take the "path leading inward."[33] Perhaps Schiller reveals this fundamental aspect of German Idealism more clearly than do systems of philosophy when he suggests that "finally, to put it quite plainly, man only plays when he is human in the full sense of the word, and he is only fully human when he plays."[34] Consequently, in German Idealism the *aesthetic principle* is raised high above aesthetics and made fundamental to life.[35] Everything which applies to the realm of imagination, art, or ideas can be resolved in emotional and spiritual terms because no action is needed to break the spell of the inner life [*Bann der Innerlichkeit*]. This marks the confluence of two distinct concepts, both developed as revolutionary critiques of art and philosophy: on the one hand, there is the transcendent, deistic concept of Kierkegaard, on the other the materialistic, atheistic outlook of Marx. Their critique begins with Hegel's concept of reality. Kierkegaard was doggedly opposed to the possibility of comprehending reality by reason, because a system can never fully grasp reality. What links Kierkegaard with the Hegelian left and with Marx is the elevation of the *factum brutum* of the given phenomenon—synonymous with negation in the philosophical system of German Idealism—to the only significant form of reality.[36] Marx's critique of Hegel, too, is directed against his assertion of the unity of reason and reality. Hegel can only reconcile reality "as a concept" and therefore transforms existence into a mysterious idea. By mystifying empiricism, the thrust of Hegel's idealistic philosophy becomes the "most crass form of materialism," because his system justifies in philosophical terms what exists in fact: "the philosophers have merely interpreted the world in a different way; our task is to change it."[37]

Lessing

Lessing stands in the midst of the tumult of philosophical disputes between rationalist Enlightenment, enlightened Pietism, Protestant orthodoxy, and the first stirrings of German Idealism. The question about the nature of history is articulated by Lessing with great acumen: how does rational Christianity, which is devoid of history, relate to the historical development of Christianity? Or stated in more general terms, what is the relation between the a priori of a system and the a posteriori of history?[38] In his parable of the rings, Lessing directs the various streams of history into the reservoir of Nathan's religiosity. He also edits the anonymous *Wolfenbüttel* fragments in which Reimarus once and for all smashes the foundations of ancient Christian eschatology by separating the historical Jesus from the idea of Christ and placing the historical figure of Jesus in history. The resurrection on which the mystery of Christianity is founded is represented as an act of deception on the part of the disciples. Lessing shares the opinion of Semler and Reimarus about the Revelation of John.

And yet, as Hegel points out, Lessing is on a different spiritual plane [*lebt in anderen Tiefen des Geistes*] than suspected by his friends and by the world in general. Arguably, Lessing's status in literary history occludes the depths of his existence, which are expressed in his *theological* writings, far away from his literary work. In the face of all objective statements of faith, he maintains his credo: "Where revealed religion is most certain of knowledge, this is precisely where it makes me most suspicious." Because, he continues, "Why can one not await a coming life as patiently as one awaits a coming day? To make this fundamental point [*dieser Grund*] against astrology is to make it against all revealed religion. Supposing there was an art of divining the future, it would be better if we did not learn it. Supposing a religion existed whose teachings about the future life were quite irrefutable, we should not lend our ear to that religion."[39]

In one stroke Lessing rises above the battle lines: above Bengel's mathematical economy of salvation, above Oetinger's phenomenology of the beyond [*des Jenseits*], above Swedenborg's topography of heaven, above the dogmatically secured truth of a Goetze, and even above Eberhard's rational counterarguments to and refutations [*aufklärerischer Aufhebung*] of hell.[40] Lessing's fundamental objection concerns not so much the *content* of their individual propositions but *how* they were arrived at. He counters an objective [*objektiv-gegenständlich*] eschatology, which passes itself off as science, with a subjective spirituality [*eine subjektive Innerlichkeit*] of the Eschaton. It is precisely with the writings of Reimarus that metaphysical Christian eschatology collapses and the possibility of transcendental eschatology, as conceived by Kant, emerges. This eschatology no longer depends on the support [*Krücken*] of scripture, which has long since become suspect; nor is it confident of possessing the truth, as generated by the rational arguments of the Enlightenment. Rather, *transcendental eschatology* requires that everything be grounded in *subjectivity*, making this the condition of possibility of cognition, as self-knowledge, self-apocalypse.[41] Within German Idealism, transcendentalism becomes "well-nigh a method of inner apocalypse."[42] All apocalypses associated with history or natural occurrences, all sounding of trumpets and symbols of wrath, all global conflagrations and new paradises are only *coups de théâtre* and parables; they are simply the orchestral arrangement for the one real apocalypse: the Apocalypse of Man.[43] Applying the conditions of transcendental eschatology, Lessing is able to refer back to the more exoteric allegories of Christian metaphysical eschatology. Here he calls on the aid of Leibniz, who "did no more nor less than what any of the old philosophers used to do in their more exoteric teachings. He observed a piece of wisdom for which apparently our philosophers (of the Enlightenment) have become much too clever. Leibniz willingly set aside his system for the sake of bringing everyone to truth according to the path on which he found them."[44] In this essay Lessing defends the eternity of hell as a way of defending Leibniz's views. "Do I intend to add to the suspicions that Leibniz only feigned his orthodoxy? Or am I seriously trying to make him appear orthodox, much to the chagrin of our philosophers? I do not intend to do either." Lessing positions Leibniz's views beyond the exoteric views of both the old Christian orthodoxy and the rationalism of the Enlightenment. "I admit that Leibniz treated the doctrine of eternal damnation in a very *exoteric* manner and that any views which he aired on the subject, *esoterically*, would have been of a different nature."[45] But Lessing, along with Leibniz, prefers precisely the old Christian eschatology to this esoteric rational conviction that one is in possession of the truth. "Moreover, I am convinced that Leibniz would have put up with the common doctrine of damnation with all of its exoteric justifications, and would even have preferred to add new ones of his own, only because he recognized that it was more in line with a great deal of the truth in his own esoteric philosophy than the opposing doctrine. He found that there was more truth even in this crude and wild concept than in the equally crude and wild concepts of the fanatical advocates of restoration [*Wiederbringer*]. This alone caused him to associate a little too much with the orthodox, rather than too little with the others."[46] Along with Leibniz, Lessing understands eternal punishment to be "that unbroken progression [*unzertrennte Forschreitung*] which links the two states of heaven and hell by an infinite number of steps without the one or the other ever losing its relative designation."[47] In this respect Lessing is already part of the eschatology of German Idealism, in which "hell is fundamental to nature, just as nature is fundamental to heaven."[48] For "the popular distinction commonly made between heaven and hell" is at odds with

the nature of the soul, because the soul is incapable of any pure sensation, that is, incapable of any such sensation which in its elementary form is anything other than pleasant or unpleasant. All this is to disregard any consideration of whether the soul should be capable of a state in which it has nothing apart from those pure sensations, whether of one type or the other. . . . Suppose the best of men still has much about him which is evil, and the worst of men is not without some good, then the consequences of evil must follow the first man to heaven, and the consequences of good accompany the other man to hell: each must still find his hell in heaven and his heaven in hell.[49]

It is only at this point that the profound implications of Lessing's final work, the Magna Carta of chiliasm, can be fully comprehended. Lessing's *Erziehung des Menschengeschlechts* [*Education of the Human Race*] ranks him together with the greatest figures of Christian theology, Origen and Joachim. Origen is the dominant source for this work. The leitmotifs of his theology, *pronoia* and *paideusis*, also permeate Lessing's eschatology.[50] Education is the only path in Origen's scheme of salvation.[51] For if the providence of God ordains the restoration of souls while retaining human freedom, then education is the only possible way.[52] There is no other way of achieving the perfection of all things and at the same time retaining human freedom. Therefore, both in Origen and Lessing providence (*pronoia*) is synonymous with education (*paideusis*). The education of every free rational being through providence is for Origen "the heart of Christianity," which is expressed "in each individual part of his theology."[53] Origen sees this education materialized "in the creation of the visible world, in philosophy, in Judaism, in the logos, in life within the Church and in future development."[54] The idea of development answers all problems arising from theodicy. Origen's real achievement is "to have transformed Christianity into educational idealism."[55]

This "summary" of Origen's system of theology may be more appropriate to Lessing because *his* eschatology can certainly be referred to as educational idealism. He outlines this concept of idealism in the *Education of the Human Race*: "Education is revelation which happens to each individual human being; revelation is education which has happened and still is happening to the whole human race.[56] . . . Education is for the individual what revelation is for the whole human race.[57] Lessing sees revelation as the education of the human race. Education ensures human freedom, freedom which does not attempt to impede revelation. "Education does not give man anything which he could not also have of his own accord [*aus sich selbst*] . . . but it gives it more swiftly and easily, just as revelation does not give mankind anything which human reason, if left to its own devices, would not have found."[58]

This idea of education implies that divine providence reaches its goal in stages. "Just as education is not indifferent about the order in which our faculties develop and is unable to teach mankind everything at once, so God has to establish a certain order and measure in the process of revelation."[59] Initially the stages of revelation lead from the Fall[60]—which indicates that man cannot hold himself to the high level determined by God—through to Israel. God chose

a single nation to receive his particular education; it was the most brutish and savage [*ungeschliffenste, das verwildertste*] of nations, with which he could start from scratch.[61] . . . In the beginning God just made himself known as the God of their fathers to familiarize them with the idea of a God who belonged specifically to their nation.[62] . . . But why educate such a raw nation, one with which God had to start from scratch? I have answered: so that in the due course of time individual members of this nation could be groomed with more certainty to educate all the other nations. He nurtured in them the future educators of the human race. Jews became these educators; only they could become this, only men from a nation which had been educated in this way.[63]

In this way Israel's history points forward to Jesus. "A better teacher must come and prise the stale textbook from the child's hands: Christ came."[64] In the meantime, the other part of the human race, the Greeks and Romans, "had advanced so far in the exercise of reason that they needed more noble incentives for their moral action than the temporal rewards and punishments which had operated hitherto.[65] . . . It was time for their actions to be influenced by the expectation of a real afterlife. And it so happened that Christ was the first reliable, practical teacher of the immortality of the soul."[66]

The idea of education also determines future development. "Education has its goal for the whole human race no less than for the individual. All education has a goal."[67] It can be said of Lessing with even greater justification than of Origen, who unites many other strands of thought, that he transformed Christianity into educational idealism. While the idea of educational idealism is first defined by Origen, it is Joachim's prophecy which becomes the goal of Lessing's eschatology. The Old and New Testaments are the primers of mankind. "But each primer is only intended for a specific age and it is damaging for a child who has outgrown it to spend any more time on it."[68] Just as we no longer need the Old Testament to teach us about the unity of God, so it is time to dispense with the New Testament along with the doctrine on the immortality of the soul.

Certainly, the age of a new eternal gospel will come, as we are promised even in the primers of the new covenant. It is even possible that certain enthusiasts of the thirteenth and fourteenth centuries (Joachim and the Spirituals) caught a ray of this new eternal gospel, but were wrong in as much as they announced its arrival to be so imminent. Arguably their conception of the three ages of the world was not an empty whim, and they certainly had no ill intentions when teaching that the new covenant would become just as outmoded as the old one had. They still thought in terms of the same divine economy, the same God. To put my words in their mouths, they still referred to the same plan of the general education of the human race.[69]

The Joachimite *ecclesia spiritualis* is not a *civitas platonica*, but is conceived as a future one. Similarly, Lessing thinks of the age of a new eternal gospel not as a utopia but as a future one. After all, the nature of utopia is to be distinguished from chiliasm, for utopia belongs to essentially politicized man and emerges from the political spirit.[70] The state is the vessel for the fulfillment of this concept of humanity, with the provision, however, that in utopia the ideal conditions, which according to Plato are only possible "in thought," are produced artificially. Only in this way is the present form of the state differentiated from its ideal. Even the ideal of utopia needs to take its bearings from the real state.[71] This explains why Greek civilization and the Renaissance are the two high points in the history of utopia. In his *Utopia* Thomas More deals with the real tradition of classical antiquity. This contrasts with chiliasm, which is never driven by political forces or forces similar to politics, but by anarchic forces. Admittedly, also the chiliastic kingdom is "on earth," and its geographical location can even be specified as the earthly Jerusalem. Despite this "indication of place" the chiliastic kingdom is no longer an earthly place, and this is what fundamentally distinguishes chiliasm from utopia.[72] A comparison between specific elements in utopia and the events in Münster convincingly illuminates the differences between utopia and chiliasm. The millennium is not being inaugurated, but it is coming. It is not to be found in any location, but it is happening [*es ereignet sich*]. It is not being discovered, but it is expected.

The philosophy of chiliasm is anarchic, and Lessing is reported to have felt the strongest aversion to "those ridiculous and ill-fated aspects of all moral and political machinery." Once, in a conversation, Lessing got so excited that he proclaimed that the whole of "bourgeois society must yet be fully abolished [*aufgehoben*] and, as far-fetched as it may sound, it nevertheless comes close to the truth: people will only be governed well when they no longer need a government."[73] This "inner transformation" is to be brought about by the free covenant of "the most noble-minded and wise" and, regardless of existing barriers between nations, religions, and citizens, they will join hands in the ideal brotherhood [*Bund*] of the Freemasons.

The motif of the Kingdom of God on earth can thus also be heard faintly in the philosophy of chiliasm. The motif of "on earth" becomes even more pronounced in the course of the history of philosophical chiliasm. In Kant, the *Ideas for a Universal History from a Cosmopolitan Point of View* amount to an "eternal peace," secured "by mutual self-interest ... it is the spirit of trade, incompatible with wars, that sooner or later controls every nation."[74] If in Hegel, world and spirit are held in equilibrium as the world spirit [*Welt-geist*], then the Hegelians of the left give predominance to the moment of the "world": the spirit of the age [*Geist der Zeit*] becomes the age's spirit [*Zeitgeist*] (Ruge) and world spirit [*Weltgeist*] becomes world ideology (Marx).

Fritz Gerlich was the first to examine Marxist doctrine from the perspective of philosophical chiliasm. "To produce evidence of this origin, we must demonstrate the connections between Lessing and Marx. They bear the names of Kant, Fichte, Hegel, and Weitling. Having arrived at Hegel, the teacher of Marx, we have reached our end: Marxism. Once the bridge between Marx and Lessing is established, then the connection with chiliasm, so fundamental to Lessing, becomes apparent. Consequently, Marxism is shown to be a child of the more recent tendencies of chiliasm—not only dogmatically but also historically."[75] It must be said that Gerlich defines the "stages" from a one-sided, oversimplified perspective, since he, like those who follow him, explores the chiliastic factor at the margins of philosophical work, rather than pointing to the Eschaton, which lies beating at the heart of German Idealism.

Kant's Philosophy of Religion

Kant is quite right to begin his *Critique of Pure Reason* with the initial thoughts of Copernicus, for the Kantian system is the philosophy of Copernican man. The Copernican world is an earth deprived of the heaven which used to be an archetype to the earth. Therefore, Copernican man gets no closer to his true nature by closing the gap between the world and the heavenly archetype [*oberen Urbild*]. Because the space between heaven and earth has become meaning-less, Copernican man seeks to revolutionize the world according to an ideal that can become reality in the course of time. The ideal is no longer the Platonic idea which dwells on high, but is to be found in the future. In the Ptolemaic world, because it has a heaven over it, *eros* holds sway, pulling the upper and lower spheres closer to each other. In the Copernican world, where upper and lower have become meaningless, the *spirit* reigns, forging ahead through the dialectic.[76] The philosophy of Copernican man is the philosophy of the spirit, and from the outset Kant shows himself to be the philosopher of the spirit.

While the world of Ptolemaic man is completed by the dialogue between I and thou, the call and response between God and man, the conversation between the interlocutors of heaven and earth, all the words [*alles Wort*] of Copernican man remain unanswered [*ohne Ant-wort*] monologues.[77] As space has become infinite and empty, only dead bodies move within it, according to unalterable laws which are merely the laws of the autonomous reason of Copernican man. An object can be known by Copernican man only insofar as it has been produced by himself. "A light goes on" for Copernican man, for Francis Bacon, Galileo, Toricelli, and all the natural scientists that follow. "They learned that reason only perceives what it has produced according to its own designs, that it must not be content to follow the lead of nature, but must advance with principles of its own judgment based on unvarying laws, and compel [*nötigen*] (!) nature to answer its questions. For otherwise random observations, made according to no preconceived plan, cannot be brought together in a necessary law, which is after all what reason seeks and needs."[78] Nature does not freely respond to man's words, but "reason must approach nature, on the one hand, equipped with the principles according to which concordant phenomena acquire the validity of laws and, on the other hand, using experiments which derive from those principles. Reason must approach nature with a view of being instructed by it, though not in the role of a pupil who listens to all that his master chooses to tell him, but in the role of a judge who compels (!) the witnesses to answer questions which he himself thinks fit to pose."[79]

This is precisely what Kant intends to do for metaphysics, which "has not yet had the good fortune of attaining the sure methods of science."[80] Kant believes that "the examples of mathematics and natural philosophy . . . are remarkable enough to reflect upon the key elements which changed their mode of thinking and which have proved so advantageous to them, and to make us try to emulate them."[81] While it has up to this point been assumed that cognition [*Erkenntnis*] must take its bearing from the object, all attempts to do so by using a priori categories have failed; Kant thus intends to move in the opposite direction.

Let us then make the experiment whether we may not be more successful in meta-physics, if we assume that the objects must conform to our cognition. This appears to accord better with the possibility of our gaining the end we have in view, that is to say, of arriving at the cognition of objects a priori, of determining something with respect to these objects, before they are given to us. We here propose to do just what Copernicus did in attempting to explain the celestial movements. When he found that he could make no progress by assuming that all the heavenly bodies revolved round the spectator, he reversed the process and tried the experiment of assuming that the spectator revolved, while the stars remained at rest. In metaphysics we may make the same experiment with regard to the intuition of objects.[82]

Since heaven no longer responds to human discourse [*Rede*], it must be made to testify, as an appointed judge compels a witness. However, heaven under *duress* [*genötigte*] is increasingly shrouded in silence, and human articulation now consists of the signs of self-reflective reason, penetrating only empty space rather than reaching God. Therefore, *prayer* as an interior, formal worship of God is "a superstitious delusion."[83] The "spirit of prayer" alone is permissible, and it can be ongoing in man. Because

in this latter desire, man seeks the "spirit of prayer" only in himself (so as to enliven his thoughts by the *idea* of God), but in the former, he seeks in his own words, which he utters quite freely, to influence God. In the sense of the spirit of prayer, prayer can be offered utterly sincerely, even if man does not presume to assert God's existence with complete certainty. In the instance where prayer is addressed directly, he assumes the highest object to be present in person. . . . For a man to be associated with the practice of talking to himself out loud immediately leads to the suspicion that he is a little mad, and so he is judged in that light (not without some justification) if he is encountered on his own in a particular activity or demeanor which could be associated with somebody who is in a trance.[84]

The *change* [*Wendung*] from Ptolemaic to Copernican humanity does not come about all of a sudden. In fact it does not begin with Copernicus; rather, its origins can be traced back to Joachim, who declares that the allegory [*das Gleichnis*] of the image and archetype in the age of the Holy Spirit has been superseded. The worldly kingdom of the spirit is ushered in to replace the union of heaven and earth, which for the Catholic Church is forged in the mystery of the Mass. The "Copernican revolution," involving the transformation from eros to spirit, first comes to philosophy with clarity in the Kantian system. *Spirit* is the watchword for all Joachimites, from the Spirituals Müntzer and Sebastian Frank, to Böhme, Lessing, and German Idealism. Armed with the "spirit," they join in battle with the sacrament of the Catholic Church, the word of the Lutheran Church, the dogma of the Orthodox Church, the dogmatism of philosophy and the systems of bourgeois society.

While the Holy Spirit of Joachim and the Spirituals is still understood as revelation, although as a kind of illumination, the spirit of reason uncovers, in the act of *re-flectio*, of reflecting on oneself, the source of its own possibilities at its boundaries [*in seiner Grenze als die Wurzel seiner eigenen Möglichkeit*]. This is because the spirit's being is autonomous and can set its own boundaries. The *nomos* is the real *autos*. Therefore, the final eschatology of the spirit is revealed to be the identity of *nomos* and *autos*. The *nomos* is identical to *autos* in autonomy. The last things are no longer the *heteros nomos*, God and the things of the world, but the assumption of one's own spiritual being. Metaphysical eschatology is superseded by transcendental eschatology. In the process of unveiling reason, the veil of the temple at Sais is lifted so that reason gains an understanding of itself in the very process of unveiling.[85] The unveiling of reason is not of the same order as other discoveries, but takes precedence over the others because it is only through the unveiling of reason that all other Eschata are legitimized. "That is how transcendental philosophy becomes the method of inner apocalypticism par excellence."[86]

When transcendental philosophy is not just a glimmer, as in the case of

Lessing, but is actually carried out, then Kant is able to draw on the exoteric allegories of metaphysical eschatology with more justification than Lessing. In so doing Kant takes note of "that cleverness for which our most recent philosophers have become far too wise," but which Lessing thinks he encounters in Leibniz.[87] Kant, too, was "prepared to put his theories aside and sought out the exoteric parables" of metaphysical eschatology because he recognized that it was more in line "with a great truth of his esoteric philosophy" than the system of rationalism was. "Obviously, he did not adopt it in the crude and wild way of many theologians. But he found that there was more truth even in this crude and wild concept than in the equally crude and wild concepts" of the Enlightenment: "And this alone caused him to associate a little too much with the orthodox, rather than too little with the others."[88]

In a nearly forgotten essay about "Das Ende aller Dinge" [The End of All Things], which bears a strong resemblance in its tendencies and motivations to Lessing's essay on Leibniz, the metaphysical statements of Christian eschatology become the *as ifs* of transcendental eschatology. The thought of "the End of all Time" has "something horrifying about it because it leads, as it were, to the edge of an abyss,"[89] the abyss of reason, "yet there is also something compelling about it, because one cannot help but keep looking back at it in horror." This thought is a valid description of the nature of "reason considered from a moral point of view."[90]

The transition from time into eternity . . . brings us up against the End of all Things, as temporal beings [*als Zeitwesen*] and objects of possible experience - which end, however, in the moral order of ends, is at the same time the beginning of a duration of just those same beings as supersensible, and consequently as not standing under conditions of time; thus that duration and its state will be capable of no determination of its nature other than a moral one.[91]

Transcendental eschatology inquires beyond the objective statements of Christian eschatology:

Why does mankind expect the world to end *in the first place*? And even if this is conceded, why does it have to be a terrifying end (for most of the human race)? . . . The reason for the first assumption seems to be that reason tells man that the continuation of the world only makes sense insofar as the rational beings inhabiting it focus on the ultimate goal of their existence. If this is unattainable then creation seems pointless to them, like a drama lacking a resolution and a reasonable purpose. This perspective arises from the view that the whole nature of the human race is so corrupt that there is no further hope; and therefore the only proper solution, the wisest, most just (according to the majority of people) solution is in fact to bring it to a dreadful end.[92]

The objective statements of eschatology assume the status of *myth*. "We are only concerned here (or are playing) with ideas created by reason itself, whose objects (if they have any) exceed our horizon, which however, though yielding much speculative knowledge, does not yet for that reason mean they should be considered empty in every respect. On the contrary, in practical terms they are put into our hands by legislative reason, not to ponder deeply on the identity and nature of their objects, but to think about the purpose of moral principles which are grounded in the ultimate goal of all things."[93] And so Kant moves on to his elucidation of the prophecy of John's Apocalypse, "that henceforth there is to be no more time," which "means nothing more than: we must consider our maxims, as if, despite all the infinitely progressing changes from good to better, our moral condition, as regards our convictions (the *homo Noumenon*, whose transformation is in heaven), were not subject to temporal changes."[94] But that "one day, a point in time will arrive when all change (and with it all time itself) will come to an end is an idea which shocks our imagination. From that moment, the whole of nature will freeze as if petrified."[95] And yet

this idea, as much as it might exceed our comprehension, is akin to reason in practical terms. Even if we assume the moral and physical condition of man's life here to be on its most favorable footing, that is, one of steady progress and striving for the highest good (which is held up as a goal), he cannot, however (even when conscious of his unchanging conviction), find any satisfaction in the prospect of a never-ending transformation in his condition (moral and physical). His present state is always going to be evil compared to the better state which he is preparing to enter; and the idea of an unending progression toward the ultimate goal is a prospect of an unending series of evils which, although it might be outweighed by the greater good, even so, does not give rise to the contentment which he can imagine on finally *reaching the ultimate purpose* [*Endzweck*].[96]

On this point Kant turns to "*mysticism* (because reason has its own secrets, as it is not easily satisfied with its immanent, that is, practical, uses, but likes to venture into the transcendental), where a kind of reason [*eine Vernunft*] does not understand itself or what it wants, but prefers to wax lyrical."[97] This is simply so "that men may at last look forward to eternal rest, which amounts to their supposedly blissful end of all things, a concept that really ushers in the loss of reason and the end of all thought."[98]

Transcendental eschatology thus ends up with the mystery of reason and reveals the *tragic dualism* of Copernican man. This tragic dilemma found expression in the myth of Prometheus.

Prometheus is not a thought devised by man but is one of the primeval thoughts [*Urgedanken*] which thrust their way into existence and consequently evolve whenever they, like Prometheus in Aeschylus, find a profound mind as their breeding ground. Prometheus is the thought in which the human race, having once conjured up the whole panoply of the gods from its innermost resources, turns back on itself and becomes aware of itself and its own fate. Prometheus is that principle archetype of humanity which we have called the *spirit*; and where previously there was weakness of spirit, he brought reason and self-awareness to the soul. He atones for the whole of humanity, and is in his suffering the pure sublime model of the human ego [*Menschen-Ichs*]. This sets itself aside from quiet communion with God and suffers the same fate, clamped by iron necessity to the rigid rock which is the randomness and inevitable reality of life, from where it surveys forlornly the unbreachable gulf, which cannot be restored, at least not immediately, and which has arisen because of an act perpetrated in the past that is irrevocable and irredeemable.[99]

Quite rightly, Schelling reminds us of Kant in this grandiose discussion of Prometheus, because Kantian philosophy is the philosophy of Promethean man. The Promethean philosophy of Copernican man is the Kantian philosophy of the ego.[100]

Let us not leave this without honoring Kant's memory, to whom we are indebted for speaking with such resolution about a course of determined action which does not enter contemporary consciousness and belongs to an earlier age, and even to the world of ideas. Without it there would not be an integrated personality, nothing eternal in man; rather, he would just consist of random, incoherent actions. This doctrine of Kant was in itself an act of his spirit, which demonstrated not only his acumen but also the moral courage which fearless sincerity requires.[101]

The most puzzling and also the most "disturbing"[102] aspect of Kantian philosophy is the relationship of Prometheus to the divine.

The world having progressed as far as Zeus, a new possibility arises for the human race that is independent of him and has its origins in a different world order, a possibility which becomes a reality through the prescience of Prometheus. Zeus had considered replacing the existing human race with a new one. But there was something within him which, after what Prometheus had done, made it absolutely impossible for him to attempt it. Zeus himself only triumphed over the blind cosmic forces through the power of the spirit and, aided by Prometheus, set up the new kingdom. And yet the punishment of Zeus is so severe and his wrath so great.[103]

Prometheus is in his right, and yet he is plagued by Zeus with unspeakable tortures lasting for an incalculable length of time. But Zeus, too, is in his right because this was the only price at which freedom and independence from God could be purchased. There is no alternative: "It is a contradiction which we are not to resolve but rather have to acknowledge. The fate of the world and that of mankind is tragic."[104]

Kant makes subjectivity the foundation of transcendental philosophy. He unmasks all objective statements belonging to the old system of metaphysics as pseudo-dialectic, and empties of its meaning a world solely dependent on natural laws by augmenting its intelligible random nature [*intelligible Zufälligkeit*]. He posits subject and object within the one *I*; "I am conscious of myself" is a thought which in itself implies the presence of a second *I*: the *I* as subject and the *I* as object. What is meant by this is not a dual personality, but rather that the *I* which thinks and sees is the person while the *I* of the object looked at by me, like all objects outside me, is the thing [*die Sache*]. The split between phenomenon and essence, which in Kantian philosophy is synonymous with the split between necessity and freedom, is carried over by Kant into the subject itself.[105] Kant divides the subject into *phenomenon* and *noumenon*; the unresolved, eternally irresolvable conflict between freedom and necessity reaches to the very interiority of man [*innerste Struktur des Menschen*]. Whereas the empirical *I* is completely bound, the intelligible *I* is utterly free, "because pure reason is not affected by any form of sensory perception."[106] Natural causality and freedom can occur in the *I* independently of and undisturbed by the other, because freedom is not a psychological characteristic but a transcendental predicate. Yet the intelligible *I* cannot be understood as the thing in itself (Hermann Cohen), which would be merely the norm. For empirical action is the product of the intelligible *I*. It is at this point that Kant introduces the *dialectic*.[107] Action is determined by empirical causality and by intelligible causality, that is, *freedom*: "It is very curious that in the world of facts, there should even be a concept of reason (which in itself cannot be demonstrated by observation, and for which there is no theoretical proof of its possibility). And this is the concept of freedom whose reality, as a particular kind of causality (whose conceptualization would be rewarding [*überschwenglich*] from a theoretical point of view), can thus be experienced through practical laws of pure reason which accord with real actions."[108]

In *Religion Within the Boundaries of Mere Reason*, Kant encompasses the dialectic of *freedom*, which man exercises as *choice* and God as *grace*. The eschatological drama of the individual and of the collective unfolds in *three stages*. "Act one" deals with "the propensity to evil alongside that of good, or with radical evil in human nature." "Act two" is about the battle between good and evil for the dominance of man. Finally, "Act three" is about "the victory of good over evil and the establishment of the Kingdom of God on earth." Together with the original propensity for good, there is also in human nature a propensity toward evil, and consequently man is evil by nature. Since the natural predisposition toward evil

must ultimately be sought in a free power of choice, and hence is imputable, this propensity is morally evil in itself. This evil is radical, since it corrupts the ground of all maxims; as natural propensity, it also is not to be extirpated by human forces, for this could only happen through good maxims—something that cannot take place if the supreme subjective ground of all maxims is presupposed to be corrupt. Yet it must be equally possible to overcome this evil, for it is found in the human being as a creature free to act.[109]

Radical evil is not to be called "malice," since in the case of malice evil as such, which is of the devil, is the driving force of the maxim. But radical evil is "perversity of the heart," which "can coexist with a will which in the abstract is good. Its origin is the frailty of human nature."[110] There is "no comprehensible reason to explain where the moral evil in us could originally have come from."[111] Therefore one can say that man "lapsed into evil through temptation and is not fundamentally corrupted," which leaves room for "hope of a return to the good from which he strayed."[112]

But this hope

surpasses every concept of ours [*übersteigt alle unsere Begriffe*]. For how can an evil tree bear good fruit? But, since by our previous admission a tree which was (in its predisposition) originally good brought forth bad fruits, and since the fall from good into evil (if we seriously consider that evil originates from freedom) is no more comprehensible than the ascent from evil back to good, then the possibility of this last cannot be disputed. For, in spite of that fall, the command that we ought to become better human beings still resounds unabated in our souls; consequently we must be capable of it, even if what we do is of itself insufficient and we thereby make ourselves receptive to a higher assistance inscrutable to us.[113]

A general training in actions compliant with the law creates an empirical virtue, *virtus phaenomenon*. The history of human evolution itself warrants only cultural progress, which is tantamount to a "change in mores," toward the principle of happiness, but does not warrant moral improvement, which is founded upon the principle of holiness. Intelligible virtue, *virtus noumenon*, "cannot come about by gradual *reform*, as long as the ground of the maxims is dubious, but by a *revolution* in man's attitude (a transition in this attitude to the maxim of holiness)." In this revolution "a new man" comes into being through "a form of rebirth," just like a new creation and transformation of the heart.[114] Moral progress is not founded upon the improvement of mores but on the transformation of the mind [*Denkensart*], and that is where a start must be made, "although man usually goes about it in a different way,"[115] starting the revolution from the base structure [*Unterbau*] of society. The divine spark in the depths of the soul, which radical evil is unable to destroy, enables the revolution to come about. "The very incomprehensibility of this predisposition, proclaiming as it does a divine origin, must work up the mind to the point of exaltation and gird it up for the sacrifices which may have been imposed upon it out of concern for duty."[116]

So Kant's anthropology leads to an aporia that becomes ever more clearly exposed as grace and that cannot be appropriated by reason "as an additional possession."[117] "For the use of reason would presuppose a rule concerning what good we ourselves must do (with a particular aim in mind) in order to achieve something; to expect an effect of *grace* means, however, the exact opposite, namely that the good (the morally good) is not of our doing, but that of another being."[118] The possibility of repentance [*Umkehr*] is dependent on grace. For "moral good does not differ from moral evil as earth does from heaven, but as heaven does from hell."[119] Therefore, "good and evil, the kingdom of light and the kingdom of darkness, cannot be thought of as adjacent realms gradually merging by stages (of greater and lesser light); rather, they are separated from each other by an enormous force."[120] The distance between "the goodness which we ought to effect in ourselves and the evil from which we start is, however, infinite, while the deed—that is, the degree to which the conduct of one's life conforms to the holiness of the law—can never be achieved in any amount of time. Nevertheless, the human being's moral constitution ought to agree with this holiness."[121] This antinomy is resolved in such a way that, although from the human point of view the continuous advance from a deficient good to something better "always remains deficient," so that the good deed appears to us "at each instant inadequate to a holy law," yet from the pure, intellectual perspective of God, who sees man's disposition, this advance toward the holy law is "judged to be a perfect whole, even with respect to the deed." Therefore, man can expect, "regardless of his constant deficiency, to be pleasing to God."[122]

If the maxim of holiness, unattainable as such, is identifiable with man's endeavors only from God's perspective, then grace increases in another aspect again, because man "*started from evil* and he will never be able to cancel out that guilt."[123] Never can man achieve "a surplus over what he is always indebted to do on himself," a surplus with which he might pay off his debt [*Schuld*].[124] "Therefore, every human being would have to expect *infinite punishment* and exclusion from the Kingdom of God."[125] But through the "revolution in disposition [*Gesinnung*] . . . the subject of sin" dies. Although man is "physically still the same person subject to punishment, he is, in his new disposition as an intelligible being, a different man in a moral sense as he stands before the divine judge and pleads his cause."[126] Here, then, is that "surplus over what is earned from works, as was sought earlier, and one which is imputed to us by *grace*. For what in our earthly life is merely in the process of becoming is imputed to us, as if we already possessed it here in full. Indeed we have no rightful claim to this, to the extent that we know ourselves, so that the accuser within us would be more likely to render a verdict of guilty. The sentence, therefore, is always one of grace."[127] Kantian philosophy, like Luther's theology, is predicated on the aporia of *grace*, which alone "makes possible the victory of good over evil and establishes the Kingdom of God on earth."

In Kant's philosophy individual eschatology is inextricably linked to the eschatology of the whole community, for dangers arise for the individual, "not only from his own crude nature, to the extent that he is individualized, but also from people with whom he has relations or intercourse."[128] If it were not possible "to establish a society to uphold the moral law, which would draw on combined forces to counteract evil, then this would place the individual in constant danger of relapsing into evil, irrespective of what he might have done to extricate himself from its sway."[129] Further, since "the duties of virtue concern the entire human race, the concept of an ethical community always refers to the ideal of a totality of human beings, and in this it distinguishes itself from a political community."[130] The ethical community is a duty of a particular kind, "not of man to man but of the human race to itself."[131]

The juridical community, in particular the state, is there to "limit the freedom of each person to the conditions under which it can coexist with the freedom of everybody else in conformity with universal law." Thus the juridical community pays attention only to the "legality of actions." In an ethical community, however, the "inner morality" of actions must be taken into account. Therefore, the supreme legislator must "be one who knows the heart so as to penetrate to the most intimate parts of everyone's disposition and, as is necessary in every community, to give to each according to the worth of his actions. But this is the concept of God as moral ruler of the world. Hence an ethical community is conceivable only as a people under divine command, that is, as a people of God, and specifically in accordance with the law of virtues."[132] God alone can establish a moral people of God. "Yet man is not permitted on this account to remain idle in the undertaking. . . . He must rather proceed as if everything depends on him, and only under these conditions can he hope that a higher wisdom will grant him perfection on the basis of his good intentions [*wohlgemeinten Bemühung*]."[133]

The wish of all who have good intentions [*aller Wohlgesinnten*] is therefore "that the Kingdom of God come, that his will be done on earth"— "but what preparations must be made so that this wish may come to pass among them?"[134] In his answer Kant reveals the Joachimite core of his "teaching on religion": "An ethical community under divine moral legislation is a church which, inasmuch as it is not the object of any possible experience, is called the church invisible. The visible church is the actual union of human beings into a whole that accords with this ideal. . . . The true (visible) church is the one which represents the moral Kingdom of God on earth, inasmuch as this is possible with human beings."

The hallmarks of the true church are, first, universality, "whence its numerical unity, for which it must be internally predisposed; to wit, though indeed divided and at variance with itself in incidental opinions, yet, as regards its essential purpose, it is founded on principles that necessarily lead it to overall union into a single church (hence, no sectarian schisms)";[135] second, "its integrity, that is, union for no incentives other than moral ones"; third, "relations according to the principle of freedom, including the internal relations of its members among themselves as well as the external relations of the church to the political power, both in a free state; fourth, "the immutability of its constitution."[136] As a church, the ethical community has "nothing in its principles that really resembles a political constitution." It could best be likened to the constitution of a household "under a common though invisible moral father."[137] In this way, the pure religion of reason ultimately rules over everything, "so that God may be all in all." The casing in which the embryo first formed into a person must be set aside if this person is now to enter the light of day. The guidelines of sacred tradition, with its appendages, statutes, and observances which served their time, are gradually becoming superfluous and ultimately even an encumbrance as this human being enters adolescence. As long as he (mankind) "was a child, he thought as a child" and knew how to combine statutes, imposed on him from outside, with scholarship and a philosophy which served the Church; "now that he is a man he lays aside childish things." "The degrading distinction between laity and clergy ceases, and equality springs from true freedom, yet without anarchy, for each indeed obeys the law (not the statutory one) which he has prescribed for himself, yet must regard it at the same time as the will of the world ruler as revealed to him through reason, and this ruler invisibly binds all together, under a common government, in a state inadequately prepared for in the past through the visible church."[138] But this is not to be expected "from an external revolution whose impact is violent and turbulent and subject to fortuitous circumstances." The principle of the pure religion of reason itself "must form the basis for the transition to the new order of things, which, once grasped on mature reflection, will be carried out, inasmuch as it is to be a human work, through gradual reform; for, as regards revolutions, which can cut short the progress of reform, they are left up to providence and cannot be introduced according to plan without damaging freedom."[139]

Kant sees the *history* of Christianity as a *falling away* from the Kingdom of God. "This history of Christianity (which, in so far as it was to be erected on a historical faith, could not have turned out otherwise), when beheld at a single glance, like a painting, could indeed justify the outcry, *tantum religio potuit suadere malorum!*"[140] Kant knows himself to be positioned in the *kairos*.

Should one now ask, which period of the entire church history known up to now is the best? I reply without hesitation: the present, and I say this because one only need allow to grow unhindered the seed of the true religious faith now being sown in Christianity—by only a few to be sure, but in the open—to be able to expect it to come continuously closer to that church which unites all human beings and constitutes the visible representation (schema) of an invisible Kingdom of God on earth.[141]

Finally Kant tries to incorporate the apocalyptic symbols into the religion of pure reason.

The appearance of the Antichrist, the chiliastic millennium, the announcement of the proximity of the end of the world—through reason they all take on their proper symbolic meaning. And the latter, introduced as an event we cannot see in advance, expresses well the necessity for us always to be ready for it, while in fact always regarding ourselves actually as the chosen citizens of a divine state.[142] . . . The separation of good from evil, which would not be beneficial on the church's approach to perfection, is seen as the final outcome once the divine state has been fully established. In addition, there is the final proof of its steadfastness, seen as a power: its victory over all its enemies who are considered to be in a state (the state of hell). This brings all earthly life to an end, in that death, the final enemy (of those who are good), is abolished. This is the beginning of eternity, which beckons for both parts, offering to the one salvation and to the other perdition, while the church form is dissolved and the vicar on earth enters together with all those people who have been raised to citizenship in heaven, so that God is all in all.[143]

Hegel's Dialectic

Kant is the Old Testament and Hegel the New Testament of German Idealism. That is how the young Hegel himself understood his relationship with Kant, whose law of duty he equated with the law of the Old Testament. Hegel seeks to derive his own system strictly from the New Testament, particularly from the sayings of Jesus in the Sermon on the Mount and St. John's Gospel. The foundations of Hegel's doctrine are still openly visible in the fragments of his *Theologische Jugendschriften* [*Early Theological Writings*], which were published by Hermann Nohl, himself inspired by Dilthey's work on the early Hegel. In his meticulous study, Theodor Hearing has tried to discern the rhythm of Hegel's progression of thought. In these early writings the structure of his system is still recognizable in a way which is barely possible later, when a fully fledged terminology gives rein to his thoughts. For this reason, the *Early Theological Writings* are fundamental to understanding all of the later works of Hegel, as well as to grasping his central theme of the dialectic, and they will be discussed here in detail.

Even if Kant regards the *shalt* of the law not as "an order given by an external agency" but as a "consequence of one's own understanding," "as respect for duty," this does not cancel the positivity of the law. When Kant turns against mere legality by showing that "the legal is universal and the force of its obligation resides within this universality,"[144] it only partially does away with the positivity, since the command of duty is universal, which remains opposed to the particular, and the latter is the oppressed when the former reigns. "Between the Shaman of the Tungus, the European prelate who rules church and state, the Voguls, and the Puritans, on the one hand, and the man who listens to his own command of duty, on the other, the difference is not that the former make themselves slaves, while the latter is free, but that the former have their lord outside themselves, while the latter carries his lord in himself, yet at the same time is his own slave."[145] The man of the command and the man of duty are both slaves, the only difference being that the former carries his lord outside himself and the latter within himself. Kant's *morality* is in effect still *legality*, for the Kantian *ought* is not sublated in being [nicht *aufgehoben im Sein*].

But Jesus, who overcomes the law with love, moves beyond Kantian morality. "Against complete subservience to the law of an alien Lord, Jesus opposes not a partial subjugation to a law of one's own, the self-coercion of Kantian virtue, but rather virtues without lordship and without submission, that is, modifications of love."[146] If Jesus

wanted to restore humanity in its entirety, he could not possibly have taken a course like this, because it simply adds on an obdurate arrogance to man's conflicted state. To act in the spirit of the laws could not have meant for him to act out of respect for duty and to contradict inclinations, for both parts of the spirit (no other words can describe this conflicted being [*Zerrissensein*]), just by being thus divergent, would have been not in the spirit of the laws but against that spirit, one part because it was something exclusive and self-restricted, the other because it was something suppressed.[147]

This spirit of Jesus, a spirit raised above morality, is present in the Sermon on the Mount, which is an attempt elaborated in several examples

to strip the laws of legality, of their legal form. It does not teach respect for the laws; rather, it exhibits that which fulfils the law and annuls it as a law, and thus is something higher than obedience to the law and makes the law superfluous. Since the commands of duty presuppose a separation (between reason and inclination) and since the dominance of the concept declares itself in a *thou shalt*, that which is raised above this separation is by contrast an *is* [*ein Sein*], a modification of life.[148]

Even when what Jesus sets against and above the laws is expressed as a "command,"

this turn of phrase is a command in a sense quite different from the *shalt* of a moral imperative. It is only the sequel to the fact that, when life is conceived in thought or given expression, it acquires a form alien to it, a conceptual form, while, on the other hand, the moral imperative, as a universal, is in essence a concept. And if in this way life appears to men in the form of something reflected, something said, then this type of expression (a type inappropriate to life), *Love God above everything and thy neighbor as thyself*, was quite wrongly regarded by Kant as a command requiring respect for the law which commands love. And it is in this confusion of the utterly accidental kind of phraseology expressive of life with the moral imperative (which depends on the opposition between concept and reality) that we find Kant's profound reduction of what he calls a *command* (love God first of all and thy neighbor as thyself) to his moral imperative. And his remark that *love*—or to take the meaning which he thinks must be given to this love, liking to perform all duties—*cannot be commanded* falls away of its own accord, because in love all thought of duties vanishes.[149]

Love, seen as an ideal which no human being can attain, is turned upside down, "for such an *ideal* in which duties are represented as willingly done, is self-contradictory since duties require an opposition, and an action which we like to do requires none."[150]

In *love* there is "unity between inclination and the law, in which the latter loses its form as law."[151] The correspondence between inclination and the law is "the *pleroma* (fulfillment) of the law," a state in which there is a synthesis of the subject and object, in which the subject and object have lost their opposition to one another: "A synthesis in which the law (which Kant calls objective for that reason) loses its universality and the subject its particularity—so both lose their opposition to one another."[152] The opposition between duty and inclination becomes unity in the modifications of love. "Since the law was opposed to love not in respect to its content but to its form, it could be assimilated into love but in that assimilation it lost its characteristic form."[153]

Whereas the principle of *respect* pervades Kantian ethics and is considered to be the principle of differentiation which secures the truth between man and man, the young Hegel sublates precisely the borderline of this differentiation in true being [*im wahren Sein*] in his *metaphysics of love*, which reveals the modifications of love. All forms of separation, all constraints on relationships, have disappeared in the true nature of love. True being exists in love alone because "union and being are synonymous."[154] But Kant would dismiss this attempt to regard love as the ground of our being as a flimsy, transient, and fantastic mode of thinking, because love is a pathological inclination and its insubstantial nature is not commensurate with our humanity.

Of course *love cannot be commanded*; of course it is *pathological*, an inclination— but this does not detract from its greatness. It does not degrade love that its essence does not dominate something alien to it [*ein ihr Fremdes*]. But this does not mean that it is something subordinate to duty and right; on the contrary, it is rather love's triumph that it lords over nothing, is without any hostile power over another. *Love has conquered* does not mean the same as *duty has conquered*, i.e. subdued its enemies; it means that love has overcome hostility.[155]

Whereas duty, by setting boundaries beyond itself, always leaves an objective law intact, the power of this objectivity is broken by love because it is boundless. Love is the "union of the spirit and the divine; to love God is to feel one's self in the all of life with no external restrictions in the infinite."[156] But Hegel sees infinity not as the absence of all limitation but rather as perfection [*Voll-*

endung]. It is not the same as the negative, bad infinity, which, unlike the true concept of infinity, does not imply a return to itself [*Rückkehr in sich selbst*].

In the fragment about love, which Herman Nohl includes in the appendix, Hegel's dialectic appears *in statu nascendi*. This fragment comes from the Frankfurt period, which Herman Nohl considers to be "the most important and epoch-making of Hegel's life."[157]

If union is synonymous with being, then "true union and real love can only come about among the living."[158] In love, "life is present as a doubling of itself and as a single and unified self; here life has run through the circle of development from an immature to a completely mature unity."[159] Hegel twice expounds his first proposition on the dialectic:

This *unity* is per-fected life because in it also reflection has come into its own; immature unity stood over against the possibility of reflection, separation; and in this process unity and separation were united, a living being, which had been opposed by itself (and now feels this) but which did not make this opposition absolute. Life senses life in love. In love all tasks are resolved: the self-destruction of the one-sidedness of reflection and the infinite opposition of the unconscious immature few.[160]

The possibility of reflection is negation as separation, which life has to go through in order to be per-fected in love as a living being.

When the unity was undeveloped there still stood over against it the world, the possibility of separation between itself and the world; as development proceeded, reflection produced more and more oppositions (unified by satisfied impulses) until it set the whole of man's life in opposition even to himself, until love completely destroys objectivity and thereby annuls and transcends reflection, depriving man's opposite of all foreign character, and life finds itself, lacking nothing else [*ohne weiteren Mangel*]. In love the separate does still remain, but as something united and not as something separate—life senses life.[161]

In this section, we find for the first time the keyword which pervades Hegel's whole work: development.[162] In the course of development, reflection produces more and more oppositions. Everything on which the spirit reflects is set up as standing apart [*als Gegen-stand*], as an object which is separated from it, over-against [*gegen-über*] it. This development finds its culmination when the whole of human nature is placed in opposition to the spirit—when love sublates reflection into the complete absence of objectivity [*Objektlosigkeit*], and when the object becomes the subject. Not only is the schema of the dialectic developed in the fragment about love, but all the stages begin to emerge in succession, as they will later be expanded in the

Phenomenology of Spirit. In statu nascendi the "logical" steps and the "real" steps are inextricable, and all attempts to understand the Hegelian dialectic either as a logical or a real process end up misunderstanding precisely the unity of the logical and real processes. The most significant elements of Hegel's opposition and union are ambiguously concrete statements about a form [*eine Gestalt*] but at the same time about universal categories. The empirical material forms the ground on which the seemingly abstract schemata of logic are built. With the turn to the universal and the abstract-logical comes the fulfillment of the concrete sphere in unification [*ineins*], because the principle of the dialectic encompasses the universal as well as the particular. That is why even in Hegel's language the lyrical, poetic, and visionary elements are so sensitively blended with concrete clarity and disciplined abstraction. His unity of style is grounded in the union of the universal and the particular in his dialectic.

The principle of differentiation which thwarts the path to union is tantamount to what is *mortal* in the dialectic of love. "Since love is a sensing of something living, lovers can be distinct only in so far as they are *mortal*.... To say that the lovers have an independence and a living principle peculiar to each of themselves means only that they may die."[163] What is in-dependent [*das Selbst-ständige*], that which op-poses [*wider-steht*] union, is op-position [*der Wider-stand*]. "But love strives to annul even this distinction, to annul this possibility (of separation) as a mere abstract possibility, to unite even the mortal element and make it immortal."[164] In the state of love [*im Sein der Liebe*], the path to union passes through shame, which Hegel defines with striking subtlety:

If the separable element persists in either of the lovers as something peculiarly his own before their union is complete, it creates a difficulty for them. There is a sort of antagonism between complete surrender or the only possible cancellation of opposition (i.e. its cancellation in complete union) and a still subsisting independence. Union feels the latter as a hindrance; love is indignant if part of the individual is severed and held back as a private property. This raging of love against (exclusive) individuality is shame.[165]

Shame is not a twitching of the mortal body, not a potent moment of independence which opposes union, but "an effect of love, which only takes an indignant form on encountering something hostile.... A pure heart is not ashamed of love, but is ashamed if its love is incomplete; it upbraids itself if there is some hostile power which hinders love's culmination."[166] What becomes apparent here is the outline of the Hegelian dialectic, which drives toward the negation of opposition in unification, which in turn is only possible in the complete surrender of love. The rhythm of the dialectic, which is learned from life, is steeped in the mystery of love: "Love acquires this wealth of life in the exchange of every thought, every kind of manifold inner experience, for it seeks out differences and devises unifications *ad infinitum*; it turns to the full variety of nature in order to drink love out of every life."[167] Once this synthesis is achieved, that which has been united cannot again become separate: "God has acted and created." Hegel represents the idea of synthesis in the symbol of *the child*: "The child is the parents themselves." The parents, "the lovers, separate again but in the child the union itself has become unseparated."[168] This symbol of the child also occurs in Hegel's later works as a representation of synthesis. Synthesis is not stasis; rather, from it comes profusion again. The child,

this unity, however, is only a point, a seed. The lovers cannot so contribute to it as to give it manifold forms in itself at the start, for in their union there is no opposition; it is free from all inner division. Everything which gives the newly begotten child a manifold life and a specific existence it must draw into itself, and set over against itself and unify with itself. The seed breaks free from its original unity, turns ever more and more to opposition, and begins to develop. Each stage of its development is a separation, and its aim in each is to regain for itself the full riches of life (enjoyed by the parents). Thus the process is: unity, separated opposites, reunion.[169]

There is no direct reference to the New Testament in this fragment, where sexuality is the basis for the discussion of love and shame. But the context in which this fragment occurs makes it quite clear that the words *love* and *life* are defined by their Johannine usage. The Johannine concept of love is "in truth the only one which really does justice to the particular structure of the Hegelian concept of love, as a pure spiritual relationship, inasmuch as it fits into his complete line of development, and also corresponds to the aforementioned analyses of the relationship of love."[170]

In the twelfth fragment, which presents the fundamental structure of the *Geist des Christentums und sein Schicksal* [Spirit of Christianity and Its Fate], Hegel uses St John's Gospel and sayings from the Sermon on the Mount to develop the principle of dialectic, which is not to negate the object but to reconcile [*versöhnen*] it. The reconciliation of fate through love is the theme of the work which Hegel encapsulates in draft form: "The forgiveness of sins is not the cancellation of punishment (because every punishment is something positive, something objective, which cannot be annulled). It is not the removal of a bad conscience, because a deed cannot become undone; rather, it is the reconciliation of fate by love."[171] Hegel's love is opposed to Kant's morality: "A return to morality does not cancel sins and their punishment, fate; the deed remains. On the contrary it becomes even more irksome; the more morality there is, the more deeply the immorality of it is felt. Punishment, its fate, is not removed because morality is still opposed by an objective force."[172] Love is the blossom of life and, in its widest sense, "the Kingdom of God, the whole tree with all essential modifications and stages of development."[173] Hegel's world is thus completely contracted into the mystery of love, and the dialectic of the entire process is summarized in the truth of love.

The substance of love, moreover, is God, and so religion can be described as the self-consciousness of God: "Religion and love are one. The beloved is not opposed to us, he is one with our being; we only see ourselves in him—and yet there again he is not us—a miracle, which we are unable to fathom."[174] If the substance of love is God, then the substance of man is love: "In ancient days the gods walked among men but the more they grew apart and distant, the more the gods distanced themselves from man. Because of this they received more sacrifices, incense, and ministration—and were more feared, until the separation went so far that reunion could only come about through force. Love can only exist in response to its equivalent, in response to the mirror image, the echo of our being."[175] Thus, *mysticism* and *Feuerbach* mix in Hegel's work in a strange way, and this sliding *middle* runs through his work. "God is love, love is God; there is no other godhead than love—only that which is ungodly, without love, must contain God in its idea, outside itself."[176] In this way love is perfected in the revelation of life and always ahead [*je voraus*] the revelation of God, as described in all its modifications by Hegel in his works. All of Hegel's system is fundamentally the philosophy of religion, the depiction of the self-revelation of God.

The dialectic, which uncovers the seal of love in the essence of life, bears the sign of the spirit as an indelible watermark. "Eternal life can be called a spirit as opposed to the abstract multitude of the dead, because spirit is the living unity of what is manifold . . . the spirit is the quickening law in union with what is manifold, which then is given new life."[177] Therefore, the law of the dialectic is dispersed throughout and applied everywhere in the *Phenomenology of Spirit*. In this work, when Hegel "equates this quickened multiplicity with a large host which is yet still linked to the life-giver, then these individual lives become organs, the infinite whole becomes an infinite all of life. When he [i.e., man] equates infinite life with the spirit of the whole outside himself, because he is limited, and at the same time sets himself apart from himself, the limited one, thus raising himself to life and reaching the most intimate union with it, then he is worshipping God."[178] The *Phenomenology of Spirit* is to be understood as prayer, as praise to God. But God is identical with the logos-spirit. "That the true is actual [*wirklich*] only as system, or that substance is essentially subject, is expressed in the representation of the absolute as spirit—the most sublime notion and the one which belongs to the modern age and its religion. The spiritual alone is the actual [*das Wirkliche*]."[179]

When one compares Hegel's early writings with the *Phenomenology of Spirit*, the first thing that strikes one is the difference of inner tempo: "For the real issue is not exhausted by stating it as an aim, but by carrying it out, nor is the result the actual [*wirkliche*] whole, but rather the result together with the process through which it came about. The aim by itself is a lifeless universal, just as the guiding tendency is a mere drive that as yet lacks an actual existence; and the bare result is the corpse which has left the guiding tendency behind it."[180] Because "the true is the whole. But the whole is nothing other than the essence which comes to completion through its development. Of the absolute it must be said that it is in essence *a result*, that only in the end is it what it truly is."[181]

Only "impatience demands the impossible, namely, the attainment of the end without the means. For one thing, the *length* of the path has to be endured, for each moment is necessary. For another, each moment has to be *lingered over*, because each is itself an individual entire shape. . . . Even the world-spirit itself has had the patience to pass through these forms in the lengthy process of time and to undertake the enormous labor of world history . . . and since there is no less laborious way by which it could attain consciousness of itself, individuals cannot by the very nature of the case conceive their substance any more easily. At the same time, they do have less trouble because all this has already been *implicitly* accomplished."[182]

The tempo in the *Phenomenology* slows down, since the opposition of the world has grown, since Hegel has recognized the enormous power of the negative and is staring this force in the face. In the *Phenomenology* he is tarrying with the negative. While in his early writings the young Hegel was caught in the raptures of love that is loath to undergo any separation and is stronger than the notion of individuality, he admits in the *Phenomenology*: "Thus the life of God and the divine cognition may well be spoken of as disporting of love with itself; but this idea sinks into mere edification, and even insipidity, if it lacks the seriousness, the suffering, the patience, and the labor of the negative."[183]

Separation and "the act of analysis [*des Scheidens*] is brought about by the power and work of the mind, the most amazing and greatest, or more accurately, absolute power."[184] Negation is the constitutive element of the dialectic. The dialectic acquires its ultimate form through the enormous power of the negative. The dialectic

is the process which generates and passes through its own moment, and this whole movement determines what is positive and what its truth is. It also includes the negative, that which would be called false, if it could be regarded as something from which one might abstract.... Appearance is the coming into being and passing away of that which itself does not come into being or pass away, but is in itself [*an sich*] and constitutes the reality and the movement of the life of truth. The true is thus the Bacchanalian revel in which no member is not drunk and, because each immediately dissipates when he drops out, the revel is just as much transparent and simple repose.[185]

Bacchanal delirium and simple repose, the union of Dionysus and Apollo, constitute the nature of truth. The growing together, *con-crevisse*, of subject and object permits the true to emerge. It is important "to understand and express truth not (only) as *substance* but also as *subject*."[186] If separated, subject and substance are abstract and thus either the vanity of subjectivity or of empiricism. Faced with this disintegration into two abstracts, Hegel combines [*mischt*] the finite and the infinite into a whole. The living substance is being, "which is in truth subject, or, what is the same, is in truth actual only in so far as it is the movement of positing itself, or is the mediation of its self-othering with itself."[187] Substance as subject is pure, simple negativity and is for this very reason the diremption of the simple [*Enztweiung des Einfachen*]. It is not the original unity but self-restoring sameness that is the true. "It is the process of its own becoming, the circle that presupposes its end as its goal, having its end also at its beginning; and only by being worked out to its end, is it actual."[188]

The distance [*Ausstand*] and "disparity which exists in consciousness between the 'I' and the substance, which is its object, is the distinction between them, the *negative* in general. It can be seen as the *lack* of both, but it is their soul or that which moves them; which is why some of the ancients conceived the *void* as the principle of motion."[189] That is how negation, generally classified by German Idealism as the lesser term because it represents descent to a worldly level, is transferred to the very core of existence. But the enormous power of the negative is only revealed in death. For death "is of all things the most dreadful, and to hold fast what is dead requires the greatest strength."[190] In death negation reaches its deepest depth and turns into perfection. For death is already the negation of negation. "In death the finite is posited as sublated [*als aufgehobenes gesetzt*]. But death is only the abstract negation of the negative in itself; it is itself nullity, revealed nullity. But the posited nothingness is at once sublated and the return to the positive. Here cessation, liberation from finiteness comes in. This liberation from finiteness is not presented to consciousness as death, but this higher view of death is found in thought."[191] But the deepest negation of death has to be endured and cannot be avoided.

The life of the spirit does not fear death and keep itself from destruction, but it endures death and is preserved in it. It discovers its truth only by finding itself in absolute diremption [*Zerrissenheit*]. It is not that force, a purely positive one, which disregards the negative, saying: this is nothing or it is not of the truth, and abandons it for something else, but rather it is only that particular force which, facing the negative, tarries with it. This tarrying with the negative is the magical power which turns it into a living being.[192]

It is the mightiness of the spirit to have death itself in its power, for the spirit contains in itself such "power of decay" that even "decay decays."[193]

The genesis of the spirit is *logic*; it is also a genesis of self-consciousness. The word *self-consciousness* [*Selbstbewusstsein*] resonates with the triple rhythm of the dialectic, which is at the center of the Hegelian system. For the *self* is linked to *existence* [*Sein*] by *consciousness* [*das Bewusst*]. The laws of logic are based on the dialectical structure of consciousness: the diremption and reconciliation [*Versöhnung*] of moments in the totality of the self. Self-consciousness is a state of becoming [*ein Werden*], and therefore it is both being and nonbeing. Self-consciousness could not be divided in two (like "I"-"I"), if it had never before been a unity, but it could not know itself as one [*das Eine*], if it had not previously been divided in two and distinct. Because self-consciousness is dialectical and a state of becoming, it is at once being and nonbeing. From this follows Hegel's dictum which forms the core of his logic: "Pure being and pure nothingness are the same."[194]

But nothing [*das Nichts*] is not the harmless nonpresence of something; rather, it is the annihilating power of death which puts an end to finitude. Finitude *exists*, but the truth of finite being is the *end* of being: "Finitude does not change like anything else; rather, it passes away. . . . The being of finite things as such contains the seed of degeneration as their being in themselves; the time of their birth is the time of their death."[195] We are not to linger over the existence of finitude in order to preserve the past; rather, there is the deeper question, "whether transitoriness [*Vergänglichkeit*] and degeneration [*das Vergehen*] degenerate? That this does not happen is sub-stantiated precisely in that view of the finite which posits degeneration as the final stage of finitude."[196] In the aftermath of the disintegration of Hegel's dialectic, the same opinion emerges with Heidegger, who as a successor to Kierkegaard is preoccupied with finitude and postulates nothingness as an absolute. Absolute spirit has power over death, so that not only is finitude "transitory and liable to degenerate, but degeneration, nothingness is not the last thing, but in its turn degenerates."[197]

In religion man casts off all finiteness and gains freedom, for in this region the spirit entertains a relationship not to something limited but to the infinite, which is a relationship of freedom and no longer one of dependence. All restrictive interests are left behind on the "sandbank of finitude," and "in this region of spirit flow the streams of forgetfulness from which Psyche drinks, and in which she drowns all sorrow."[198] This is the "region in which all the enigmas of the world are solved, all the contradictions of deeper-reaching thought have their meaning unveiled, and where the voice of the heart's pain is silenced—the region of eternal truth, of eternal rest, of eternal peace."[199]

The "manifold works of the sciences, the arts, the issues of political life, relationships which relate to man's freedom and his will,"[200] all issue from man as *homo spiritualis*, spiritual man. But all of these manifold situations find their final center in the idea of God. "In religion man places himself in a relation to this center, in which all other relations converge, and in so doing he raises himself to the highest level of consciousness."[201]

As in everything, the spirit must also run its course in religion because this is an essential element in the Hegelian idea of the spirit. For the spirit "is only spirit, inasmuch as it is for itself the negation of all finite forms, as this absolute ideality."[202] However, because there are not two kinds of spirit, a divine spirit which would be utterly distinct from a human one, the way of the spirit is the life of God. The process of the spirit producing itself, the course of this spirit, contains distinct moments. But the way is not yet the goal, and the spirit has not reached the goal without completing the course. While it is completing the different stages of this process, the spirit is not yet complete; its knowledge of itself is not yet true; it is not yet revealed to itself.[203] The development of God is ruled by the same logical necessity that operates in the universe.[204] "Finitude is the essential moment of the infinite in the nature of God, and so one can say: God himself is the one who becomes finite."[205] Finitude is a moment in the divine life and God is "this movement in itself and only because of that is he the living God. This persistence of finitude must not be held onto, but sublated: God is the movement toward finitude and therefore its sublation to itself; in the 'I,' as the one who sublates himself as finite, God returns to himself, and is only God in the act of this return. Without a world God is not God."[206]

In these three stages of the dialectic "the idea of the divine unfolds. Spirit is divine history, the process of distinguishing [*des Sichunterscheidens*], *dirimirens* and taking this back in itself [*in sich Zurücknehmens*]: that is the divine history."[207] Indeed, the unrivaled Ferdinand Christian Baur, who had mastery of philosophy and theology as fully as Hegel did, draws attention to Hegel's close relationship to Gnosis, "a much closer one than one would suppose, given the length of time separating the two."[208] All Gnostic systems, primarily the Valentinian and Pseudo-Clementine, "generally share this characteristic; their principle is the same, as are the moments through which they pass in their development."[209]

The apex is the absolute spirit. The aeons of Valentinian Gnosis, through which the primeval aeon itself is reflected, are the pure entities in which the spirit reflects its own being, the independent movement of the spirit being in itself. In the aeons, distinctness is already manifest in unity, the distinction of the spirit from itself is a path to being other and to finality.[210] Because God is spirit, "no darkness, no coloring or mixture enters this pure light";[211] neither does it enter the Gnostic light of the father, *lumen paternum*.

Although God is the process, he is eternal identity in his movement to himself. The "holy spirit is eternal love."[212] Love, like the Gnostic syzygy, is a distinction between two things, which however are not in themselves at all distinct. The feeling and the consciousness of this identity is love. The Gnostic pleroma, the realm of the aeons (which, although distinctive, are yet the same),[213] is divided by this distinction which is sublated in the identity of the absolute spirit with itself. In the first form of the Gnostic pleroma, in the kingdom of the Father, as Hegel called this sphere, the distinction does not yet become actual. "The absolute eternal idea is (for now) in itself and for itself God in his eternity, before the creation of the world, outside the world."[214] The division only becomes apparent in the second form: the Kingdom of the Son of the World. The world, this *being other* of God [*das Anderssein Gottes*], "divides itself on himself [*spaltet sich an ihm selbst*] into these two facets: physical nature and finite spirit."[215] Similarly, in the Gnostic systems the light world of the pleroma divides into the created, actual, and finite world through the falling away of Sophia-Achamoth, who for that reason is distinguished, as the lower Sophia, from her mother, the higher Sophia. Hegel's finite spirit is identical with the Gnostic psyche. "The Demiurge, the principle of the psychic, is there with man, who, in as much as he is created by him, is only of a psychic nature, and nothing other than finite spirit, as he knows of nothing else, apart from external nature, in whose sphere he moves and which he faces as its ruler."[216] In the third form the sublation of negation is completed, the negation of negation. "That is the way, the process of reconciliation, in which the spirit has unified with itself what it has made distinct in its *diremption*, its judgment, and now as holy spirit is in the community of the spirit."[217]

Through finitization [*Verendlichung*], the absolute spirit attains self-knowledge as absolute spirit in the negation of finitude. In the Gnostic systems the same turning point is defined by the fact that man is not merely regarded as psyche but recognizes the spark of pneuma in himself. Psyche differs from pneuma in that pneuma is conscious of its identity with the absolute spirit. This knowledge, which is the crucial knowledge of Gnosis, must help natural consciousness overcome and sublate finitude. In the *pneumatic* "'I', the 'I' that sublates itself as finite, God returns to himself and is" for Hegel as for Gnosis "only God as this act of returning."[218] Tertullian gives direct confirmation of this fact for Valentinian Gnosis: "God is only God because he takes back to himself what he in *enthymesis* and *ektroma* (Achamoth), in his *diremption* (separation), had made distinct from himself, and by the negation of negation, mediates with himself."[219] The spirit is raised up through pneuma. The *pneumata* are those who are conscious through Gnosis of the idea of the absolute. *Pneumatikoi* are the community of the elect who Sophia leads to her heavenly bridegroom, to union with pleroma, to the kingdom of the aeons with which *ecclesia*, as one of the aeons, is identified. The community of the spirit brings about "the transition from mere humanity to divine humanity" and is "the explanation for the reconciliation [*Explication der Versöhnung*], that is, that God is reconciled with the world."[220]

The system of Gnosis and that of Hegel are grounded, therefore, in the supposition that the idea of the divine finds its explanation and completion in the three stages of dialectic. "Spirit is the divine history, the process of becoming distinct from self, *dirimirens*, and taking it back into itself: that is divine history."[221]

Discussions of Joachimite prophecy and Hegelian philosophy have revealed the connection between the Joachimite theology of history and the Hegelian philosophy of history. The Christian concept of the Trinity is seen essentially in historical terms and is equated with the dialectical principle of history. Working from the principles of *love* and *freedom*, which are identical in the essence of the spirit, Joachim and Hegel construct world history from the perspective of an end to fulfillment. They both consider the history of the spirit to be synonymous with the course of history. Just as Joachim's exegesis interprets the metaphysical fate of Christ, including the resurrection, in terms of a historical dialectic, Hegel, too, in his philosophy of religion, builds his dialectical, historical speculations on the foundation of death and resurrection.

The principle of the dialectic is active in death and resurrection. At first, Hegel offers Christ's fate as an example. "It is the lot of finite humanity to die; death is the ultimate proof of being human, absolute finitude, and although Christ died—the ultimate death of a criminal, not just a normal death, but a death of shame and disgrace on the cross—humanity appeared in him to the utmost degree."[222] However, the principle of death affects the very heart of God:

God has died, God is dead—that is the most terrible thought, that all that is eternal, all that is true, is no more; that negation itself is in God; this is accompanied by the most acute pain, the feeling of complete hopelessness [*Rettungslosigkeit*], the surrender of all that is most worthy.—But this is not the end, for now comes the reversal [*Umkehrung*]; the same God survives this process and this is only the *death of death*. God rises again to life, and thus it turns into the opposite. This is resurrection.[223]

Death and resurrection, however, are not "miracles," isolated events in the fate of Christ, but "as it is in the one instance, it is for all; as it is once, it is always."[224] Resurrection, "the transcendence of the negative, is not a departure from human nature but its ultimate test [*Bewährung*] in death and in the fullness of love. The spirit is only spirit when it is the negative of a negative, which then contains the negative in itself. When the Son of Man sits at the right hand of the Father, then the honor of human nature and its identity with the divine have, in this elevation, attained the highest level in the spirit's eyes."[225] The absolute history of the idea of the divine is not a unique event, but something which has happened in itself [*an sich*] and which continues to happen forever.[226] The third stage, the rise of the community, consists of the outpouring of the Holy Spirit. "The endurance [*das Bestehen*] of the community is its continuous *everlasting development*, which is based on its eternal knowledge of the spirit."[227] The knowledge of the community develops in stages, so that there are three steps or stages in the kingdom of the spirit: "The first stage is one of direct unhampered religion and faith; the second the stage of understanding for those referred to as educated: the stage of reflection and enlightenment; and finally the third stage is that of philosophy."[228]

Right at the end of the philosophy of religion, which is not a separate part of the whole system but constitutes its core and its main theme, Hegel finishes "with a discord" [*Mißton*] which blows apart the whole system, forcing it into a new position which is taken up by Marx and Kierkegaard. This discord is the question of reality. For if the rise and endurance [*Entstehen und Bestehen*] of the community is accounted for in the kingdom of the spirit, then *decay* [*Vergehen*] must also be considered. "To speak of decay would be to finish on a discordant note. But what can be done? This discord exists in *actuality* [*Wirklichkeit*]."[229] As in the days of the Roman emperors, when the universal unity of religion disappeared, the divine was made profane, political life lacked all guidance and trust, reason found its sole refuge in the form of private law, and welfare became individualized and an end in itself, so too now, says Hegel, "moral views in the form of individual opinion and conviction lacking any objective truth have become the norm, and the obsession with private law and pleasure is commonplace."[230] Reconciliation manifested as unity of the spirit is destroyed and the power of the state avails for nothing, since "decay has set in too deeply. When the Gospel is no longer preached to the poor, when the salt becomes ineffectual and all fundamentals are surreptitiously removed, then the people, their powers of reasoning stunted, only have a notion of the truth and can do nothing to assuage their spiritual thirst."[231] However, it is Hegel's aim to remove this "discord" in philosophical knowledge. The purpose of his lectures is precisely to reconcile reason with religion in the philosophy of religion, with the state in the philosophy of the state, and with society in the philosophy of law; "to recognize the need for reason in its manifold formulations; and to rediscover truth and the absolute in religion, the state, and society."[232]

"But this reconciliation is itself only partial and has no universality outside itself."[233] Here Hegel raises the theme which dominates Marx's whole critique: "Philosophy is in this respect a separate shrine [*ein abgesondertes Heiligtum*] and its servants a priestly line which is set apart, unable to conform to the world; its task is to guard the heritage of truth. It is the task of the present empirical age to decide how it finds a way out of its dilemma and what form it will take; it is not the immediate and practical task of philosophy."[234]

Marx and Kierkegaard

Hegel's Legacy

The end of the philosophy of religion and the emergence of *discord* marks the point at which the entire Hegelian system bursts apart, as much with respect to its factual as to its historical consequences. The explosive material is already latent in the principle of Hegel. Even though in the Hegelian system the power of the state coincides with the divinations of religion and the principles of philosophy, as he reconciles actuality with spirit, the state with religious conscience, and religious conscience with philosophy, yet this reconciliation is still touched by death. For philosophy is the "reconciliation of corruption."[235]

Philosophy only comes about

when a people [*ein Volk*] has left behind its concrete life, separation and division of classes have emerged, and the community [*das Volk*] is approaching its fall; when a gulf has arisen between inward strivings and external reality, and the old forms of religion etc. are no longer satisfying; when the spirit manifests indifference to its living existence or whiles away in it unsatisfied, and moral life is dissolved.... When philosophy with its abstractions paints a gloomy picture [*grau in grau*], the freshness and life of youth has gone, the reconciliation is not a reconciliation in the actual but rather in the ideal world.[236]

This has been a repeated phenomenon throughout the history of philosophy: Ionian philosophy only emerges when the Ionian states decline; Socrates and Plato are at odds with the Athenian state; in Rome, philosophy only becomes widespread under the despotic rule of the Caesars with the decline of the Roman Republic; the downfall of the Roman emperors coincides with the rise of Neoplatonic philosophy. Similarly, in the fifteenth and sixteenth centuries, as the medieval framework collapses, the philosophy of the modern age begins. This means that Hegel's reconciliation is also inevitably a reconciliation with the corruption of the bourgeois, Christian world.

With immense effort Hegel achieves the situation of *a global mean* [*Weltmitte*]. His successors reject the *mediation* [*Vermittlung*] of bourgeois society, Christian religion, and the principles of philosophy as an attempt at harmonization and even "the most crass materialism." The mystical union of reason and actuality which culminates with Hegel is separated out by Marx and Kierkegaard into the two ends of outwardness [*Äusserlichkeit*] and inwardness [*Innerlichkeit*]. Hegel's efforts to unite these ends were of a "conceptual nature." In contrast to Hegel's universalism within the one-sided element of the concept, Marx and Kierkegaard advocate the categorical one-sidedness of *interest* within the universal element of actuality.

Around 1840 Hegel's reconciliation came to an end. The year 1843 saw the publication of the following texts, which were meant to have a revolutionary impact: Feuerbach's *Grundsätze der Philosophie der Zukunft* [*Principles of the Philosophy of the Future*]; *Das entdeckte Christentum* [Christianity Discovered], by Bruno Bauer; Kierkegaard's *Either-Or*; and *The Critique of Hegel's Philosophy of Law*, by Karl Marx. They all share the theme of the dissolution of the bourgeois, Christian world as laid out by Hegel's philosophical theology of Protestantism. The measure of the caustic critique, the fierce controversy concerning reason and actuality, can only be taken by the resolute nature of Hegel's reconciliation. In the end Hegel grounds his reconciliation of God and man, reason and actuality, in the incarnation of God. That which happened in Christ happens forever in man: "As the one is, so are all; what happened once is for all time."[237] This unity of divine and human nature is plainly split in two for Marx as for Kierkegaard. According to Hegel, Christendom and worldliness meet, but Christianity is seen by Marx and Kierkegaard as an "inverted world" [*verkehrte Welt*]. Actuality, which for Hegel is the home of reason, seems for Marx and Kierkegaard to subsist in the shadow of *self-alienation*.

Hegel presents his classical formulation of the unity of reason and actuality in his preface to *The Philosophy of Law*: "The reasonable is actual, and the actual is reasonable."[238] The task of philosophy is to re-flect on [*nach-zu-denken*] actuality with reason. The correspondence of idea with actuality is the very measure of truth. But not everything that there is [*da ist*] is actuality to the same degree or in the same way. Hegel distinguishes *actuality* from merely passing, transient, and therefore meaningless existence. An actuality dependent on mere chance does not deserve the name of actuality in the "emphatic" sense. This unity of reason and actuality, however, later becomes highly questionable. Hegel's propositions unifying the reason of actuality and the actuality of reason are separated out into the "right" or the "left," into conservatism or revolution—the former in the element of religion and the latter in the element of society. The splitting of the unity arises from turning Hegel's concrete (*con-crevisse* = having grown together) philosophy into an abstract one-sidedness [*Vereinseitigung*]. The *right* mystifies reality into something supralogical, demanding that reason conform to a reality beyond logic. The *left*, on the other hand, devalues reality, claiming that it is sublogical and demanding that sublogical reality conform to reason, the idea. But in Hegel both the conservative and the revolutionary moments carry equal weight [*gleich gültig*].

In the same way that Joachim of Fiore in spite of his revolutionary theology and prophecy, is still able to fit into the medieval establishment, Hegel willingly subordinates himself to the Prussian state and blends in with bourgeois society, thus preventing the revolutionary tendencies of his philosophy from breaking out. Only the conservative aspect of Hegel's philosophy is relative; its revolutionary character is absolute. For Hegel, like Joachim, conceives of the course of world history as a progression [*Prozess des Fortschritts*] and, consequently, as a constant negation of any system that currently exists. Just as the young generation of Spirituals regards itself as fulfilling the promise of the *ordo spiritualis*, so the Hegelian left aims to change reality through the guidance of Hegelian reason. What the Spirituals and the Hegelian left have in common is that they draw on the revolutionary consequences of Joachimite theology and Hegelian philosophy, respectively. Just as the Catholic Church excludes the Spirituals from the system of the medieval world and persecutes them as heretics, so too does bourgeois society exclude the Hegelian left.[239] Feuerbach has to give up his university lectureship at Erlangen; Ruge loses his post as a lecturer at Halle. To avoid imprisonment, Ruge flees Germany for Paris, but in Paris he is also persecuted and he takes refuge in Switzerland, before finally fleeing to England. Stirner, who started as a schoolteacher, sinks into petty bourgeois poverty in Berlin and has to eke out his days as a milkman. Bruno Bauer is removed from his lectureship because of his radical research into the Gospels and lives for many years in a shed he builds near Berlin. Karl Marx's plan to qualify as a lecturer [*habilitieren*] in Bonn comes to nothing. Persecuted by the police states of the Continent, Marx flees from one country to another before finding his final place of exile in England. Kierkegaard cannot commit to taking up a post as a pastor after his theological exams, and lives in Denmark where, derided as an oddity, he is at loggerheads with both church and state. Behind the Hegelian left lurks Schopenhauer, scornful of the professorial philosophy taught by the philosophy professors. From Schopenhauer, who also withdraws from academic life, the route leads straight to Nietzsche, who, "six thousand feet above men and time," outlines the standards of a new world.

The confusion surrounding Hegel is substantively caused by the fundamental ambivalence of *sublation* [*Aufhebung*], an ambivalence which it shares with Joachim's *transire*. It is difficult today to imagine the seriousness of the dispute: "One must recall that historical moment in order to appreciate the real power and authority a philosophical system can exert. Imagine the pathos and conviction of the Hegelians in 1830 who, in bitter earnestness, rehearsed the question of what world history would consist of once the world spirit in Hegelian philosophy had broken through to its goal, to knowledge of itself."[240] While conservative philosophers initially try to accommodate Hegel within the system of Protestant Christianity, they end up having to concede one tenet after another until finally, like the Christian philosopher Franz von Baader, they reject Hegel altogether. In the anonymously published *Posaune des jüngsten Gerichts über Hegel den Atheisten und Antichristen* [Trumpet Call of the Last Judgment for Hegel, the Atheist and Antichrist], Bruno Bauer demonstrates to the "well disposed" [*den Wohl gesinnten*] that not only the bad Hegelians of the left but even Hegel himself was in fact an "atheist" and "Antichrist": "O, the poor, wretched people . . . who were happy to hear that religion and philosophy coincide, who thought that they still held on to their God, when they heard and accepted that religion is the self-consciousness of the absolute spirit."[241] In reality Hegel's *explanation* of religion amounts to its *destruction*.[242] Therefore, Bauer warns against Hegel's magic word: reconciliation. Many have been drawn away from the true God by Hegel's magic word and have been led toward atheism. According to Hegel, the reconciliation of reason with religion in fact means acknowledging that there is no God and that in religion the "I" only ever deals with itself, while it thinks itself to be dealing with a living, personal God. Self-consciousness is that magical means by which

the ego is duplicated as in a mirror and, finally, when for centuries it has identified its reflection as God, discovers that the image in the mirror is itself. The wrath and punitive justice of God are therefore nothing other than the ego itself clenching its fist and threatening itself in the mirror. God's grace and mercy, moreover, are nothing other than the ego offering its hand to its own image. Religion sees this reflection as God; philosophy negates the illusion and shows man that there is nobody behind the mirror and that it is only its own reflection to which the ego has hitherto related.[243]

In this fight over Hegel's philosophy of religion, Bruno Bauer and Kierkegaard expose the crisis in Christian religion. While Ruge exposes the crisis in the philosophy of law, Karl Marx brings it to a head in his own critique of Hegel's philosophy of law. Marx and Kierkegaard extract the extreme consequences from the collapse of Hegel's philosophy: Marx destroys the bourgeois, capitalist world and Kierkegaard the bourgeois, Christian world.

Like the Spirituals were once steered by Joachim's theology, so the

Hegelian left is encouraged by Hegel's philosophy no longer to strive for an inner reform of existing society but to proclaim its transformation. In knowledge of the fulfillment, of the full end of the Christian world through Hegel's philosophy, his heirs—Feuerbach and Ruge, Stirner and Bauer, Kierkegaard and Marx—proclaim the transformation. By describing the nature of the state and of society, Hegel, like Joachim and the Spirituals, enables a future group to reject the claims of bourgeois society and to legitimate their own claims on the grounds of philosophy and the logic of history. Hegel supplies the young generation with the arguments needed to deny bourgeois society its raison d' être in history. He enables this new group to set itself up as messengers of the true essence [*des wahren Wesens*] and to revolutionize the status quo along the lines of the Hegelian idea. Thus Hegel forges the weapons to be used by the Hegelian left to fight bourgeois society, just as Joachim did for the Spirituals.

Marx and Kierkegaard

Much as the inner light of the Spirituals' mysticism becomes a devouring flame in Müntzer's theology, so too does the spark of Hegel's philosophy ignite Marx's revolutionary blaze. "Its inner self-sufficiency and its perfection are destroyed. What was an inner light becomes a consuming flame which turns outward. As a consequence, the world's becoming philosophical coincides with philosophy becoming worldly, its realization coincides with its disappearance."[244] Hopes that once soared freely suddenly become mundane and of this world; the innermost dreams of the spirit are turned outward and realize the course of history with particular force.

Yet, whereas Thomas Müntzer's critique of the medieval world fused the two elements of the religious and the social, Marx and Kierkegaard carry out their critiques separately at the end of the bourgeois world. It is at this point, shortly before 1848, that Marx in his *Communist Manifesto* (1847) and Kierkegaard in his *Literary Pronouncement* (1846) declare the final breakdown of bourgeois society. Far apart as they seem, they are still close allies in their radical attack on bourgeois society, finding their inspiration in Hegel. It is to the credit of Karl Löwith that he first recognized the full implications of the historical connection between Marx and Kierkegaard, and his excellent analysis is used here with appreciation. The contrast between Marx and Kierkegaard, as Löwith shows, simply illustrates the two sides of an *identical* critique and a shared subversion of bourgeois society. To revolutionize the bourgeois, capitalist world, Marx pins his hopes on the masses of the proletariat, the economic life of the masses, while Kierkegaard, in his fight against the bourgeois, Christian world, places all his bets on the *individual*. This corresponds to Marx's view of bourgeois society as a mass of "alienated individuals" [*vereinzelten Einzelnen*], in which man is alienated from the true nature of his species; Kierkegaard, on the other hand, sees Christianity as the massive proliferation of Christendom in which nobody takes the emulation of Christ seriously. Marx directs his critique at the self-alienation experienced by people as capitalism, and Kierkegaard directs his critique at the self-alienation experienced by Christians as Christianity.[245]

At the age of eighteen Marx stands at a crucial turning point. In a letter to his father, which ranks among his most important texts, he gives details of his significant transformation of mind·

There are moments in life which like boundary marks denote the end of one period while at the same time clearly pointing in a new direction. At such times of transition we feel compelled to gaze upon the past and present with the eagle eye of thought, so as to become aware of our real situation. World history itself likes this kind of retrospection, which often gives it the semblance of being retrogressive and static, while it is simply leaning back to comprehend itself, to penetrate its own spiritual accomplishments through the process of thought [*geistig*].[246]

When making this comparison with world history, Marx is not just thinking of his rewarding year of work in Berlin; he is also depicting the world historical situation in which the spiritual world finds itself after Hegel's death.

With a zeal for work which exceeds all measure, Marx throws himself into the most diverse subjects. Although he had to study jurisprudence, he felt "above all a compulsion to wrestle with philosophy." He combined these two subjects in such a way that, alongside his purely legal studies, "he tried to carry out a philosophy of law within the legal field. By way of introduction I supplied a few metaphysical propositions and extended this unfortunate opus into the area of public law, a work of almost three hundred pages."[247] At the end of this work, Marx realized that he "could not achieve his goal without philosophy. Therefore, I was once more able to throw myself into her arms with a good conscience and I wrote a new, fundamental metaphysical system, which, when I had completed it, compelled me repeatedly to recognize its faults [*Verkehrtheit*] as well as those of all my earlier efforts."[248]

In the course of 1837, Marx's studies find a magnetic center: Hegel. "I had read fragments of Hegel's philosophy, whose grotesque melody of the rocks [*Felsenmelodie*] was irksome to me."[249] Marx tries to break Hegel's spell and writes a dialogue, *Kleanthes oder vom Ausgangspunkt und notwendigen Fortgang der Philosophie* [Cleanthes; or, On the Starting Point and Necessary Continuation of Philosophy].

In this philosophical essay art and science were united, up to a point, although they had become completely separate domains. At a brisk pace I entered into the work, a philosophical-dialectical development of the Godhead, in its manifestations as pure concept, as religion, as nature, as history. My last sentence was the beginning of the Hegelian system, and this work—for which I familiarized myself to some extent with the natural sciences, Schelling, and history, and which has caused me endless trouble and is written in such a common way (since it is really meant to be a new logic) that I can now barely think my way back into it—this same treatise, this my dearest child, nurtured in moonlight, bears me like a false Siren into the bosom of the enemy.[250]

This ambiguous resistance to Hegel drives Marx into the arms of the Young Hegelians. "While out of sorts, I became familiar with Hegel from beginning to end, and with most of his students as well. Through several meetings with friends in Stralow I ended up in a doctor's club [*Doktorclub*]."[251] A sentence from a letter written to Marx by Bruno Bauer, a man his senior, then at the center of the doctor's club, testifies to the Young Hegelian Society's enthusiastic atmosphere: "The catastrophe will be frightful and must be a huge one; I would almost say, it will be of a larger dimension than that which occurred when Christianity first came upon the world."[252] While Marx binds himself ever tighter to "the current world philosophy" of the Young Hegelians, he is overcome by "a true fit of irony [*eine wahre Ironiewut*], as could so easily happen after that many negations."[253] He becomes increasingly aware of the reason for his animosity to Hegel and the difference between himself and the Young Hegelians in the Society. His dissertation on Epicurus and Democritus includes a discussion of Hegel's successors. In the context of Aristotle's complete system, Epicurus and Democritus are perceived to be the materialistic and atheistic epigones. This is an obvious comparison to Hegel's complete system and *his* materialistic and atheistic successors. It is really the same theme which he treated earlier in *Cleanthes; or, On the Starting Point and Necessary Continuation of Philosophy.*

As in history of philosophy there are nodal points which raise philosophy in itself to concretion, subsuming abstract principles to a totality and thus breaking the continuity of the straight line, so there are also moments in which philosophy turns its gaze to the outside world and no longer conceptualizes it, but rather, in the way a practical person spins intrigues with the world, emerges from the transparent kingdom of Amenthes [thoughtlessness] and throws itself on the breast of the worldly siren.[254]

To the extent that philosophy has run its course and now engages with *totality*, there is no longer any possibility of continuing in a straight line. Two completely unrelated totalities oppose one another: the *totality* of a worldless [*weltlose*] philosophy and the totality of an unphilosophical world. *Diremption* has come to a head. "And so it is a fragmented [*zerrissene*] world which opposes a philosophy total in itself." But also this philosophy is thereby fragmented and full of contradictions. The objective universality of the perfected world philosophy thus comes full circle, becoming merely the subjective forms of consciousness to be found in various private philosophies. "However, one must not be blown off course by this storm, coming as it does after a great philosophy, a world philosophy."[255]

"Anyone who does not grasp this historical necessity must consequently deny any possibility of human life in the aftermath of a total philosophy," or he must consider *mediocrity* as the normal manifestation of the absolute spirit. "Without this necessity it is incomprehensible how, after Aristotle, a Zeno, an Epicurus, or even a Sextus Empiricus could come forth; or after Hegel, the fundamentally groundless and paltry efforts of the more recent philosophers."[256] It is not a matter of adapting Hegel's system to reality, which is what the Young Hegelians such as Ruge and his ilk are doing. "A propos of Hegel, it is pure ignorance on the part of his followers when they explain away certain features of his system as compromises [*Akkomodation*]."[257] It is conceivable that Hegel himself was guilty of this or that seeming inconsistency for the sake of this or that compromise. He may himself have been conscious of this. But what Hegel could not have been conscious of is that in the last analysis the possibility of this compromise is rooted in the shortcomings of his principle itself. There can be no talk of Hegel's compromise with religion and the state, because "this lie is the lie at the heart of his principle."[258]

At times like this, half-wits like Ruge and the other Young Hegelians "take the opposite view of valiant commanders. They believe that they are able to repair the damage by decreasing their forces, by dispersal, by a peace treaty with the real needs, while Themistocles, when Athens was threatened with devastation, persuaded the Athenians to leave it for good and found a new Athens on the sea, on the basis of another element."[259] When philosophy (= Athens) is threatened with devastation, Marx (= Themistocles) intends to persuade the Athenians to leave it for good, and to found a new Athens on the basis of another element. This other element is *reality* [*Wirklichkeit*]. "It is a psychological law that once the theoretical intellect has achieved freedom within itself, it turns into practical energy and, emerging from the shadow kingdom of Amenthes as will, it directs itself against the external reality of the world from which it is excluded."[260] To the extent that philosophy as will turns itself outward against the world of appearance, it becomes *one* side of the world opposed by another; inspired by the desire to realize itself, philosophy enters into a tense relation with the world. "What was an inner light becomes a consuming flame which turns outward. As a consequence, the world's becoming philosophical coincides with philosophy becoming worldly, its realization coincides with its disappearance."[261]

Marx then significantly extends the nature of Hegelian sublation [*Aufhebung*] by drawing both reason *and* actuality into the process of sublation: you cannot sublate philosophy without making it real [*verwirklichen*], but you cannot realize [*verwirklichen*] philosophy without sublating it.[262] In the concluding comments to his critique of Hegel's philosophy of law, Marx postulates the emancipation of humanity: "*Philosophy* is the *head* of this emancipation; its *heart* is the *proletariat*. Philosophy cannot be realized without the sublation of the proletariat; the proletariat cannot be sublated without the realization of philosophy."[263]

A critique of Hegel's philosophy of law presupposes a critique of religion, for the "critique of religion is a prerequisite of all criticism."[264] Beyond the intellectual critique of religion, which Marx regards as essentially having been brought to an end in Germany by the writings of Feuerbach and Bruno Bauer,[265] his struggle against religion is indirectly a struggle against "that world whose spiritual aroma is religion."[266] ... Religion is the sigh of the oppressed creature, the heart [*das Gemüt*] of a heartless world, the spirit of a dispirited world. It is the opium of the people. The sublation [*Aufhebung*] of religion, itself the illusory happiness of the people, is the demand for their real happiness. To call on them to give up their illusions about their condition is to call on them to give up a condition that requires illusions."[267] The critique of religion brings disillusioned man to his senses.

The task of history is, once the truth of the beyond has disappeared, to establish the truth about the here and now. Once the sacred form of human self-alienation has been unmasked, it is the task of philosophy, which is in the service of history, to unmask self-alienation in its profane form. Thus the critique of heaven is transformed into a critique of earth, the critique of religion into the critique of law, and the critique of theology into the critique of politics.[268]

In this way Marx's adjudication against religion ends up with the element of society.

Kierkegaard's decision in *Either/Or* is an adjudication for *eternity* against time, especially against *his* own time. Thus he joins the ranks of Feuerbach, Bauer, Stirner, and Marx. Kiergekaard shares with Marx the stringency and force as well as the incisiveness of his critical analysis. But there is more: in fact, the *individual* in Kierkegaard crosses swords with the *human species* in Karl Marx.

"In these times everything is political," begins Kierkegaard's preface to his comments on the individual.[269] Only religion is different from politics, as different as heaven is from earth, by virtue of its starting point and its final goal. For politics begins on earth in order to remain on earth, while religion, "deduces its origins from above, and transfiguring the earthly [*das Irdische verklärend*], seeks to raise it up to heaven."[270]

And yet there is a connection between religion and politics. Kierkegaard aims essentially at the same relationship between religion and politics as Marx, though admittedly in inverse valuation [*freilich wertet er umgekehrt*]. For even a politician can recognize that "the religious is the transfigured rendering of that which the politician has thought of in his happiest moment, assuming that he really loves humanity and people, even if he finds the religious dimension impractical, too elevated and too ideal."[271] But, in fact, no form of politics or secularity [*Weltlichkeit*] is able to think through or fully implement the concept of human *equality*, which Marx deals with particularly. To achieve complete equality in the medium of *secularity* would mean attempting to realize it within a medium whose essence is *disparity* [*Verschiedenheit*], and would thus be a complete contradiction in terms. "With the aid of eternity, the religious alone is able fully to attain human equality, an equality not of this world, true equality, the only possible human equality, and that is why—let this be said to its glory—the religious is true humanity."[272]

What the times *demand*—the demand of the times is the slogan of the Hegelian left, especially of Ruge and Marx—cannot be specified, since

fire has broken out within the secular world [*in der Weltlichkeit*], kindled by an inner combustion, whose origin and cause have been secular frictions within secularity. What the times *need* most urgently, however, can be put neatly into one word: eternity. The misfortune of our time is precisely that it has become only "time," temporality [*Zeitlichkeit*], which, impatient as it is, refuses to hear of eternity. Then, well-meaning or frenzied, it even tries to make the eternal superfluous by false emulation, which will fail in all eternity. For the more one thinks it possible to dispense with the eternal, or hardens one's heart against it, the more fundamentally one needs it.[273]

Because his times have become stranded on the sandbank of temporality, Kierkegaard calls it a time of disintegration.

For Kierkegaard criticism of the age amounts to a critique of Hegel. He opposes the Hegelian system with an absolute negativity, using a concept of irony which cannot be dialectically sublated. In the quantitative dialectic of world history the absolute ethical distinction, along with the determination that arises from it, are neutralized. Kierkegaard establishes that Hegel's system is an absolute system, complete but without an *ethics*.[274] The *quantitative* dialectic of world history is opposed by the *qualitative* dialectic of the individual, which requires the subject's infinite concentration.[275] If becoming a subject were not the ultimate task, then ethics would be in a state of despair, "but what does the system care, a system which is so consistent as not to allow ethics to be part of it?"[276] But ethical quality condemns even the most astonishing quantity, recognizing in the quantitative dialectical process of historical judgment "a demoralizing aesthetic distraction."[277] The critique of Hegel, on the other hand, is also a criticism of the times. "For in our age the issue is not of one particular scholar or thinker who dedicates himself to world history; rather, the whole age is crying out for world history." An age is immoral when it is too closely in touch with world history. "Spoiled by the constant company of world history, one is led to concentrate exclusively on what is significant, to become preoccupied with contingencies and outcomes of world historical importance, instead of attending to what is most essential, what concerns the innermost heart: freedom and the ethical."[278] The ethical, however, is the absolute, which carries its infinite value in itself and "does not need any adornment in order to be presentable. But this alarming adornment is precisely world history."[279] It is alarming because it conceals *desperation*.

In the midst of the jubilation about our age and the nineteenth century, one hears an undercurrent of concealed contempt for human life; in the midst of the importance of our generation, there is a *despair* about being human. Everything, everything has to be part of it; people want to delude themselves world-historically in the totality; nobody wants to be an individually existing person. Maybe this is why so many people, even those who have seen the anomalies in his philosophy, cling to Hegel. They fear that if they were to become individually existing persons, they would disappear without a trace, so that even the daily paper would give them a second look, let alone literary reviews and the speculative thinkers of world history. They fear that if they were to become individually existing persons they would have to live forgotten and deserted like a country dweller and, if we drop Hegel, without even the possibility of receiving letters from anyone. It is undeniable that if one does not have any strong ethical or religious passion, one is forced to despair at being an individual human being—that is all.[280]

Amid the bravado of the generation one can detect in the individual traces of anxiety and despair. "Just as people in the desert have to travel in large caravans for fear of robbers and wild animals, so individuals today have a horror of existence because it is godforsaken; they dare to live only in great herds and cling together en masse in order at least to be something."[281]

Self-Alienation

In adjudicating against Hegel's reconciliation of reason and reality, Marx and Kierkegaard opt for reason and turn *reconciliation* into *critique*. Marx's critique is directed against both Hegel's philosophy of law and *bourgeois capitalism*, while Kierkegaard's critique is directed against Hegel's philosophy of religion and *bourgeois Christianity*. Their common denominator is the critique of the *bourgeois Christian world*, and their common principle is making *reality actual* [*die Wirklichkeit wirklich zu machen*].[282]

Marx does not challenge Hegel's interpretation of actuality as the union of essence and existence, but does accuse him of crass materialism because Hegel mystifies empiricism. In his critique of Hegel's philosophy of the state, Marx goes after Hegel's "pantheistic mysticism" paragraph by paragraph. Everywhere Hegel posits the agent of production [*das Produzierende*] as the product of its product.[283] Empirical reality appears in Hegel's *Philosophy of Right* as it is and is even declared to be rational; it is not, however, rational by virtue of its own reason, but rather because a new foundation is supplied to empirical facts. "The fact which is taken as a point of departure is not conceived as a fact as such, but as a mystical result. The real becomes a phenomenon, but the idea has no other content but this phenomenon. . . . The entire mystery of the *Philosophy of Right* and of Hegelian philosophy in general is contained in these paragraphs."[284] Throughout, Hegel turns the idea into the subject while turning the actual, real *subject* into the *predicate*. Hegel's "reconciliation" may not "remedy the difficulties, but he certainly brings it into a clearer perspective."[285] Kierkegaard, like Marx, engages critically with Hegel's concept of reality: "Whenever one hears philosophers speak about reality, it is just as misleading as when one looks through the window of a junk dealer and reads the words on a sign, 'Get your washing wrung here.' If you wanted to have your washing put through the wringer, you would be deceived. The sign is only there to be sold."[286] Reality is not to be treated as if it were a branch of logic; logic cannot assimilate reality because it cannot allow for what is coincidental in reality. "What reality is cannot be expressed in the language of abstraction. Reality is an inter-est [*inter-esse*] between the abstraction's hypothetical unity of thought and being."[287] Actual reality [*wirkliche Wirklichkeit*] is the ground on which Marx and Kierkegaard stand. This reality is based on the interest which unfolds in the *passion* for action. Passion—contrary to the closed circle, to the solution [*Schluss*] of the Hegelian system—drives the process of *re-solution* [*Ent-schluss*], which facilitates a decision for either this or that.[288] But a decision in this precise sense is the leap, for Marx, from the realm of necessity to that of freedom; for Kierkegaard, from the world to God. Revolutionary humanity is an existence in the state of leaping [*im Sprung*], a fractured [*zer-sprungene*] existence longing for unity.

The difference between Marx and Kierkegaard lies in the positions of *inside* and *outside*. Marx pins his hopes for a proletarian revolution on the economic situation of the masses, while for Kierkegaard it is the individual that underpins the religious revolution of bourgeois Christianity. This contrast corresponds to the difference in their interpretation of self-alienation.[289] Marx sees bourgeois society to be a society of isolated individuals in which man is alienated from his species; Kierkegaard sees in bourgeois Christendom a Christianity of the masses in which man is alienated from his individuality. In the response to Hegel's reconciliation of bourgeois society, state, and Christianity, Marx directs his critique against the self-alienation of man in bourgeois capitalism, while Kierkegaard directs his critique against man's self-alienation in bourgeois Christendom.[290] Both critiques are grounded in the disintegration [*Zerfall*] of God and the world, which is the original precondition for self-alienation, as has been shown in the studies on apocalypticism and Gnosis.

The main theme of Marx's critique of bourgeois society is man's *self-alienation*. Marx analyzes the nature of self-alienation within the elements of state, economy, and society. In the state and society, self-alienation is governed by the *division* between bourgeois society and the political state. Once upon a time they were identical, since bourgeois society was political society. This identity has disappeared, and Hegel presupposes it to have disappeared. Only the division between the bourgeois and political states presently articulates the true condition of political society.[291] The universal law dividing bourgeois society from the political state cuts right down the middle of whomever is a member of these groups. As an actual citizen he finds himself part of a bureaucratic, social organization; as a private individual, the bourgeois man stands outside the state. Thus, in order to behave as an actual citizen, he has to step outside of his bourgeois reality. "One's existence as a citizen is an existence outside one's communal existence, which is therefore purely individual."[292] The real person is the private person under the present constitution [*Staatsverfassung*].

The separation between "man" and "citizen" is set out in the declaration of human rights in the French Revolution. *Droits de l'homme*, human rights, are distinguished as such from *droits du citoyen*, citizens' rights. A *citoyen*, as distinct from an *homme*, is a member of bourgeois society. The fact that a member of bourgeois society is plainly a human being and that his rights are called human rights is explained by the nature of political emancipation. "Liberty" as a *citizen*'s human right "is the right to do everything which does not harm others. The limits within which each individual can act without harming others are determined by law, just as the boundary between two fields is marked by a stake. Liberty is a question of man regarded as an isolated monad, withdrawn into himself."[293] The human right to liberty is not founded on a bond, on the *communio* of man with man, but on the separation of man from man. The practical consequence of the human right to liberty is the right to *private ownership of property* [*Privateigentum*]. This right entitles one arbitrarily (*à son gré*), without regard for other human beings, to dispose of one's possessions. The human right to private property is the right to self-interest. The human rights to liberty and private ownership of property are the basis of bourgeois society, a society in which everybody regards the other not as a realization of but as a limitation on his freedom.

The forms of self-alienation found within the elements of state, society, and religion are but the result of one fundamental self-alienation that governs human life. Human life in a society based on private property is lived in *labor*. The subjective nature of private property, private property personified, is *labor*. According to Engels, Marx called Adam Smith the Luther of political economy. Just as Luther abolished the external trappings of heathen

Catholicism by making religiosity part of man's spiritual nature, so for Smith the classical national economy abolishes the thoughtless materiality of wealth by incorporating private property into man himself and allowing man to recognize himself in its essence. As a result man becomes a function of private property, just as Luther made him a function of religiosity.

"Under the guise of recognizing man, the national economy, whose principle is labor, is merely the next logical step in the denial of man."[294] Man no longer stands outside private property in a state of tension with regard to its external nature, but man himself is the fraught nature of private property. "What was previously being external to oneself—man's actual externalisation—has merely become the act of externalising—the process of alienating."[295] Since the classical national economy, under the guise of recognizing man in his independence and autonomy, incorporates private ownership into the very nature of man, it must, "as it develops, throw this hypocrisy to one side and reveal itself in all its cynicism, which it does by . . . making work more one-dimensionally, and hence more relentlessly and effectively, into the sole constituent of wealth."[296] Growing cynicism about Smith's national economy spreads through Say as far as Ricardo, not because they are able more clearly and definitively to see the consequences for industry, but mainly because they have an increasing awareness of how these factors intensify man's alienation. The self-alienation of man becomes increasingly apparent as the science of the national economy develops more robustly and effectively. The ruptured reality of industrialized capitalism confirms the national economy's principle of rupture. In industrialized capitalist society, all wealth has become the wealth of labor, and industry is the perfected form of labor, just as industrial capital is the perfected form of private property.[297] Only now is private property able to perfect its dominance of men and become a world-historical power of the most universal form.[298]

Alongside the critique of classical national economy, with its implicit critique of bourgeois, capitalist society, comes the critique of Hegel. For "Hegel concurs with the concept of modern national economy" when he conceives of labor as the essence of man.[299] But because Hegel finds the redeeming nature of man in labor, he only sees its positive and not its negative side. Hegel knows and acknowledges only abstract intellectual work. In philosophy, for Hegel, the laboring man is able to recover himself through the element of externalization.[300] In philosophy, man in his self-knowledge is separated from himself, an act of externalization which Hegel conceives to be the essence of philosophy.

The outstanding achievement of Hegel's *Phenomenology* and its outcome—the dialectic, negativity as the principle that moves and creates the outcome—is that Hegel grasps the self-creation of man as a process, understanding objectification as the loss of the object, as externalization and as sublation of this externalization. He thus grasps the essence of labor and understands objective man—true because real man—to be the result of his own labor. The real, active orientation of man to himself as a species-being is only possible insofar as he brings forth all of his species-powers—as a result of history—and relates to them as objects, which is only possible in the form of alienation.[301]

But at the same time Hegel's one-sidedness and *limitations* become clear. For the purpose of philosophy is to transcend the object of consciousness. Objectivity as such is the alienation of man, and does not accord with man's self-consciousness. Reappropriation does not aim to sublate human nature, which is a function of self-alienation. It is not *alienation* but *objectivity* that must be sublated. Hegel's dialectic postulates man as a spiritual being, not as an object. Man, for Hegel, is synonymous with his self-consciousness. All *alienation* of man is thus nothing but the alienation of his self-consciousness. The alienation of self-consciousness does not reflect the real alienation of human nature. Real alienation is for Hegel nothing but the "phenomenon" of the alienation of man's spiritual nature [*des innersten Wesens*], of self-consciousness.

The process of self-alienation is presented in the *Phenomenology*. "The *Phenomenology* is, therefore, an occult critique, one that to itself is still an obscure and mystifying criticism, but inasmuch as it keeps in view man's alienation, even though man appears only in the shape of spirit, there lie concealed in it all the elements of criticism, already prepared and elaborated in a manner often rising far above the Hegelian standpoint."[302] Individual sections of the *Phenomenology* contain the critical elements for entire realms, like religion, the state, and bourgeois life, but admittedly in an alienated form. For the real process of history is only depicted as the phenomenon of the process, which comes about through self-consciousness. Therefore, Hegel's dialectic is a dialectic of the idea, not of actuality. What Hegel burns in the dialectical fire of the idea is not actual religion, the actual state, actual society and nature, but religion itself as already an object of knowledge, as theology and dogma. It is not the state and society which undergo sublation, but jurisprudence and political science; it is not nature which is sublated in its objectivity, but the natural sciences.[303] Hegel conceives of labor as man's act of self-creation. But this act is simply formal because human nature itself is regarded only as an abstract spirit, a self-consciousness. The dialectical process must have a carrier. The subject can be God as absolute spirit, while real man and real nature are reduced to predicates and symbols of what is hidden. Subject and predicate are reversed in Hegel's dialectic. The absolute idea in turn sublates itself and must give itself up again as an abstraction; therefore, the absolute idea arrives "at an essence which is its complete opposite, *nature*."[304] In fact, Hegel's logic concludes "that the absolute idea is nothing for itself and that only *nature* is something."[305] But Hegel is still referring to nature as an abstraction. "*Nature* as nature—that is, insofar as it is sensuously [*sinnlich*] distinct from that secret sense [*Sinn*] concealed within it—nature as separate and distinct from these abstractions is nothing, a nullity demonstrating its nullity; it is senseless [*sinnlos*] or has only the sense of an externality which has been superseded."[306] The externality of nature is its flaw [*Mangel*], for the absolute is the spirit.

Marx opposes Hegel's dialectic of the *spirit* with his dialectical materialism of *nature*. The subject of dialectical processes is now "man who in- and ex-hales all the forces of nature."[307] The objective nature of man creates objects because it is posited by these objects, because it innately is nature. Man is immediately a being of nature. "As an objective, sensuous being man is "therefore a suffering being, and because he feels his suffering [*Leiden*], he is a passionate [*leidenschaftliches*] being."[308] Passion is the energizing, striving force in human nature. Man is not only a natural being, but a human natural being, which means being a member of a species and having to assert and occupy himself [*sich bestätigen und betätigen*] as a member of a species in both his being and his knowledge. All things natural must emerge, and man too has his act of emergence: history. "History is true natural history of man."[309] Marx reveals that *economics* is the foundation of nature. "As is the case with every historical and social science, it must be borne in mind with the study of economic categories that . . . economics as a science did not just begin at the point when it was first mentioned."[310]

The self-alienation of man now appears not as a *logical* but as an *economic* process. Marx diagnoses money as the source of self-alienation. Money is the real spirit of all things.[311] "Money lowers all the gods of mankind and transforms them into a commodity. Money is the universal, self-constituting value of all things. Therefore, it has robbed the whole world, both the human world and nature, of its own peculiar value. Money is the essence of man's work and existence, alienated from man, and this alien essence dominates him, and he worships it."[312] Right from his first analysis of self-alienation

Marx takes aim at the bourgeois, Christian world. Money in bourgeois society is the embodiment of value, which conflates and exchanges [*verwechselt und vertauscht*] all things. Thus money is "the overall conflation and exchange of all things, the world turned upside-down, the conflation and exchange of all natural and human qualities."[313]

It is not by chance, therefore, that Marx calls his critique of political economy *Capital* and begins this work with an analysis of commodities. For the *problem of commodities* is not an isolated one; rather, it is the structural problem of bourgeois society and capitalism in general. Commodities have always been traded, but in bourgeois society the inner and outer life are both determined by them. Commodities are the constitutive form of society, the universal category of all social being.[314]

At first glance commodities appear to be straightforward. Analysis shows, however, that it is "a very tricky area, full of metaphysical sophistry and theological pitfalls."

The form of wood, for instance, is altered by making a table out of it. Nonetheless, the table remains wood, that common, everyday thing. But as soon as it steps forth as a commodity, it is changed into a natural supernatural thing [*ein sinnlich übersinnliches Ding*]. It not only stands with its feet on the ground, but, in relation to all other commodities, it stands on its head, and evolves whims from its wooden brain far more wonderful than if it had begun to dance of its own accord [*als wenn er aus freien Stücken zu tanzen begänne*].[315]

The "mystical character of the commodity" derives from the commodity form itself.

The mystery of the commodity form, therefore, is simply that it takes the social characteristics of men's own labor and reflects them back to men as the objective characteristics of the products of labor themselves, as the social properties of nature belonging to these things. It thus also reflects the social relation of the producers to the totality of labor as a social relation of objects, one that exists independently of the producers. Through this quid pro quo the products of labor become commodities, natural supernatural or social things. It is only the specific social relation of men themselves that here assumes for them the phantasmagoric form of a relation of things. Hence in order to find an analogy we must take flight to the obscure region of the religious world. Here the products of the human mind appear endowed with their own life, as independent forms that enter into relations with one another and with men. In the commodity world, the same holds for the products of the human hand. This I call the fetishism that clings to the products of labor as soon as they are produced as commodities, and which therefore is inseparable from commodity production.[316]

The fetish character of the world of commodities arises from the peculiar character of the labor that produces the commodities.

The transcendence [*Aufhebung*] of self-alienation follows the same course as self-alienation.[317] Communism is the positive expression of annulled [*aufgehobenen*] private property. In its first form, communism is "only a general, perfected form of private property.... It regards direct, physical ownership as the sole purpose of life and existence; the function of the worker is not abolished [*aufgehoben*], but extended to all men."[318] The relationship of private ownership continues to be a relationship to the community, to the material world. "This form of communism—since it negates the personality of man in every sphere—is but the logical expression of private property, which is this negation. General envy constituting itself as power is the disguise in which greed reestablishes itself and satisfies itself, only in another way."[319] In this first form communism is "only a manifestation of the vileness of private property, which wants to set itself up as the positive community system."[320] In its second form, as political communism which abolishes [*Aufhebung vollzieht*] the state, it has come to terms with its concept but not yet with its essence. Political communism regards itself as a stage in the reintegration or restoration of man within himself, as transcendence [*Aufhebung*] of his self-alienation. But to the extent that he has not yet grasped the positive nature of private property or understood the real nature of human needs, he is still ensnared and infected by it. Only in its third form is communism to be seen "as the positive transcendence [*Aufhebung*] of private property as human self-alienation, and therefore as the real appropriation of the human essence by and for man; communism therefore is the complete return of man to himself as a social (i.e., human) being—a return accomplished consciously which embraces the entire wealth of previous development. This communism, as fully developed naturalism, equals humanism and as fully developed humanism equals naturalism."[321] Communist naturalism or humanism is different from both idealism and materialism; at the same time it is the truth that binds them together.[322]

"Just as atheism as the supersession [*Aufhebung*] of God is the emergence of theoretical humanism, so communism as the supersession of private property is the vindication of real human life as man's property, the emergence of practical humanism. Through the supersession [*Aufhebung*] of religion, atheism is self-mediating humanism; through the supersession of private property, communism is self-mediating humanism.... Only when we have superseded this mediation—which is, however, a necessary precondition—will positive humanism, positively originating in itself, come into being."[323] Atheism and communism are the real becoming [*das wirkliche Werden*] of history; "they are rather the first real emergence, the realization become real for man, of his essence as something real."[324]

Marx goes on to suggest that "naturalism alone is capable of grasping the act of world history."[325] He depicts the definitive form of communism fully in Hegelian tones. This form of communism "is the genuine resolution of the conflict between man and nature, and between man and man, the true resolution of the conflict between becoming and being, between objectification and self-affirmation, between freedom and necessity, between individual and species. It is the solution of the riddle of history and knows itself to be the solution."[326] Working on the premise of the positive supersession [*Aufhebung*] of private property, man produces man, himself and others. Just as society itself produces man as man, so it is also produced by him.

The human essence of nature exists only for social man; for only here does nature exist for him as a bond with other men, as his existence for others and their existence for him, as the vital element of human reality; only here does it exist as the basis of his own human existence. Only here has his natural existence become his human existence and nature become man for him. Society is therefore the perfected unity in essence of man with nature, the true resurrection of nature, the realized naturalism of man and the realized humanism of nature.[327]

Kierkegaard's critique of secularized Christendom is also concerned with the self-alienation of man. But in contrast to the "fantastic theories about society" as developed by Karl Marx, Kierkegaard's concern is to decipher the faded "original text [*Urschrift*] of the individual, human relations of existence. . . . That the idea of socialism in the community should ever become the means of redeeming our times is out of the question." The principle of community and of association, "which can have its validity at best in relation to material interests, is not affirmative in our times but negative—an evasion, a distraction, a delusion: its dialectic is that by strengthening individuals it [i.e., the principle] also enervates them; it strengthens numerically through joining together, but ethically speaking, that is a weakening."[328]

The human equality that socialism aims to achieve cannot be realized in the element of reality. Not even the idea of human equality can be thought through in all its implications because the essence of worldliness is disparity

[*Verschiedenheit*]. In the *world* humans are *unequal*, but before *God* they are *equal*. In the *world* they are a *multitude*, but before *God* they stand as *individuals*. As an individual, man stands in a relationship to divinity [*Gottheit*]. Considered in a secular, temporal, and social context, it seems absurd that only the individual is able to attain humanity, for it is more plausible that several people together would reach this goal. This is true for all earthly and sensual goals [*sinnlichen Zwecken*]. When worldliness predominates, then secular ideology "abolishes God, eternity, and the relationship of man with the divine, or transforms it into a fable and replaces it with modernity. Consequently, being human comes to mean a specimen of a species endowed with reason, so that this species is of a higher order than the individual, or so that it is only exemplary, not made up of individuals."[329] In the element of eternity "only one reaches the goal, which implies that each is able to, and each should become this particular one, but only one reaches the goal." Precisely this imperative to be individual applies *to all* in equal measure; it makes no distinction with regard to any single one. Nobody is excluded from this call to individuality.[330]

It is the original sin of Christendom to have forgotten that the cause of Christianity rests with the individual.[331] The individual is "the strait through which time, history and the whole race must pass."[332] The view that the absolute can be realized within society ultimately has "recourse to the delusion of the temporal world [*Zeitlichkeit*] that some righteous fellows, or the whole of humanity, are able to impress God to such an extent that they can be Christ himself."[333] When Marx builds a society without God, and Kierkegaard places the individual alone before God, their common assumption is the disintegration of God and the world, the division [*die Entzweiung*] of the divine and the secular.

The Eschatology of Marx and Kierkegaard

Once self-alienation is revealed to be the leitmotif in the analyses of Marx and Kierkegaard, elements inevitably emerge which determine the eschatological drama of history in each of their views. The entire socioeconomic catalog of Marx's analyses simply serves as the orchestration of the theme of self-alienation[334]—the fall into exile and the path to redemption. *Social economy* is for Marx the *economy of salvation*. Kierkegaard, for his part, seeks to eclipse eighteen centuries as if they had never existed and to live as Christ's contemporary. With Kierkegaard the apocalypticism of early Christianity [*urchristliche Apokalyptik*] becomes reality again.

As early as his critique of Hegel's *Philosophy of Right*, Marx entertains the positive possibility of universal emancipation

in the formation of a class with radical chains, a class of civil society which is not a class of civil society, a class which is the dissolution of all classes; a sphere which has a universal character because of its universal suffering and which lays claim to no particular right because the wrong it suffers is not a particular wrong but wrong in general; a sphere of society which can no longer lay claim to a historical title but merely to a human one, which does not stand in one-sided opposition to the consequences but in all-round opposition to the premises of the German political system; and finally, a sphere which cannot emancipate itself without emancipating itself from—and thereby emancipating—all other spheres of society, which is, in a word, the total loss of humanity and which can therefore redeem itself only through the total redemption of humanity. This dissolution of society as a particular class is the proletariat.[335]

The proletariat assumes the role of Christ. In Christ, too, the destiny of mankind [*das Menschenlos*] found its ultimate expression [*auf den äussersten Punkt erschienen*].[336]

In *The Holy Family* Marx explains in more detail the soteriologico-economic framework of the socioeconomic relationship between the bourgeoisie and the proletariat.

The propertied class and the class of the proletariat present the same human self-alienation. But the former class feels at ease and strengthened in this self-alienation; it recognizes alienation as its own power and has in it the semblance of a human existence. The class of the proletariat feels annihilated in alienation; it sees in alienation its own powerlessness and the reality of an inhuman existence. It is, to use an expression of Hegel, in abasement [*Verworfenheit*] the indignation at that abasement, an indignation to which it is necessarily driven by the contradiction between its human nature and its condition of life, which is the outright, resolute, and comprehensive negation of that nature.[337]

While the propertied class is forced to sustain itself and its antithesis, that is, the proletariat, the proletariat is forced to abolish [*aufheben*] itself and the antithetical determinant which makes it into the proletariat—private property. The propertied class is the positive side of this antithesis, the conservative party, or self-sufficient private property. The proletariat is the negative side of the antithesis, the revolutionary party, or private property in the state of dissolution [*das sich selbst auflösende Privateigentum*].

"From the point of view of its national, economic movement, private property is, of course, continually being driven toward its own dissolution, but only by an unconscious development which is independent of it and which exists against its will; this is limited by the nature of things—only, that is, by creating the proletariat as proletariat, misery [*Elend*] conscious of its own physical and spiritual misery, and dehumanization [*Entmenschung*] conscious of its own dehumanization, and hence striving to supersede itself [*sich selbst aufhebende*].The proletariat executes the judgment which private property, in creating the proletariat, suspends over itself."[338] Therefore, the proletariat can be the redeemer, "since the abstraction of all humanity, even of the semblance of humanity, is practically complete in the fully formed proletariat; since the conditions of life of the proletariat sum up all the conditions of life of society today in their most inhuman and acute form; since man has lost himself in the proletariat, yet at the same time is driven directly to revolt against that inhumanity."[339] Evidently, *proletariat* does not denote the concrete mass of the proletariat but a *historical dialectical entity*. "It is not a question of what this or that proletarian, or even the whole proletariat, at the moment considers as its aim. It is a question of what the proletariat is, and what, in accordance with this being, it will historically be compelled to do."[340]

In every political upheaval Marx glimpsed the summer lightning of impending catastrophe. He closely followed events in all countries at all times, seeking to determine their potency for the drama of world history— much along the lines of apocalypticism. At first, Marx believes himself to have recognized the crucial hour of world history in the year 1848. In 1852 Marx contributes the *Eighteenth Brumaire of Louis Napoleon* to the socio-economic history of salvation. In the din of the Parisian commune, Marx still believes he hears the end of the bourgeois, Christian world. The limping gait of the revolution in Europe does not cause him to doubt his prophecy, but it continuously deepens his rancor against man's actual unreasonableness and high-handedness. Marx draws further away and buries himself more deeply in order to discover the law, the path leading from the bourgeois, Christian world to the classless society. The "ultimate purpose" of his work is "to discover the special law of motion governing modern society." Like the ancient apocalyptics, Marx believes that the stages of end history [*Endgeschichte*] can "neither be left out nor decreed away," but like them he tries "to shorten and ease the birth pangs."[341] The socioeconomic apocalypse is *Capital*, the revelation of the last things. The dull rumble of impending catastrophe is audible throughout the inventory of socioeconomic analyses, as the dramatic tension rises from chapter to chapter.

The subject of this drama, as the title suggests, is capital. Marx depicts the collapse of capitalist society and the dawn of classless society as a mighty apocalypse: *capital* and *labor* are the two antithetical poles of bourgeois society. The proletariat markets itself through its own productive force as a commodity and sells itself to capital. In doing so, a law emerges which results from the overall exchange of goods and triggers an uncanny surge in the automatism of production, precipitating the dissolution of the entire structure of bourgeois society: the law of *surplus value* [*Mehrwert*]. The proletariat is eternally damned to go on producing its labor force, as if a blind instrument in the accumulation of capital, and to reproduce its own instruments of torture.

But all methods for the production of surplus value are at the same time methods of accumulation; and every extension of accumulation becomes again a means for the development of these methods. It follows therefore that as capital accumulates, the lot of the laborer, be his payment high or low, must grow proportionally worse. The law, finally, that always equilibrates the relative surplus population, or industrial reserve army, to the extent and energy of accumulation, this law rivets the laborer to capital more firmly than the wedges of Vulcan did Prometheus to the rock. It establishes an accumulation of misery, corresponding to the accumulation of capital. Accumulation of wealth at one pole is, therefore, at the same time, accumulation of misery, agony of toil, slavery, ignorance, brutality, mental degradation, at the opposite pole, that is, on the side of the class that produces its own product in the form of capital.[342]

The accumulation of surplus value introduces capital to movements of *concentration*. This concentration is caused by the dynamics of the internal laws of capitalist production.

Hand in hand with this concentration, or this expropriation of many capitalists by few, develop, on an ever extending scale, the co-operative form of the labor-process, the conscious technical application of science, the methodical collective cultivation of the soil, the transformation of the instruments of labor into instruments of labor only usable in common, the economizing of all means of production by their use as the jointly owned means of production of combined, socialized labor. Along with the constantly diminishing number of the magnates of capital, who usurp and monopolize all advantages of this process of transformation, grows the mass of misery, oppression, slavery, degradation, exploitation; but with this too grows the revolt of the working class, a class always increasing in numbers, and disciplined, united, organized by the very mechanism of the process of capitalist production itself.

The monopoly of capital becomes a fetter on social production. "Concentration of the means of production and socialization of labor at last reach a point where they become incompatible with their capitalist integument.

This integument is burst asunder. The knell of capitalist private property sounds."[343] At the end of this chapter, in which Marx outlines the historical tendencies of capitalist accumulation, he refers back to the *Communist Manifesto* of 1847. Twenty years spent in the intensive study of economics in England have only confirmed Marx's prophecy and proven his social economics to be an economics of salvation. "The advance of industry, whose involuntary promoter is the bourgeoisie, replaces the isolation of the laborers, due to competition, by the revolutionary combination, due to association. The development of modern industry, therefore, cuts from under its feet the very foundation on which the bourgeoisie produces and appropriates products. What the bourgeoisie therefore produces, above all, are its own grave-diggers. Its fall and the victory of the proletariat are equally inevitable."[344] With the dawn of the classless society, the leap from the "realm of necessity" into the "realm of freedom" is accomplished.

The global upheavals in 1848 confirm for Kierkegaard that his diagnosis is correct: the human race is ill and, in a spiritual sense, fatally so.[345] The century's catastrophes and revolutions are only an introduction and form "the rough notes, not the main part of the book."[346]

Kierkegaard agrees with Marx.

Guilty of all of this is the conceited, semieducated bourgeoisie, who are flattered by the press into thinking they are democratic; they imagine that they, the general public, should be in charge. But perhaps history has never before experienced such a rapid arrival of nemesis, for in the same twinkling of an eye, at the same stroke of the clock, that the bourgeoisie resolutely grasped at power, the fourth estate rose up. Now, it will certainly be said that it is guilty, but that is untrue: it is only the innocent victim, who will be pulled to pieces, shot down, and cursed—and it will be claimed to be in self-defense, and so it is in a sense, because the bourgeoisie overthrew the state.[347]

The historical emergence of the fourth estate is for Kierkegaard, as for Marx, the most crucial event of the century—it marks the very turning point of history. Face to face with Marx, Kierkegaard recognizes the decisiveness of the moment. The one thing that is needed [*was nottut*] is Kierkegaard's anticommunist manifesto, in which he stands face to face [*Aug in Aug*] with Marx. It shall be discussed in detail, because this manifesto is only to be found in print in a remote corner of a newspaper.

Kierkegaard remarks that Europe is, in a worldly sense, losing its way "with ever greater, passionate haste" in problems which can only be answered in a godly way [*göttlich beantworten lassen*].

No real progress has been made in the endeavor to make the fourth estate, that is, all men, attempt to solve the problem of equality between man and man in the secular sphere [*Weltlichkeit*], in the sphere whose nature is disparity. . . . A barrier stands eternally before it, and the borders of eternity mock all human efforts. They mock the arrogance that counters its supreme and glorious rights, the arrogance that seeks to explain in temporal and worldly terms that which should be a mystery to the temporal sphere [*Zeitlichkeit*] and which only eternity can and will explain.[348]

The real issue here is eternity, "its prospect at every moment, its gravity, its bliss, its balm." Only when we recognize "what the issue really is, only then does the new era begin."[349]

To be sure, some time must still be "wasted on what are only convulsions," for there is deep-seated "superstition" in man's power to redeem and bestow happiness on the basis of his worldly intelligence. The quantitative dialectic of world history, the finite dialectic of reason, will in any case be able to "form an incredible number of combinations."[350] But all worldly apocalypses and experiments must fail because worldliness is essentially disparity, relativity. Human equality will not be achieved in the element of disparity and brokenness [*Gebrochenheit*]. The worldly theorists, however, will hardly notice "that misfortune has not been due to random errors and deficiencies in this combination but essentially due to the need for something quite different: religiousness."[351] As a result, the human race becomes "ever more confused, like a drunken man, the more restlessly he rushes about, the more intoxicated he becomes, even when he gets nothing more to drink."[352] When the human race is finally weary of suffering and bloodshed, only then will it finally take note, only then will *change* come [*kommt es zum Umschlag*]. This change marks a turning point of great consequence, as was the case in the Copernican age, but in reverse: "What appeared to be political, and was falsely assumed to be so, will prove to be a religious movement."[353] From this moment on, "as the fourth estate is established, it will become clear that there can be no earthly rule, even when the crisis is overcome."[354] Until now, emperors, kings, popes, generals, diplomats "have been able to rule and direct the world at a critical moment. But from this time on, as the fourth estate is established, it will become clear that only martyrs can rule the world at the critical moment."[355] The victor [*Siegesherr*] in the new age is the martyr. The martyr is the ruler of the future race. "Blood will need to be shed to regain eternity, but it is blood of a different kind. It is not that shed by the thousands of victims who die in battle [*Schlachtopfer*], no, it is the precious blood of individuals—of martyrs, of these mighty dead who can do what no living person who orders the slaughter of thousands can and what these mighty dead could not do when alive but only when dead: command the obedience of a fanatical throng [*rasende Menge*], precisely because this fanatical throng was allowed, in their disobedience, to slay the martyrs."356

As it becomes apparent that the sociopolitical revolution is being transformed into a religious revolution, so it also becomes apparent that *spiritual leaders* [*Geistliche*] are needed. For if the battle is to be joined and, crucially, if it is to be won, then "it has to happen through spiritual leaders; neither soldiers, policemen, diplomats, nor policy makers have the understanding."357 Spiritual leaders are needed who can disperse the throng and make them into individuals—spiritual leaders who would not make too many demands on learning and would wish for nothing less than to rule; spiritual leaders who, when required, would be enormously eloquent and no less powerful in their silence and endurance; spiritual leaders, if possible, with a knowledge of the human heart, who would be no less well versed in how to practice forbearance when passing judgment or sentences; spiritual leaders who would know how to use authority guided by the art of making sacrifices; spiritual leaders who would be prepared, trained, and educated to obey and to suffer, so that they would be able to calm, admonish, edify, stir, but also compel— not by force, no, but by nothing less than through their own obedience—and above all able to suffer patiently all the unpleasantness of the sick without being disturbed, just as little as the doctor is disturbed by the patient's cursing and lashing out during an operation. For the human race is ill and, in a spiritual sense, fatally so. But as so often happens, when the patient is asked to indicate the place where it hurts, he points to the wrong place [*verkehrte*]—and so it is with the human race at the moment. It thinks that a political or social revolution would help. "But, in truth, it is eternity which is needed—is there any need for more compelling evidence than this terrible sigh (out of hell) which has been heard from socialism: God is evil; just deliver us from him, and we will find relief. So it admits what it lacks, for the demonic always contains the truth in inverted form."358

When the catastrophe breaks out and transforms into a religious movement, then spiritual leaders are needed "for the greatest of all dangers, which is far closer than one possibly thinks." For "the strength of communism is evident and consists of the same ingredients of religiousness, and even Christian religiousness, but in demonic combination."359 And so Kierkegaard has the presumption to prophesy the Antichrist: like mushrooms after rain, demonically infected figures will appear, "who will boldly make themselves apostles, on a level with the apostles, some having the task of fulfilling Christianity, and soon even becoming founders of a religion themselves, founders of a new religion, which is alleged to meet temporal and worldly demands in a different way from the asceticism of Christianity." The most dangerous thing is when the demonic figures [*die Dämonischen*] themselves become apostles—like thieves masquerading as policemen—the founders of a religion that will find disastrous support in such a critical time because, viewed from the perspective of eternity, it is true to say about this time that religiousness is needed, true religiousness; whereas, viewed from the demonic perspective, the same age says of itself that religiousness is needed, but demonic religiousness.[360] "The one thing that is needed" [*Das Eine, was not tut*] is Kierkegaard's *antikommunist manifesto*, in which he crosses swords with Marx and calls for a resolution. Kierkegaard's prophecy concerning the religious revolution of martyrs stands in opposition to Marx's prophecy of the proletarian world revolution. Inwardness and outwardness are divided between Marx and Kierkegaard into worldly revolution [*weltliche Umkehrung*] and religious repentance [*religiöse Umkehr*]. Kierkegaard has made it absolutely clear that Christian life is inwardness and must therefore be acosmic and antiworldly. Marx has replaced the truth of the world beyond with the truth of this world, and has shown that the atheistic roots of communism are constitutive. The fusion [*Ineins*] of inside and outside can only be attained if one is prepared to abandon the territory which holds Marx and Kierkegaard, even in their opposition, captive.

Epilogue

With Hegel on the one hand and Marx and Kierkegaard on the other, this study is not simply closed but is essentially resolved. For the entire span of Western existence is inscribed in the conflict between the higher (Hegel) and the lower (Marx and Kierkegaard) realms, in the rift between inside (Kierkegaard) and outside (Marx).

While existence means the same as ecstasy, the former in Latin and the latter in Greek, existence also means the minimum of vegetative life in the sense of "naked existence." Human life spans the interval between the maximum as ecstasy and the minimum as naked existence. The higher realm of Hegel's ecstasy is abased into the lower realm of naked existence of Marx and Kierkegaard. The ecstasy of Hegel's love is banished by the plight of existence—by anxiety and guilt (Kierkegaard), by hunger and misery (Marx), by despair and death. The maximum and the minimum are absolute measures and as such the end. Torn asunder in the oppositions of upper [*Oben*] and lower realm [*Unten*], inside and outside, Hegel's philosophy and the prophecy of Marx and Kierkegaard come to an end. The history of their time is experienced by them as a straining toward this end.

The de-cision which Marx and Kierkegaard call for deepens the rift and makes it absolute. That is why this call for a decision marks the beginning of a crisis that is still shaking our present age. For crisis is scission [*Scheidung*] arising from the call for decision [*Entscheidung*]. Just as the crisis of the Renaissance and Reformation smashes the framework of the Middle Ages, so, too, the crisis marked by Marx's and Kierkegaard's call for decision smashes the framework of the modern age. Once the framework of the modern age is smashed, the aeon demarcated by the milestones [*Marksteine*] of antiquity–Middle Ages–new age comes to an end. Hegel had already conceived of his philosophy as the endpoint and fulfillment [*volles Ende*] of the Western spirit. But philosophy is the "spiritual dimension of world history." The "latest philosophy" is the result of all earlier philosophies: "nothing is lost, all principles are preserved."[361] Hegel's fulfillment, however, is a reconciliation of destruction, for it is the final act before a great reversal, before the complete break with the classical, Christian Western tradition. This awareness of the end of history is formative not only for Hegel and his successors but also for his opponents. Even if Burckhardt doubts Hegel's construction of reason, he nonetheless affirms his situation at the end of history. For Burckhardt's final motif is his insight that Old Europe is coming to an end.

While the elemental decision [*Entscheidung der Elemente*] in the crisis of the Reformation and the Renaissance was clearly defined as *re-*, as going back either to the purely Christian or to pure antiquity, at the end of the modern age classical antiquity and Christianity are inextricably intertwined and therefore are *both* transposed to the end [*ins Ende gestellt*]. Certainly Kierkegaard wishes to reestablish early Christianity on a general basis, and Marx has the same desire for the Greek polis. However, is Kierkegaard's individual not the "I" as discovered by the Renaissance? Is not Marx's proletariat the messianic community of apocalypticism? Thus, classical antiquity and Christianity cross over and blur together in Western culture [*im Abendländischen*], and in this way both classical antiquity and Christianity are framed as fulfillment [*in die Vollendung gestellt*]—completed in the end [*als volles Ende*].

In bringing to an end the classical, Christian world, an epoch of two and a half millennia, Hegel is in fact concluding the history of the Western spirit. A new epoch is beginning, which introduces a new aeon that is post-Christian in a more profound sense than that of the calendar. This epoch, in which the threshold of Western history is crossed, regards itself primarily as the no-longer [*Nicht-Mehr*] of the past and the not-yet [*Noch-Nicht*] of what is to come. To all weak spirits longing for shelter and security, this age appears wanting. For the coming age is not served by demonizing or giving new life to what-has-been [*das Gewesene*], but by remaining steadfast in the no-longer and the not-yet, in the nothingness of the night, and thus remaining open to the first signs of the coming day. How many are liberated [*aufgesprengt sind*] to what is to come is not important. Who they are is the question that determines their position, for they are the ones who measure out existence [*die Masse des Seins vermessen*] by interpreting the signs of what is to come.

It is as legacy and task, as no-longer and not-yet, that the opposition between high [*Oben*] and lower realm [*Unten*], the rift [*Riss*] between inside and outside as the outline [*Grundriss*] of being, is passed on to the new generation at the end of the Western aeon. But what is needed to seal this fragmentation is the *coincidentia oppositorum*. For the opposites coincide *before* and *in* God, who is beyond what is higher and beneath what is lower, descending and ascending, so that he brings all to fulfillment. God encompasses both the inside and outside; he is the inner spirit of each thing because he is everything.[362] Because everything is in God, everything is *ek-sistent*; everything has its center outside itself, in God. Only man can turn away from God's center and be *in-sistent*. Man becomes stiff against God and finds the center of things in himself. Forgetting the divine measure, man becomes more and more presumptuous [*vermisst sich*] and takes himself as the measure [*nimmt sich selbst zum Mass*]: man is the measure of all things. By making himself as subject the measure of all things, man conceals the true correspondence of things and constructs fabrications [*Gemächte*]; he fills the world with purposes and safeguards, fashions it into a protective shell, and walls himself in.[363] These fabrications conceal the correspondence of things with and in God, and push God out into the realm of "mystery." Thereby, the intricate web of things becomes a mystery, as it is increasingly forced by manipulation and human technology into a new, false measure.

The question is why this error which hurls man to utter remoteness from God [*Gott-ferne*] is so particularly prevalent in him. In erring as he does, the *essence of man* is revealed as the shadow of God. Precisely because man is the *shadow of God* he is able to succumb to this idea and, more crucially, to succeed in making himself into the measure of all things. The shadow is the serpent beguiling man into misrecognizing himself as godlike . . . ultimately as God—and God as only a shadow of himself. As man makes himself into the measure of all things, the shadow takes center stage, and the correspondence of things with God becomes obscured. This is the darkness and night of the world [*Umnachtung der Welt*].

If, looking into the beauty of night, man does not mistake it but sees the darkness for what it is; if he recognizes his protective shells as mirages [*Verstellungen*]; if he perceives his insistence as dogged resistance [*Versteifung*] and unmasks his self-made measures for the lies and errors they are—then day will dawn in this human world, and the transition from insistence to existence will follow. When day dawns all measures will turn upside down. Man will then be brought home by God and will *ex-ist*, since he will find his center in God. For man is nothing in himself unless he is part of God. Then the veil enshrouding the world will lift, the mists will be dispersed, the arrogant [*vermessene*] measures of man will disintegrate, and those ordained by God will be revealed. The measure of God is the holy [*das Heilige*]. First of all, the holy is separation [*Aussonderung*] and setting apart [*Absonderung*]; being holy means being set apart. The holy is the terror that shakes the foundations of the world. The shock caused by the holy [*das Heilige*] bursts asunder the foundations of the world for salvation [*das Heil*]. It is the holy that passes judgment in the court of history. History exists only when truth is separated from error, when truth is illuminated from mystery. History is elucidated from the mystery of error to the revelation of truth.

Notes

All translations of quotations used by Jacob Taubes are my own, unless otherwise stated.—Trans.

1. Weininger, 101.
2. Hos. 11:1–2, 7–9.
3. Berdyaev, 91–92.
4. Heidegger, 13.
5. Ibid., 23.
6. Ibid.
7. Balthasar, I:175 ff.
8. Ibid.
9. Faust, I:342.
10. Balthasar, III:406.
11. Karl Barth, I:2, 64.
12. Schelling, III:628.
13. Gen. 3:8.
14. Jonas, 126.
15. Ibid., 120, 137.
16. 1 Cor. 13:12.
17. Ibid.
18. Reisner, 1929, 66.
19. Berdyaev, 107.
20. Kierkegaard, 1923, I:29.
21. Marx, 1932a, I:79.
22. Ibid., 17.
23. Löwith, 493.
24. Jonas, 146 ff.
25. Ibid., 149.

26. Ibid., 150.
27. Otto, 5.
28. "New covenant": Jer. 31:31.
29. Tillich, 1926, 8.
30. Schweitzer, 1926, 153. Cf. ibid.,
    397 ff.
31. Anaximander, *Simplicius zu
    Aristoteles Physik* 24, 13 ff., cited
    in Diels = 12A9.
32. Tillich, 1933, 28 ff.
33. Ibid., 32.
34. Ibid., 36.
35. Ibid.
36. Balthasar, I:13.
37. Tillich, 1926, 22.
38. Berdyaev, 46.
39. Deut. 6:12.
40. Balthasar, I:5.
41. 1 Cor. 15:28.
42. Rosenzweig, II:194.
43. Hegel, 1832–45, II:13.
44. Weber, 6.
45. Baeck, 362.
46. Isa. 40:3.
47. Exod. 24:7.
48. Kohn, 12. [This author does not

appear in the bibliography of
the original.—Trans.]
49. Talmud, *babylonischer*, Berak-
    hot 13a.
50. Baron, I:5.
51. Weiser, 22 ff.
52. Schelling, XI:109.
53. Gen. 11:4 ff.
54. Gen. 12:2.
55. Schelling, XI:111.
56. Ibid., 155.
57. Gen. 12:1.
58. Schelling, XI:157 ff.
59. Hegel, 1907, 247.
60. Weber, 299.
61. Baron, I:85 ff.
62. Talmud, *babylonischer*, Sanhe-
    drin 21b.
63. Wellhausen, 1895, 392.
64. Josephus Flavius, *Contra Api-
    onem*, II:16.
65. Buber, 106.
66. Wellhausen, 1900, 2 ff.
67. Ibid., 14.
68. Buber, 142.
69. Ibid., 143.
70. Kautsky, II:52.
71. Buber, 111 ff.
72. Hehn, 256.
73. Weber, 121.
74. Ibid., 299.
75. Buber, 81; cf. 92.
76. Weber, 3 ff.
77. Ibid., 87.
78. Müller, 71.
79. Exod. 21:4–5.
80. Talmud, *babylonischer*, Kiddu-
    shin 22b.
81. Lev. 25:55.
82. Ibid.
83. Weber, 299.
84. Ibid., 127.
85. Ibid., 338.

86. Buber, 111 ff.
87. Weber, 339.
88. Ibid., 342.
89. Ibid.
90. Ibid.
91. Otto, 5.
92. Ibid., 4.
93. Reitzenstein, 937.
94. Jonas, 74.
95. Spengler, II:225–399.
96. Jonas, 73.
97. Ibid., 74.
98. Meyer, II:95 and *passim*.
99. Baron, I:76.
100. Meyer, I:23.
101. Baron, I:76.
102. Spengler, II:242.
103. Meyer, II:72.
104. Otto, 5.
105. Jonas, 92.
106. Lidzbarski, 1925a, 1.
107. Jonas, 96.
108. Ibid., 247.
109. Ibid., 96.
110. Ibid.
111. Ibid.
112. Ibid., 98.
113. Otto, 29.
114. *Hermetica*, IV:4.
115. Lidzbarski, 1925b, 433.
116. Jonas, 98.
117. *Hermetica*, IV:8.
118. Lidzbarski, 1925a, 243.
119. Lidzbarski, 1925b, 10 ff.
120. Ibid., 13.
121. Lidzbarski, 1925a, 35.
122. Harnack, 1921, 136.
123. Ibid., 139.
124. Jonas, 105.
125. Lidzbarski, 1925b, 338.
126. Jonas, 106 ff.
127. Lidzbarski, 1925b, 393.
128. Ibid., 261.

129. *Pistis Sophia*, cited in Jonas, 112.
130. Lidzbarski, 1925b, 393 ff.
131. *Seelenhymnus der Thomasakten*, cited in Jonas, 114.
132. *Hermetica*, IV:1.
133. Lidzbarski, 1925b, 113.
134. Ibid., 20 ff.
135. Lidzbarski, 1925a, 62.
136. Lidzbarski, 1925b, 126.
137. Ibid., 287.
138. Lidzbarski, 1925a, 58.
139. Jonas, 120.
140. Lidzbarski, 1925b, 258.
141. Ibid., 244.
142. Ibid., 122.
143. Ibid.
144. Ibid., 197.
145. Jonas, 124.
146. Lidzbarski, 1925a, 67.
147. Lidzbarski, 1925b, 273.
148. Hilgenfeld, 12.
149. Volz, 6.
150. Ibid., 135.
151. Ibid., 11.
152. Geffcken, 1902, 571. [This does not appear in the bibliography of the original.—Trans.]
153. 2 Bar. 56:2.
154. Volz, 141.
155. Lommel, 130.
156. Apocalypse of Enoch 89:59.
157. Ibid., 93.
158. Ibid., 79.
159. Lommel, 130.
160. Ibid., 133.
161. Ibid., 147.
162. 4 Ezra 4:26.
163. Ibid.
164. Leisegang, 1924, II:1273.
165. Koepgen, 150.
166. Leisegang, 1926, 60 ff.
167. Baur, 1835, 668 ff.

168. Jonas, 261.
169. Lommel, 143.
170. Jonas, 260.
171. Ibid.
172. Rom. 7.
173. Jonas, 211.
174. Ibid., 164.
175. Ibid., 260.
176. Harnack, 1921, 158 ff.
177. Ibid., 139.

BOOK II

1. Meyer, II:139 ff.
2. Ibid., 156 ff.
3. Bickermann, 18.
4. Volz, 11.
5. Baumgartner, 69.
6. Ibid., 70 ff.
7. Boll, 1 ff.
8. Gunkel, 1895, 20 ff.
9. Jeremius, 712.
10. Eisler, 660 ff.
11. 1 Cor. 3:24.
12. Von Gall, 165.
13. Nietzsche, VII:235.
14. Eisler, 680.
15. Herford, 224.
16. Fuchs, 5 ff.
17. Tacitus, V:13.
18. Josephus, *Bellum Judaicum*, book II:1.2.
19. Josephus, *Antiquities of the Jews*, book XVII:9.3.
20. Matt. 11:12.
21. Josephus Flavius, *Antiquities of the Jews*, book XVIII:5.2.
22. Luke 1:24.
23. Talmud, *babylonischer*, Ta'anit 23b.
24. Matt. 3:1, Mark 1:4, Luke 3:3.
25. Matt. 3:5.
26. Otto, 58.

27. Matt. 3:6.
28. Schweitzer, 1926, 424.
29. Apocalypse of Enoch 91:5–10.
30. Matt. 24:37.
31. Matt. 3:11.
32. Dibelius, 56.
33. Acts 19:2.
34. Eisler, 107.
35. Kähler, 32.
36. Ibid.
37. Otto, 5.
38. Origen, *Contra Celsum*, VII:9.
39. Otto, 5.
40. Mark 1:14–15.
41. Mark 1:4.
42. Mark 1:14.
43. Cf. Otto, 52.
44. Matt. 3:2.
45. Luke 3:7.
46. Matt. 10:6.
47. Mark 1:14.
48. Goguel, 165; Otto, 60.
49. Matt. 11:2.
50. Acts 19:1 ff.
51. Lidzbarski, 1925a, 104.
52. Matt. 11:11.
53. Matt. 11:13.
54. Matt. 5:21–22.
55. Matt. 17:12.
56. Schweitzer, 1926, 16.
57. Otto, 34.
58. Ibid.
59. Ibid., 24 ff.
60. Ibid.
61. Ibid., 41.
62. Matt. 6:10.
63. Otto, 80.
64. Luke 10:18.
65. Otto, 32.
66. Luke 11:20.
67. Otto, 78.
68. Ibid., 32.
69. Ibid., 41.
70. Ibid.
71. Matt. 11:5.
72. Eisler, 208.
73. Matt. 19:30.
74. Talmud, *babylonischer*, Baba Batra 10b.
75. Eisler, 163 ff.
76. Otto, 46.
77. Rom. 1:3.
78. Mark 12:35 ff.
79. Eisler, 180.
80. Littmann, 27.
81. Eisler, 190.
82. Schweitzer, 1926, 394.
83. Mark 1:27.
84. Matt. 11:4–6.
85. Schweitzer, 1926, 394.
86. Matt. 16:20.
87. Otto, 184.
88. Matt. 16:17.
89. Eisler, 216.
90. Pieper, 34.
91. Ibid., 10.
92. Eisler, 217 ff.
93. Luke 9:1.
94. Luke 10:1.
95. Gal. 2:8.
96. Luke 14:33.
97. Mark 10:21.
98. Mark 9:34.
99. Matt. 10:38.
100. Matt. 7:24.
101. Matt. 7:28–29.
102. Matt. 11:12.
103. Matt. 5:12.
104. Eisler, 243.
105. Jer. 2:2.
106. Hos. 12:10.
107. Eisler, 248.
108. Mark 8:4.
109. Matt. 6:25–33.
110. Mark 13:7.
111. Windisch, 177.

112. Matt. 24:26.
113. Exod. 14:12.
114. Matt. 10:23.
115. Schweitzer, 1926, 406 ff.
116. Mark 6:30–33.
117. Matt. 11:20–24.
118. Matt. 11:25–30.
119. Mark 8:31.
120. Otto, 207.
121. Ibid., 212.
122. Isa. 53:11–12.
123. Mark 10:45.
124. Schweitzer, 1926, 437.
125. Spengler, II:256.
126. Petras, 23 ff.
127. Ibid.
128. Baur, 1837, 21 ff.
129. Ibid., 30 ff.
130. Petras, 25.
131. Ibid., 26.
132. Bauer, 1877, 11 ff.
133. Matt. 5:21–22.
134. Bauer, 1877, 221.
135. Ibid., 4 ff.
136. Ibid., 221 ff.
137. Ibid., 302.
138. Ibid.
139. Ibid., 219 ff.
140. Ibid., 327.
141. Petras, 29 ff.
142. Seneca, *Epistle* 41.
143. Lucretius, *De rerum nat.* V:18.
144. Bauer, 1877, 222.
145. Eisler, 735.
146. Col. 2:12.
147. Lidzbarski, 1925a, 104.
148. Acts 18:24 ff.
149. 1 Cor. 12:12, 13.
150. Poehlmann, I:527.
151. Schweitzer, 1930, 102 ff.
152. Rom. 5:12, 18, 19.
153. Ibid., 5:14, 15.
154. 1 Cor. 15:44–49.
155. Kittel, ed., *Theologisches Wörterbuch*, "Adam."
156. Gen. 1:27.
157. Gen., 2:7.
158. Col. 1:15.
159. Isa. 53.
160. Rom. 6:3, 4.
161. 1 Cor. 15:16–19.
162. 1 Cor. 15:20.
163. Petras, 42.
164. 1 Cor. 12:13.
165. Gal. 2:10.
166. Petras, 44 ff.
167. Bauer, 1877, 171 ff.
168. Ibid., 58.
169. Petras, 44 ff.
170. Ibid., 34.
171. Ibid., 44 ff.
172. Matt. 10:23.
173. Otto, 203.
174. Acts 1:3.
175. Mark 10:29.
176. Origen, *Contra Celsum*, VII:9.
177. Luke 10:8–12.
178. Kittel, 71.
179. James 4:4.
180. James 5:1–9.
181. Troeltsch, 48.
182. Luke 13:30.
183. 1 Cor. 15:23 ff.
184. Acts 8:12.
185. 1 Cor. 2:2.
186. Schweitzer, 1930, 113.
187. Werner, 200.
188. 1 Cor. 7:20.
189. Eisler, 757 ff.
190. Ibid.
191. Origen, *Contra Celsum*, V:16.
192. Vischer, 126.
193. Ibid., 71.
194. Ibid., 132 (Harnack).
195. Rev. 12:1–2.
196. Schürer, II:448.

197. Vischer, 27.
198. Lohmeyer, 1919, 33.
199. Rev. 20: 4:3 and 20:6.
200. Rev. 20:1–21:5.
201. Rev. 17:5.
202. Mark 13:22.
203. Werner, 107.
204. Ibid.
205. Ibid.
206. 2 Thess. 2:1 ff.
207. Ibid.
208. 2 Thess. 3:11.
209. 2 Pet. 3:3 ff.
210. Werner, 111.
211. 1 Clement 23:3.
212. Harnack, 1909, I:188.
213. Werner, 698.
214. Frick, 82.
215. Clement of Alexandria, *Quis dives salvetur*, book XXI:3.
216. Clement of Alexandria, *Stromata*, book IV:26.172; cf. Frick, 90.
217. Koch, 329 ff.
218. Völker, 14.
219. Origen, ed. Balthasar, 1938, 117 ff.
220. Ibid., 69 ff.
221. Ibid., 74 ff.
222. Ibid., 86 ff.
223. Koch, 36 ff.
224. Ibid., 38.
225. Ibid., 28.
226. Ibid., 120.
227. Origen, *Peri euches*, 26; Koetschau, II:363.
228. Origen, *Commentary on the Epistle to the Romans*, 3:10.
229. Koch, 31.
230. Ibid., 31–32.
231. Ibid., 77.
232. Ibid., 32.
233. Völker, 62 ff.
234. Ibid., 234.
235. Koch, 37; Jonas, 260.
236. Werner, 149.
237. Judas 14.
238. Köhler, 258 ff.
239. Werner, 151.
240. Eisler, 761.
241. Origen, *Ser.*, 56.
242. Origen, *De Princ.*, IV:24.
243. Nigg, 75.
244. Werner, 112.
245. Tertullian, *Apol.*, 39.
246. 1 Tim. 2:2 ff.
247. Geffcken, 1920, 31.
248. Ibid., 19.
249. Ibid., 11; Spengler, II:243 ff.
250. Spengler, II:243 ff.
251. Geffcken, 1920, 16.
252. Ibid., 11; Spengler, II:243 ff.
253. Geffcken, 1920, 29.
254. Ibid., 35.
255. Ibid., 36.
256. Ibid., 204; Spengler, II:243 ff.
257. Ibid.
258. Spengler, II:310.
259. Geffcken, 1920, 202.
260. Ibid., 214.
261. Ibid., 200.
262. Ibid., 226 ff.
263. Ibid., 74.
264. Koch, 300.
265. Geffcken, 1920, 113.
266. Ibid.
267. Ibid., 134.
268. Spengler, II:311; Geffcken, 1920, 140.
269. Salin, 47.
270. Horten, 12.
271. Frick, 138 ff.
272. Augustine, *The City of God*, XX:9.
273. Ibid.
274. Eger, 47. [This author does not

appear in the bibliography of
the original.—Trans.]
275. Tillich, 1930, 238.
276. Ibid.
277. Cf. Eicken, 1 ff.
278. Troeltsch, 112.
279. Nigg, 142 ff.
280. Ibid.
281. Balthasar, I:24.
282. Ibid.
283. Ibid.
284. Balthasar I:25.
285. Benz, 3.
286. Rosenstock, 20. [This author
does not appear in the bibliography of the original.—Trans.]

BOOK III

1. Rosenstock, 23.
2. Ibid.
3. Reisner, 1935, 99 ff.
4. Rosenstock, 3 ff.
5. Reisner, 1935, 99 ff.
6. Balthasar, I:25.
7. Ibid., I:145.
8. Schelling, IV:342.
9. Marx, 1932a, I:26.
10. Hegel, 1832–45, XII:235.
11. Reisner, 1935, 99 ff.
12. Löwith, 464.
13. Ibid., 472.
14. Ibid., 475.
15. Marx, 1932a, I:263.
16. Frick, 136.
17. Grundmann, 19 ff.
18. Ibid., 43.
19. Benz, 6.
20. Ibid.
21. Lasson, II:722.
22. Ibid.
23. Benz, 10.
24. Ibid., 9.

25. Lasson, II:937.
26. Löwith, 49.
27. Benz, 21.
28. Grundmann, 150.
29. Benz, 23.
30. Ibid.
31. Grundmann, 117.
32. Löwith, 47.
33. Ibid.
34. Ibid., 56 ff.
35. Ibid.
36. Hegel, 1842, XV:689.
37. Löwith, 68.
38. Hegel, *Encyclopedia*, § 552.
Cited in Löwith, 62.
39. Benz, 26 ff.
40. Lasson, II:877 ff.
41. Ibid.
42. Ibid., 881.
43. Lessing, "Die Erziehung des
Menschengeschlechts,"
§ 86–90.
44. Benz, 33.
45. Löwith, 94 ff.
46. Ibid.
47. Ibid.
48. Benz, 46 ff.
49. Ibid.
50. Ibid.
51. Ibid.
52. Ibid., 175 ff.
53. Ibid.
54. Ibid., 177.
55. Ritschl, I:30.
56. Benz, 179.
57. Ibid., 180.
58. Ibid., 181.
59. Rosenstock, 107 ff.
60. Benz, 245.
61. Ibid., 248.
62. Ibid., 259.
63. Ibid.
64. Ibid.

65. Ibid.
66. Ibid., 260.
67. Ibid.
68. Ibid., 262.
69. Ibid., 263.
70. Ibid., 291.
71. Ibid.
72. Ibid.
73. Ibid., 292.
74. Ibid., 293.
75. Ibid., 312.
76. Ibid., 357.
77. Ibid., 358.
78. Ibid., 361.
79. Bloch, 71.
80. Troeltsch, 411.
81. Bloch, 52.
82. Volpe, cited in Troeltsch, 387 ff.
83. Ibid., 362.
84. Ibid.
85. Ibid., 808.
86. Bloch, 241.
87. Troeltsch, 391.
88. Ritschl, I:13.
89. Volpe, cited in Troeltsch, 391.
90. Troeltsch, 407.
91. Holl, 424.
92. Ritschl, I:30.
93. Holl, 425.
94. Ritschl, I:23.
95. Ibid., 31.
96. Ibid., 29.
97. Ibid., 32.
98. Ibid., 35.
99. Marx, 1932a, I:17.
100. Mannheim, 192.
101. Holl, 425.
102. Bloch, 134.
103. Ibid., 136.
104. Mannheim, 193.
105. Freund, 9.
106. Brandt, 132.
107. Holl, 425.

108. Reisner, 1935, 99 ff.
109. Ibid., 105.
110. Ibid., 132.
111. Ibid.
112. Ibid., 133.
113. Ibid., 132.
114. Ibid., 133.
115. Bloch, 186.
116. Luther, II:199.
117. Bloch, 181.
118. Reisner, 1935, 139.
119. Bloch, 186.
120. Troeltsch, 439.
121. Bloch, 198 ff.
122. Troeltsch, 447.
123. Ibid., 453.
124. Ibid., 470.
125. Bloch, 79 ff.
126. Brandt, 71.
127. Ibid., 59 ff.
128. Ibid.
129. Ibid., 61.
130. Ibid., 164.
131. Ibid., 169.
132. Ibid., 168.
133. Ibid., 187.
134. Ibid., 195.
135. Ibid., 189.
136. Ibid., 191 ff.
137. Ibid.
138. Ibid.
139. Ibid., 129.
140. Ibid., 193.
141. Ibid., 197.
142. Ibid., 200.
143. Ibid., 198.
144. Bloch, 145.
145. Freund, 112.
146. Ibid.
147. Brandt, 192.
148. Freund, 113.
149. Ibid., 114.
150. Ibid., 115.

151. Ibid., 116 ff. [Trans. modified.—Trans.]
152. Ibid.
153. Brandt, 62.
154. Ibid., 126.
155. Ibid., 180.
156. Ibid., 62.
157. Ibid., 167.
158. Ibid., 146.
159. Ibid., 178.
160. Ibid., 127.
161. Ibid.
162. Ibid., 166.
163. Ibid.
164. Kierkegaard, 1909–22, VII:61 ff. [Trans. modified.—Trans.]
165. Löwith, 490 ff.
166. Kierkegaard, 1923, I:284.
167. Löwith, 490 ff.
168. Ibid.
169. Kierkegaard, 1909–22, VI:274.
170. Löwith, 495.
171. Kierkegaard, 1909–22, VI:279.
172. Kierkegaard, 1923, I:407.
173. Löwith, 499.
174. Kierkegaard, 1923, I:400.
175. Löwith, 203.
176. Brandt, 75.
177. Ibid., 170.
178. Bloch, 112.
179. Brandt, 170.
180. Troeltsch, 813 ff.
181. Bloch, 117.
182. Troeltsch, 813 ff.
183. Ibid.
184. Bloch, 125.
185. Troeltsch, 813 ff.
186. Bloch, 166.
187. Troeltsch, 818.
188. Ibid.
189. Ibid.
190. Ibid., 821.

191. Ibid., 823.
192. Ibid., 824 ff.
193. Nigg, 214.
194. Troeltsch, 828.
195. Ritschl, I:130.
196. Balthasar, I:37.
197. Weiß, 42.
198. Ibid., 43.
199. Ibid.
200. Balthasar, I:38.
201. Ritschl, II:132.
202. Weiß, 52.
203. Ibid.
204. Ibid., 53.
205. Ibid.
206. Nigg, 283.
207. Balthasar, I:33.
208. Ibid., I:38.
209. Ibid.
210. Ibid., I:39.

BOOK IV

1. Bloch, 138.
2. Brandt, 170.
3. Jung, 51.
4. Brinkmann, 17.
5. Sudhof, I:491 and II:672.
6. Ibid.
7. Brinkmann, 131.
8. Kant, 1838, II:17.
9. Lukács, 123.
10. Ibid.
11. Ibid.
12. Ibid., 124.
13. Balthasar, I:28 ff.
14. Ibid.
15. Ibid.
16. Ibid., I:31.
17. Ibid., I:34.
18. Hirsch, 20.
19. Lasson, II:938.
20. Lukács, 131.

21. Ibid.
22. Balthasar, I:35.
23. Ibid., I:39.
24. Ibid.
25. Balthasar, I:34.
26. Ibid.
27. Ibid.
28. Nigg, 297.
29. Lukács, 126.
30. Ibid.
31. Balthasar, I:36.
32. Lukács, 132.
33. Ibid., 134.
34. Schiller, "Über die ästhetische Erziehung des Menschen," Letter XV.
35. Lukács, 153.
36. Löwith, 202.
37. Marx, 1932a, II:5.
38. Thielicke, 54.
39. Lessing, VI:418.
40. Thielicke, 28 ff.; Balthasar, I:48 ff.
41. Balthasar, I:92.
42. Ibid.
43. Ibid., I:5.
44. Lessing, VI:354.
45. Ibid., VI:357.
46. Ibid.
47. Ibid., VI:367 ff.
48. Schelling, VII:483.
49. Lessing, VI:367 ff.
50. Koch, 13.
51. Origen, *Contra Celsum*, III:49.
52. Koch, 31.
53. Ibid., 159.
54. Ibid.
55. Ibid., 160.
56. Lessing, *Erziehung des Menschengeschlechts*, § 2.
57. Ibid., § 1.
58. Ibid., § 4.
59. Ibid., § 5.
60. Ibid., § 6.
61. Ibid., § 8.
62. Ibid., § 11.
63. Ibid., § 18.
64. Ibid., § 53.
65. Ibid., § 55.
66. Ibid., § 57.
67. Ibid., § 58.
68. Ibid., § 51.
69. Ibid., § 86, § 88.
70. Freyer, 80 ff.
71. Ibid.
72. Ibid.
73. Adler, 263.
74. Kant, 1838, V:443.
75. Gerlich, 175.
76. Bloch, 138.
77. Reisner, 1935, 103 ff..
78. Kant, 1838, II:15. [Second Preface to the *Critique of Pure Reason*, 2005, 17 (trans. modified).—Trans.]
79. Ibid. [Ibid. (trans. modified).—Trans.]
80. Ibid. [Ibid. (trans. modified).—Trans.]
81. Ibid., II:17. [Ibid., 18 (trans. modified).—Trans.]
82. Ibid., II:17 ff. [Ibid. (trans. modified)—Trans.]
83. Ibid., IV:381.
84. Ibid., IV:381 ff.
85. Balthasar, I:92.
86. Ibid.
87. Lessing, VI:354.
88. Ibid., VI:357.
89. Kant, 1838, VI:393 ff. ["The End of All Things," 221 (trans. modified).—Trans.]
90. Ibid. [Ibid. (trans. modified).—Trans.]
91. Ibid. [Ibid. (trans. modified).—Trans.]

92. Ibid., VI:397 ff.
93. Ibid., VI:399.
94. Ibid., VI:400 ff.
95. Ibid., VI:401.
96. Ibid., VI:402 ff.
97. Ibid.
98. Ibid.
99. Schelling, XI:482.
100. Kroner, I:44 ff.
101. Schelling, XI:483 ff.
102. Ibid.
103. Ibid.
104. Ibid.
105. Lukács, 137.
106. Kant, 1838, II:433.
107. Sannwald, 93.
108. Kant, 1838, VII:356 ff.
109. Ibid., VI:197 ff. [Kant, 1998, 59.—Trans.]
110. Ibid. [Ibid., 60.—Trans.]
111. Ibid., VI:205 ff.
112. Ibid.
113. Ibid. [Kant, 1998, 66.—Trans.]
114. Ibid., VI:209 ff.
115. Ibid., VI:211.
116. Ibid., VI:213. [Kant, 1998, 69.—Trans.]
117. Ibid., VI:215.
118. Ibid., VI:216. [Kant, 1998, 72 ff.—Trans.]
119. Ibid., VI:222.
120. Ibid.
121. Ibid., VI:230 ff. [Kant, 1998, 84.—Trans.]
122. Ibid. [Ibid., 85.—Trans.]
123. Ibid., VI:36 ff.
124. Ibid.
125. Ibid. [Kant, 1998, 89.—Trans.]
126. Ibid., VI:238 ff.
127. Ibid., VI:240 ff. [Kant, 1998, 91.—Trans.]
128. Ibid., VI:261.
129. Ibid., VI:262.
130. Ibid., VI:265.
131. Ibid., VI:267. [Kant, 1998, 107.—Trans.]
132. Ibid., VI:268 ff. [Ibid., 110.—Trans.]
133. Ibid., VI:270. [Ibid., 111.—Trans.]
134. Ibid., VI:271 ff. [Ibid.—Trans.]
135. Ibid. [Ibid., 122.—Trans.]
136. Ibid. [Ibid.—Trans.]
137. Ibid.
138. Ibid., VI:295 ff. [Kant, 1998, 127.—Trans.]
139. Ibid. [Ibid., 128.—Trans.]
140. Ibid., VI:307. [Ibid., 135.—Trans.]
141. Ibid., VI:308. [Ibid.—Trans.]
142. Ibid., VI:313.
143. Ibid., VI:312. [Kant, 1998, 139.—Trans.]
144. Hegel, 1907, 265. [Hegel, 1996, 211.—Trans.]
145. Ibid. [Ibid.—Trans.]
146. Ibid., 293.
147. Ibid., 266. [Hegel, 1996, 212.—Trans.]
148. Ibid. [Ibid. (trans. modified).—Trans.]
149. Ibid., 267. [Ibid.—Trans.]
150. Ibid. [Ibid., 213.—Trans.]
151. Ibid., 268. [Ibid., 214.—Trans.]
152. Ibid.
153. Ibid., 277.
154. Ibid., 383.
155. Ibid., 295 ff. [Hegel, 1996, 247.—Trans.]
156. Ibid.
157. Haering, I:306.
158. Hegel, 1907, 379. [Hegel, 1996, 305 (trans. modified).—Trans.]
159. Ibid. [Ibid. (trans. modified).—Trans.]

160. Ibid. [Ibid. (trans. modified).—Trans.]
161. Ibid. [Ibid.—Trans.]
162. Haering, I:374.
163. Hegel, 1907, 379. [Hegel, 1996, 305.—Trans.]
164. Ibid., 380. [Ibid.—Trans.]
165. Ibid. [Ibid., 306.—Trans.]
166. Ibid.
167. Ibid. [Ibid., 307.—Trans.]
168. Ibid., 381. [Ibid.—Trans.]
169. Ibid. [Ibid. (trans. modified).—Trans.]
170. Haering, I:432.
171. Hegel, 1907, 393.
172. Ibid.
173. Ibid., 394.
174. Ibid., 396.
175. Ibid.
176. Ibid., 391.
177. Ibid., 347.
178. Ibid.
179. Hegel, 1832–45, II:19. [Hegel, 1977, 14.—Trans.]
180. Ibid., II:5. [Ibid., 2–3.—Trans.]
181. Ibid., II:16. [Ibid., 11.—Trans.]
182. Ibid., II:23 ff. [Hodgson, 99. —Trans.]
183. Ibid., II:15. [Hegel, 1977, 10.—Trans.]
184. Ibid., II:25.
185. Ibid., II:36 ff.
186. Ibid., II:14.
187. Ibid., II:15. [Hegel, 1977, 10.—Trans.]
188. Ibid. [Ibid.—Trans.]
189. Ibid., II:29. [Ibid., 21 (trans. modified).—Trans.]
190. Ibid., II:26. [Ibid., 19.—Trans.]
191. Ibid., XI:176 ff.
192. Hegel, 1907, 347.
193. Hegel, 1832–45, XI:323.
194. Ibid., III:78.

195. Ibid., III:137 ff.
196. Ibid., III:139.
197. Ibid., III:410.
198. Ibid., XI:5.
199. Ibid., XI:3.
200. Ibid.
201. Ibid., XI:4.
202. Ibid., XI:83.
203. Ibid., XI:75.
204. Ibid., XI:110.
205. Ibid., XI:193.
206. Hegel, 1969, 192.
207. Hegel, 1832–45, XII:218.
208. Baur, 1835, 670.
209. Ibid., 675.
210. Ibid.
211. Hegel, 1842, XII:228.
212. Ibid., XII:227.
213. Irenaeus, II:73.
214. Hegel, 1842, XII:218.
215. Ibid.
216. Baur, 1835, 678.
217. Hegel, 1842, XII:219.
218. Ibid., XI:194.
219. Baur, 1835, 681.
220. Hegel, 1842, XII:307.
221. Ibid., XII:319.
222. Ibid., XII:298.
223. Ibid., XII:300.
224. Ibid., XII:309.
225. Ibid., XII:300.
226. Ibid., XII:303.
227. Ibid., XII:330.
228. Ibid., XII:354.
229. Ibid.
230. Ibid., XII:355.
231. Ibid.
232. Ibid.
233. Ibid., XII:356.
234. Ibid.
235. Ibid., XIII:66. [Hegel, 1995, 50.—Trans.]

236. Ibid. [Ibid. (trans. modified).—Trans.]
237. Ibid., XII:309.
238. Ibid., VIII:17.
239. Löwith, 95 ff.
240. Haym, 4.
241. Baur, 1841, 71.
242. Löwith, 468 ff.
243. Baur, 1841, 148.
244. Marx, 1932a, I:17.
245. Löwith, 205 ff.
246. Marx, 1932a, I:1.
247. Ibid., 3.
248. Ibid., 6.
249. Ibid., 7.
250. Ibid., 8.
251. Ibid.
252. Landshut, 10.
253. Marx, 1932a, I:8.
254. Ibid., I:12.
255. Ibid., I:13.
256. Ibid., I:14.
257. Ibid., I:15.
258. Ibid., I:337.
259. Ibid., I:14.
260. Ibid., I:16.
261. Ibid., I:17.
262. Ibid., I:270 ff.
263. Ibid., I:280.
264. Ibid., I:263.
265. Barth, 103 ff.
266. Marx, 1932a, I:264 ff.
267. Ibid.
268. Ibid.
269. Kierkegaard, 1925, 424 ff.
270. Ibid.
271. Ibid.
272. Ibid.
273. Ibid.
274. Kierkegaard, 1909–1922, VI:203.
275. Ibid., VI:210.
276. Ibid., VI:213.
277. Ibid., VI:214 ff.
278. Ibid.
279. Ibid., VI:221 ff.
280. Ibid., VII:52.
281. Ibid.
282. Löwith, 205 ff.
283. Marx, 1932a, I:25.
284. Ibid., I:26.
285. Ibid., I:90.
286. Kierkegaard, 1909–1922, I:29.
287. Ibid., VII:13.
288. Löwith, 202 ff.
289. Ibid.
290. Ibid.
291. Marx, 1932a, I:113.
292. Ibid., I:120.
293. Ibid., I:248. [Marx, 1978, 43.—Trans.]
294. Ibid., I:288 ff.
295. Ibid.
296. Ibid.
297. Ibid., I:291.
298. Ibid.
299. Ibid., I:329.
300. [In line with most translators of Hegel, I translate *Entäusserung* consistently as "externalization," which runs counter to the common practice of translating Marx's use of the term as "alienation."—Trans.]
301. Marx, 1932a, I:328. [Marx and Engels, 1964, 202 (trans. modified).—Trans.]
302. Ibid., I:322. [Marx, 1963, 290.—Trans.]
303. Ibid., I:399.
304. Ibid., I:342.
305. Ibid.
306. Ibid., I:345.
307. Ibid., I:332.
308. Ibid., I:334.
309. Ibid., I:335.

310. Marx, 1903, 394.
311. Marx, 1932a, I:357.
312. Ibid., I:260.
313. Ibid., I:360.
314. Lukács, 94 ff.
315. Marx, 1932b, 83.
316. Ibid., 84 ff.
317. Marx, 1932a, I:292.
318. Ibid.
319. Ibid., I:293 ff.
320. Ibid.
321. Ibid.
322. Ibid., I:333.
323. Ibid., I:340.
324. Ibid.
325. Ibid., I:333.
326. Ibid., I:293 ff.
327. Ibid., I:297.
328. Kierkegaard, 1925, 54.
329. Ibid., 429.
330. Ibid., 436.
331. Ibid., 449.
332. Ibid., 445.
333. Ibid., 452.
334. Barth, 164 ff.
335. Marx, 1932a, I:278. [Marx, 1975, 254.—Trans.]
336. Hegel, 1842, XII:298.

337. Marx, 1932a, I:376 ff.
338. Ibid.
339. Ibid.
340. Ibid.
341. Marx, 1932b, 36.
342. Ibid., 596 ff.
343. Ibid., 706 ff. [Marx, 1977, 799.—Trans.]
344. Ibid. [Ibid., 799 ff.—Trans.]
345. Kierkegaard, 1927, 6.
346. Ibid., 1.
347. Ibid., 7.
348. Ibid., 1.
349. Ibid.
350. Ibid., 2.
351. Ibid., 3.
352. Ibid., 4.
353. Ibid.
354. Ibid.
355. Marx, 1932b, 36.
356. Kierkegaard, 1927, 4.
357. Ibid., 6.
358. Ibid.
359. Ibid., 7.
360. Ibid.
361. Hegel, 1842, XV:617 ff.
362. Augustine, 1934, 227.
363. Heidegger, 22.

Bibliography

Any works mentioned in the Notes but not listed in the original German bibliography have been added, whenever possible, and marked with an asterisk (*). Any published English titles used for the translation have also been added to the original German source. Multiple entries under a single author's name are listed chronologically.—Trans.

Adler, Georg. *Geschichte des Sozialismus und Kommunismus von Plato bis zur Gegenwart.* Leipzig, 1899.

Apocalypses. *See* Riessler, Paul.

Augustine. *De civitate dei.* Leipzig, 1825.

———. *Die Gestalt als Gefüge.* Ed. E. Przywara. Leipzig, 1934.

*———. *City of God.* Trans. Marcus Dods. New York, 1950.

Baeck, Leo. *Aus drei Jahrtausenden, Gesammelte Aufsätze.* Berlin, 1938.

Balthasar, Hans Urs von. *Apokalypse der deutschen Seele.* 3 vols. Salzburg, 1937–39.

Baron, Salo Wittmayer. *A Social and Religious History of the Jews.* 18 vols. New York, 1937.

Barth, Hans. *Wahrheit und Ideologie.* Zurich, 1945.

Barth, Karl. *Kirchliche Dogmatik.* 31 vols. Munich, 1932.

Bauer, Bruno. *Die Posaune des jüngsten Gerichts über Hegel den Atheisten und Antichristen: Ein Ultimatum.* Leipzig, 1841.

———. *Das entdeckte Christentum, eine Erinnerung an das 18. Jahrhundert und ein Beitrag zur Krisis des 19.* Zurich, 1843.

———. *Christus und die Cäsaren, der Ursprung des Christentums aus dem römischen Griechentum.* Berlin, 1877.

Baumgartner, Walther. "Ein Vierteljahrhundert Danielforschung." *Theologische Rundschau,* n.f., 11 (1939): bks. 2–4.

Baur, Ferdinand Christian. *Die christliche Gnosis oder die christliche Religionsphilosophie.* Tübingen, 1835.

———. *Das Christliche des Platonismus oder Sokrates und Christus: Eine religionsphilosophische Untersuchung.* Tübingen, 1837.

Benz, Ernst. *Ecclesia spiritualis, Kirchenidee und Geschichtstheologie der franziskanischen Reformation.* Stuttgart, 1934.

Berdyaev, Nikolay. *Der Sinn der Geschichte.* Darmstadt, 1925.

Die Bibel, oder die ganze heilige Schrift des Alten und Neuen Testaments. Trans. Martin Luther. Berlin, 1925.

The Bible. New Revised Standard Version. Oxford, 1962.

Bickermann, Elia. *Die Makkabäer.* Berlin, 1935.

Bloch, Ernst. *Thomas Münzer als Theologe der Revolution.* Munich, 1921.

*Boll, Franz J. *Aus der Offenbarung Johannis: Hellenistische Studien zum Weltbild der Apokalypse, von Franz Boll.* Leipzig-Berlin, 1914.

Bornkamm, Heinrich. *Mystik, Spiritualismus und die Anfänge des Pietismus im Luthertum.* Giessen, 1926.

Bousset, Wilhelm. *Die jüdische Apokalytik.* Berlin, 1903.

———. *Die Religion des Judentums im neutestamentlichen Zeitalter.* Berlin, 1906.

———. *Hauptprobleme der Gnosis.* Göttingen, 1907.

Brandt, Otto. *Thomas Münzer, sein Leben und seine Schriften.* Jena, 1933.

Brinkmann, Donald. *Mensch und Technik: Grundzüge einer Philosophie der Technik.* Bern, 1946.

Buber, Martin. *Das Königtum Gottes.* Berlin, 1932.

Charles, Robert Henry. *A Critical and Exegetical Commentary on the Revelation of St. John.* Edinburgh, 1920.

*Clement of Alexandria. In *Migne Patrologia Graeca*, vols. 8–9. Paris, 1857.

Dibelius, Martin. *Die urchristliche Überlieferung von Johannes dem Täufer.* Göttingen, 1911.

Diels, Hermann. *Fragmente der Vorsokratiker.* 3 vols. Berlin, 1910–12.

*Eger, Hans. *Die Eschatologie Augustins.* In Greifswalder Theologische Forschung, vol. 1. Greifswald, 1933.

Eicken, Heinrich von. *Geschichte und System der mittelalterlichen Weltanschauung.* Stuttgart, 1887.

Eisler, Robert. *Jesus basileus ou basileusas: Die messianische Unabhängigkeitsbewegung vom Auftreten Johannes des Täufers bis zum Untergang Jakobs des Gerechten.* Vol. 2. Heidelberg, 1930.

Faust, August. *Der Möglichkeitsgedanke: Systemgeschichtliche Untersuchungen.* 2 vols. Heidelberg, 1931–32.

Feuerbach, Ludwig. *Briefwechsel und Nachlass.* Ed. K. Grün. 2 vols. Heidelberg, 1874.

———. *Grundsätze der Philosophie der Zukunft.* Ed. H. Ehrenberg. Stuttgart, 1922.

Freund, Michael. *Thomas Münzer, Revolution als Glaube: Auswahl aus den Schriften Thomas Münzers und Martin Luthers zur religiösen Revolution und zum deutschen Bauernkrieg.* Potsdam, 1936.

Freyer, Hans. *Die politische Insel: Eine Geschichte der Utopien von Plato bis zur Gegenwart.* Leipzig, 1936.

Frick, Robert. *Die Geschichte des Reich Gottes Gedanken in der alten Kirche bis zu Origenes und Augustin.* Giessen, 1928.

Fuchs, Harald. *Der geistige Widerstand gegen Rom in der antiken Welt.* Berlin, 1938.

Gall, August von. *Basileia tou theou: Eine religionsgeschichtliche Studie zur vorkirchlichen Eschatlogie.* Heidelberg, 1926.

*Geffcken, Johannes, ed. *Die Oracula Sybillina.* 8 vols. Leipzig, 1902.

Geffcken, Johannes. *Der Ausgang des griechisch-römischen Heidentums.* Heidelberg, 1920.

Gerlich, Fritz. *Der Kommunismus als Lehre vom tausendjährigen Reich.* Munich, 1920.

Goguel, Maurice. *Das Leben Jesu.* Trans. Robert Binswanger. Zurich, 1934.

Grundmann, Herbert. *Studien über Joachim von Floris.* Leipzig, 1928.

Gunkel, Hermann. *Schöpfung und Chaos in Urzeit und Endzeit: Eine religionsge schichtliche Abhandlung über Gen.1 und Apok. Jo 12.* Göttingen, 1895.

———, ed. *Religion in Geschichte und Gegenwart.* Tübingen, 1926.

*Haering, Theodor L. *Hegel: Sein Wollen und sein Werk; Eine chronologische Ent wicklungsgeschichte der Gedanken und der Sprache Helgels von Dr. Theodor L. Haering.* 2 vols. Leipzig-Berlin, 1929–38.

Harnack, Adolf von. *Lehrbuch der Dogmengeschichte.* 3 vols. Tübingen, 1909.

———. Marcion. *Das Evangelium vom fremden Gott.* Leipzig, 1921.

*Haym, Rudolf. *Hegel und seine Zeit.* Berlin, 1857.

Hegel, Georg Wilhelm Friedrich. *Werke.* 2nd ed. 18 vols. Berlin, 1832–45.

———. *Theologische Jugendschriften.* Ed. Herman Nohl. Tübingen, 1907.

———. *Vorlesungen über die Philosophie der Religion.* Frankfurt am Main, 1969.

*———. *The Phenomenology of Spirit.* Trans. A. V. Miller. Oxford, 1977.

*———. *Lectures on the Philosophy of History.* Trans. E. S. Haldane. Lincoln, Neb., 1995.

*———. *Early Theological Writings.* Trans. T. M. Knox. Philadelphia, 1996.

Hehn, Johannes. *Die biblische und babylonische Gottesidee.* Berlin, 1913.

Heidegger, Martin. *Vom Wesen der Wahrheit.* Frankfurt am Main, 1943.

Hennecke, Edgar. *Neutestamentliche Apokryphen.* Tübingen, 1924.

Herford, R. Travers. *Die Pharisäer.* Trans. Walter Fischel. Leipzig, 1928.

Hermetica. The ancient Greek and Latin writings which contain religious or philo sophical teachings ascribed to Hermes Trismegistus. Ed. and trans. Walter Scott. 4 vols. Oxford, 1924–36.

Hilgenfeld, Adolf. *Die jüdische Apokalyptik in ihrer geschichtlichen Entwicklung.* Jena, 1857.

Hirsch, Emanuel. *Die Reich-Gottes-Begriffe des neueren europäischen Denkens.* Göt tingen, 1921.

*Hodgson, Peter C., ed. *G. W. F. Hegel: Theologian of the Spirit.* Trans. Peter C. Hodgson. Minneapolis, 1997.

Holl, Karl. *Gesammelte Aufsatze zur Kirchengeschichte*. Vol. 1, *Luther*. Tübingen, 1923.

Hölscher, Gustav. "Die Entstehung des Buches Daniel." *Theologische Studien und Kritiken* 92 (1919): 114–38.

Horten, Max. *Die religiöse Gedankenwelt des Volkes im heutigen Islam*. Halle, 1917.

Irenaeus. *Adversus Hareses: 5 Bücher gegen die Häresien*. Trans. E. Klebba. 2 vols. Kempten, 1912.

Jeremias, Alfred. *Das Alte Testament im Lichte des alten Orients*. Leipzig, 1930.

Jonas, Hans. *Gnosis und spätantiker Geist*. Vol. 1. Göttingen, 1934.

Josephus, Flavius. *Gesammelte Werke*. 7 vols. Ed. Benedikt Niese. Berlin, 1887.

Jung, C. G. "Erlösungsvorstellung in der Alchemie." *Eranos Yearbook* 4 (1936): 13 ff.

Kähler, Martin. *Der sogenannte historische Jesus und der geschichtlich biblische Christus*. 2nd ed. Leipzig, 1928.

Kant, Immanuel. *Gesamtausgabe*. 10 vols. Ed. Gustav Hartenstein. Leipzig, 1838.

*———. "The End of All Things." In *Religion and Rational Theology*, trans. Allen W. Wood, 217–32. Cambridge, 1996.

*———. *Religion Within the Boundaries of Mere Reason*. Trans. and ed. Allen W. Wood and George Di Giovanni. Cambridge, 1998.

*———. *Critique of Pure Reason*. Trans. J. M. D. Meiklejohn. New York, 2005.

*Kautsky, Karl. *Vorläufer des neueren Sozialismus*. 2 vols. Stuttgart, 1898.

Kierkegaard, Søren. *Gesammelte Werke*. 12 vols. Trans. Wolfgang Pfeiderer, Christoph Schrempf, H. C. Ketels, H. Gottsched, and A. Dorner. Jena, 1909–22.

———. *Die Tagebücher*. Trans. Th. Häcker. 2 vols. Innsbruck, 1923.

———. *Werke*. Trans. and ed. Hermann Ulrich. Berlin, 1925.

———. *Das Eine was nottut*. Trans. Hermann Ulrich. *Zeitwende*, no. 1 (Munich, 1927).

Kittel, Gerhard. "Der geschichtliche Ort des Jakobusbriefes." *Zeitschrift für Neutestamentliche Wissenschaft* 41 (1942): 71–105.

———, ed. *Theologisches Wörterbuch zum Neuen Testament*. Stuttgart, 1933.

Koch, Hall. *Pronoia und Paideusis: Studien über Origines und sein Verhältnis zum Platonismus*. Berlin, 1932.

Köhler, Walther. *Dogmengeschichte als Geschichte des christlichen Selbstbewusstseins*. Zurich, 1938.

*Kohn, Hans. *Nationalismus: Über die Bedeutung des Nationalismus im Judentum und in der Gegenwart*. Vienna, 1922.

Koepgen, Otto. *Die Gnosis des Christentums*. Salzburg, 1940.

Kroner, Richard. *Von Kant bis Hegel*. 2 vols. Tübingen, 1921–24.

Landshut, Siegfried. *Karl Marx*. Lübeck, 1932.

*Lasson, Georg. *Hegel als Geschichtsphilosoph*. 4 vols. Leipzig, 1920.

Leisegang, Hans. *Die Gnosis*. 7 vols. Leipzig, 1924.

———. *Gnosis*. In *Religion in Geschichte und Gegenwart*, by Hermann Gunkel. Tübingen, 1926.

———. *Denkformen*. Berlin, 1928.

Lessing, Gotthold Ephraim. *Gesammelte Werke*. Ed. Georg Witkowski. 7 vols. Leipzig, 1911.

Lidzbarski, Mark. *Das Johannisbuch der Mandäer*. Giessen, 1925a.

———. *Ginza: Der Schatz oder das grosse Buch der Mandäer*. Göttingen, 1925b.

Littmann, Enno. *Zigeuner-Arabisch*. Bonn, 1920.

Lohmeyer, Ernst. *Christuskult und Kaiserkult*. Tübingen, 1919.

———. *Die Offenbarung des Johannes*. Tübingen, 1926.

Loisy, Alfred. *L'apocalypse de Jean*. Paris, 1923.

Lommel, Hermann. *Die Religion Zarathustras nach dem Awesta dargestellt*. Tübingen, 1930.

Löwith, Karl. *Von Hegel bis Nietzsche*. Zürich, 1941.

Lucretius. *De rerum natura*. Latin and German edition by Hermann Diels. Berlin, 1923–24.

Lukács, Georg von. *Geschichte und Klassenbewusstsein: Studien über marxistische Dialektik*. Berlin, 1923.

Luther, Martin. *Sämtliche Deutsche Werke*. 65 vols. Erlangen, 1826–57.

Maimon, Salamon. *Versuch über die Transcendentalphilosophie*. Berlin, 1790.

Mannheim, Karl. *Ideologie und Utopie*. Bonn, 1930.

Marx, Karl. *Zur Kritik der politischen Oeconomie*. Ed. Karl Kautsky. Stuttgart, 1903.

———. *Der historische Materialismus: Die Frühschriften*. Ed. Siegfried Landshut. 2 vols. Leipzig, 1932a.

———. *Das Kapital*. Vol. 1. Ed. Korsch Karl. Berlin, 1932b.

*———. "Economic and Philosophical Manuscripts." In *Reader in Marxist Philosophy: From the Writings of Marx, Engels, and Lenin*, ed. Howard Selsam and Harry Martel. New York, 1963.

*———. *On Historical Materialism*. Moscow, 1972.

*———. "Critique of Hegel's Philosophy of Right." In *Marx's Early Writings*, trans. Gregor Benton. New York, 1975.

*———. *Capital*. Vol. 1. New York, 1977.

*———. "On the Jewish Question." In *The Marx-Engels Reader*, ed. Robert Tucker, 26–52. New York, 1978.

*———. *The Communist Manifesto*. Ed. Frederic L. Bender. New York, 1988.

Marx, Karl, and Friedrich Engels. *Gesamtausgabe*. Frankfurt am Main, 1927–35.

*———. *Marx and Engels: Collected Works*. Trans. T. B. Bottomore. London, 1964.

Meyer, Eduard. *Ursprung und Anfang des Christentums*. 3 vols. Stuttgart, 1921–23.

Müller, David Heinrich. *Über die Gesetze Hammurabis*. Vienna, 1903.

Nietzsche, Friedrich. *Gesammelte Werke*. 23 vols. Munich, 1922–29.

Nigg, Walter. *Das ewige Reich*. Zurich, 1945.

Otto, Rudolf. *Reich Gottes und Menschensohn*. Munich, 1935.

Origen. In *Migne Patrologia Graeca*, vols. 11–17. Paris, 1857.

*———. *Werke.* Ed. Paul Koetschau. 12 vols. Leipzig, 1899–1955.

———. *Geist und Feuer: Ein Aufbau aus seinen Schriften.* Ed. Hans Urs von Balthasar. 2nd ed. Salzburg, 1938.

Petras, Otto. *Post Christum, Streifzüge durch die geistige Wirklichkeit.* Berlin, 1935.

Pieper, Werner. "Der Pariastamm der Sieb." *Le Monde Oriental* 17 (1923): 1–75.

Poehlmann, Robert von. *Geschichte der sozialen Fragen des Sozialismus in der antiken Welt.* 2 vols. Munich, 1912.

Reimarus, Hermann Samuel. *Von dem Zwecke Jesu und seiner Jünger.* Ed. Gotthold Ephraim Lessing. Braunschweig, 1878.

Reisner, Erwin. *Die Geschichte als Sündenfall und Weg zum Gericht: Grundlegung einer christlichen Metaphysik der Geschichte.* Mannheim, 1929.

———. *Die christliche Botschaft im Wandel der Epochen.* Mannheim, 1935.

Reitzenstein, Richard. *Das iranische Erlösungsmysterium.* Bonn, 1921.

Riessler, Paul. *Altjüdisches Schrifttum ausserhalb der Bibel.* Augsburg, 1928.

Ritschl, Albrecht. *Geschichte des Pietismus.* 3 vols. Bonn, 1880–86.

*Rosenstock, Eugen. *Revolution als politischer Begriff in der Neuzeit.* Breslau, 1931.

Rosenzweig, Franz. *Stern der Erlösung.* 3 vols. Berlin, 1930.

Salin, Edgar. *Civitas dei.* Tübingen, 1926.

Sannwald, Adolf. *Der Begriff der Dialektik und die Anthropologie.* Mannheim, 1931.

Schelling, Friedrich Wilhelm Joseph von. *Sämtliche Werke.* Ed. K. F. A. Schelling. 14 vols. Stuttgart and Augsburg, 1856–61.

Schiller, Friedrich. *Kleinere prosaische Schriften.* 3 vols. Leipzig, 1792.

Schürer, Emil. *Geschichte des jüdischen Volks im Zeitalter Jesu Christi.* 2 vols. Leipzig, 1890.

Schweitzer, Albert. *Geschichte der Leben-Jesu-Forschung.* Tübingen, 1926.

———. *Die Mystik des Apostel Paulus.* Tübingen, 1930.

Seneca. *Ad Lucilium epistolae morales.* Rome, 1937.

Spengler, Oswald. *Untergang des Abendlandes.* 2 vols. Munich, 1919–23.

Sudhof, Karl. *Versuch einer Kritik der Echtheit der paracels. Schriften.* 2 vols. Berlin, 1894–96.

Susmann, Margarethe. "Ezechiel." *Neue Wege* 36 (1942): 9.

Tacitus. *Gesammelte Werke.* Ed. Karl Halm. 4th ed. 6 vols. Leipzig, 1887.

Talmud, der babylonische. Trans. Lazarus Goldschmidt. Berlin, 1929.

Tertullian. *Liber Apologeticus.* Ed. Henry Annesley Woudham. Cambridge, 1850.

Thielicke, Helmut. *Vernunft und Offenbarung: Eine Studie über die Religionsphilosophie Lessings.* Gütersloh, 1936.

Tillich, Paul. *Das Dämonische: Ein Beitrag zur Sinndeutung der Geschichte.* Tübingen, 1926.

———. *Religiöse Verwirklichung.* Berlin, 1930.

———. *Die sozialistische Entscheidung.* Potsdam, 1933.

Troeltsch, Ernst. *Die Soziallehren der Christlichen Kirchen und Gruppen.* Tübingen, 1912.

Vischer, Eberhard. *Die Offenbarung Johannis: Eine jüdische Apokalypse in christlicher Bearbeitung mit Nachwort von A. Harnack.* Leipzig, 1886.

Voelker, Walther. *Das Vollkommenheitsideal des Origines.* Tübingen, 1931.

Volz, Paul. *Die Eschatologie der jüdischen Gemeinde im neutestamentalischen Zeitalter.* Tübingen, 1934.

Weber, Max. *Gesammelte Aufsätze zur Religionssoziologie.* Vol. III. Tübingen, 1921.

Weininger, Otto. *Über die letzten Dinge.* Vienna, 1920.

Weiser, Arthur. *Glaube und Geschichte im alten Testament.* Stuttgart, 1931.

Weiß, Johannes. *Die Idee des Reiches Gottes in der Theologie.* Giessen, 1901.

Wellhausen, Julius. *Die religiös-politischen Oppositionsparteien im Alten Islam.* Berlin, 1894.

——. *Prolegomena zur Geschichte Israels.* Berlin, 1895.

——. *Ein Gemeinwesen ohne Obrigkeit.* Berlin, 1900.

Werner, Martin. *Die Entstehung des christlichen Dogmas: Problemgeschichtlich dargestellt.* Bern, 1941.

Windisch, Hans. "Die Sprüche vom Eingehen in das Reich Gottes." *Zeitschrift für Neutestamentliche Wissenschaft* 27 (1928): 165 ff.

Cultural Memory | *in the Present*

Regina Mara Schwartz, *Sacramental Poetics at the Dawn of Secularism: When God Left the World*

Gil Anidjar, *Semites: Race, Religion, Literature*

Ranjana Khanna, *Algeria Cuts: Women and Representation, 1830 to the Present*

Esther Peeren, *Intersubjectivities and Popular Culture: Bakhtin and Beyond*

Eyal Peretz, *Becoming Visionary: Brian De Palma's Cinematic Education of the Senses*

Diana Sorensen, *A Turbulent Decade Remembered: Scenes from the Latin American Sixties*

Hubert Damisch, *A Childhood Memory by Piero della Francesca*

Dana Hollander, *Exemplarity and Chosenness: Rosenzweig and Derrida on the Nation of Philosophy*

Asja Szafraniec, *Beckett, Derrida, and the Event of Literature*

Sara Guyer, *Romanticism After Auschwitz*

Alison Ross, *The Aesthetic Paths of Philosophy: Presentation in Kant, Heidegger, Lacoue-Labarthe, and Nancy*

Gerhard Richter, *Thought-Images: Frankfurt School Writers' Reflections from Damaged Life*

Bella Brodzki, *Can These Bones Live? Translation, Survival, and Cultural Memory*

Rodolphe Gasché, *The Honor of Thinking: Critique, Theory, Philosophy*

Brigitte Peucker, *The Material Image: Art and the Real in Film*

Natalie Melas, *All the Difference in the World: Postcoloniality and the Ends of Comparison*

Jonathan Culler, *The Literary in Theory*

Michael G. Levine, *The Belated Witness: Literature, Testimony, and the Question of Holocaust Survival*

Jennifer A. Jordan, *Structures of Memory: Understanding German Change in Berlin and Beyond*

Christoph Menke, *Reflections of Equality*

Marlène Zarader, *The Unthought Debt: Heidegger and the Hebraic Heritage*

Jan Assmann, *Religion and Cultural Memory: Ten Studies*

Jacob Taubes, *The Political Theology of Paul*

Jean-Luc Marion, *The Crossing of the Visible*

Eric Michaud, *The Cult of Art in Nazi Germany*

Anne Freadman, *The Machinery of Talk: Charles Peirce and the Sign Hypothesis*

Stanley Cavell, *Emerson's Transcendental Etudes*

Stuart McLean, *The Event and Its Terrors: Ireland, Famine, Modernity*

Beate Rössler, ed., *Privacies: Philosophical Evaluations*

Bernard Faure, *Double Exposure: Cutting Across Buddhist and Western Discourses*

Alessia Ricciardi, *The Ends of Mourning: Psychoanalysis, Literature, Film*

Alain Badiou, *Saint Paul: The Foundation of Universalism*

Gil Anidjar, *The Jew, the Arab: A History of the Enemy*

Jonathan Culler and Kevin Lamb, eds., *Just Being Difficult? Academic Writing in the Public Arena*

Jean-Luc Nancy, *A Finite Thinking*, edited by Simon Sparks

Theodor W. Adorno, *Can One Live after Auschwitz? A Philosophical Reader*, edited by Rolf Tiedemann

Patricia Pisters, *The Matrix of Visual Culture: Working with Deleuze in Film Theory*

Andreas Huyssen, *Present Pasts: Urban Palimpsests and the Politics of Memory*

Talal Asad, *Formations of the Secular: Christianity, Islam, Modernity*

Dorothea von Mücke, *The Rise of the Fantastic Tale*

Marc Redfield, *The Politics of Aesthetics: Nationalism, Gender, Romanticism*

Emmanuel Levinas, *On Escape*

Dan Zahavi, *Husserl's Phenomenology*

Rodolphe Gasché, *The Idea of Form: Rethinking Kant's Aesthetics*

Michael Naas, *Taking on the Tradition: Jacques Derrida and the Legacies of Deconstruction*

Herlinde Pauer-Studer, ed., *Constructions of Practical Reason: Interviews on Moral and Political Philosophy*

Jean-Luc Marion, *Being Given That: Toward a Phenomenology of Givenness*

Theodor W. Adorno and Max Horkheimer, *Dialectic of Enlightenment*

Ian Balfour, *The Rhetoric of Romantic Prophecy*

Martin Stokhof, *World and Life as One: Ethics and Ontology in Wittgenstein's Early Thought*

Gianni Vattimo, *Nietzsche: An Introduction*

Jacques Derrida, *Negotiations: Interventions and Interviews, 1971-1998*, ed. Elizabeth Rottenberg

Brett Levinson, *The Ends of Literature: The Latin American "Boom" in the Neoliberal Marketplace*

Timothy J. Reiss, *Against Autonomy: Cultural Instruments, Mutualities, and the Fictive Imagination*

Hent de Vries and Samuel Weber, eds., *Religion and Media*

Niklas Luhmann, *Theories of Distinction: Re-Describing the Descriptions of Modernity*, ed. and introd. William Rasch

Johannes Fabian, *Anthropology with an Attitude: Critical Essays*

Michel Henry, *I Am the Truth: Toward a Philosophy of Christianity*

Gil Anidjar, *"Our Place in Al-Andalus": Kabbalah, Philosophy, Literature in Arab-Jewish Letters*

Hélène Cixous and Jacques Derrida, *Veils*

F. R. Ankersmit, *Historical Representation*

F. R. Ankersmit, *Political Representation*

Elissa Marder, *Dead Time: Temporal Disorders in the Wake of Modernity (Baudelaire and Flaubert)*

Reinhart Koselleck, *The Practice of Conceptual History: Timing History, Spacing Concepts*

Niklas Luhmann, *The Reality of the Mass Media*

Hubert Damisch, *A Theory of /Cloud/: Toward a History of Painting*

Jean-Luc Nancy, *The Speculative Remark: (One of Hegel's bon mots)*

Jean-François Lyotard, *Soundproof Room: Malraux's Anti-Aesthetics*

Jan Patocka, *Plato and Europe*

Hubert Damisch, *Skyline: The Narcissistic City*

90 A   B   1-list   4   20
90 B   B   12   Them Judais   4
RS 190 SP 11   4   M   4
RS C 108 SP 13   4   Theme
RS 190 Sec.   4   Theme M   20
4   M